CHANGE AND CONTINUITY IN INDIA'S VILLAGES

✵

SOUTHERN ASIAN INSTITUTE SERIES

COLUMBIA UNIVERSITY

CHANGE AND CONTINUITY IN INDIA'S VILLAGES

EDITED WITH AN
INTRODUCTION BY
K. ISHWARAN

COLUMBIA UNIVERSITY PRESS

NEW YORK AND LONDON 1970

K. Ishwaran is Professor of Sociology
at York University,
Toronto, Canada.

Copyright © 1970 Columbia University Press
SBN: 231-03323-0
Library of Congress Catalog Card Number: 79-110604
Printed in the United States of America

Southern Asian Institute Series

The Southern Asian Institute of Columbia University seeks a deeper understanding of that vast and tumultuous area stretching from West Pakistan in the west to Indonesia and the Philippines in the east. To understand the problems facing its leaders and its diverse peoples requires sustained training and research. Our publications are intended to share with others whatever concepts and propositions might be useful in forwarding economic and political development, in accommodating tradition and change, and in the search of each people for international security.

THIS BOOK
IS DEDICATED TO THE MEMORY OF
MAHATMA GANDHI
AND
JAWAHARLAL NEHRU
WHO INSPIRED THE SILENT REVOLUTION
THAT HAS AWAKENED THE TEEMING
MILLIONS IN VILLAGE INDIA

*Peasants have never been subdued by the
sword, and never will be. They do not know
the use of the sword, and they are not
frightened by the use of it by others. . . . Those
who defy death are free from all fear.*
M. K. Gandhi, *Hind Swaraj*

*I do not know, but I do feel, that
there is some magic in this moment of
transition from the old to the new, something
of that magic which one sees when the night
turns to day.*
Jawaharlal Nehru, *Independence and After*

Preface

THE ORTHOGRAPHY OF Indian words followed here is close to the original phonetics. This practice has been followed uniformly throughout the volume. For instance, in the word Nāmahaḷḷi, the dash above indicates a long vowel, and the dot below indicates a lingual.

The transliteration system is based on standard romanized words found in dictionaries of native languages and on prevalent pronunciation.

Indian terms are italicized on the first appearance only in each paper.

As editor, I wish to thank all the contributors for the time and effort they so generously offered.

I should like to thank Professor S. N. Eisenstadt for increasing the value of this volume by his succinct summary of the main findings of the papers.

I must place on record the assistance I have received in many ways from York University, Toronto.

Finally, I thank all my friends, too many to be named individually, for sustaining my enthusiasm.

York University, Toronto
January, 1970

K. ISHWARAN

Contents

CHANGE AND CONTINUITY IN INDIA'S VILLAGES

K. ISHWARAN

Introduction

I

AFTER CENTURIES OF COMPARATIVE isolation, the Asian village has emerged as an important element in the social, political, and economic processes of Asian nations. This development has been more than a merely political one. It has involved nothing less than the complex procedure of a total restructuring of the national societies of Asia.

Village society has come into closer relations with not only the national system but also the wider global community. No doubt this change was already under way even in the colonial period, but seldom as a deliberate process. With national liberation, a policy of deliberate socioeconomic development was begun with vast consequences for change in village Asia. The hopes and aspirations of the Asian countries are vitally linked to the efforts in the promoting of this development. Social scientists and planners have increasingly turned their attention to such processes. The importance of the study of peasant society and the changes that have overtaken it comes from the fact that the majority of the Asian people live in villages. In a very real sense, the battle for free Asia is being fought in her villages.

Broadly, the changes in Asian village society can be described as national-oriented and global-oriented. However, the two kinds of change are deeply related since the global diffusion of ideas, ideologies, and technology filters through the national systems. There have been profound changes, and they have created challenging problems. To meet such challenges, a number of institutional devices and mechanisms have been developed. The term "modernization" might be used to describe these adjustments. They include the processes of industrialization, urbanization, increased social and political mobilization, and an increasing ideological commitment to secularism.

India occupies an important place, not only in an Asian context, but also in a global context. In terms of her population, natural resources, technological skills, and political organization, she deserves special attention from all those interested in the peace and prosperity of the developing world. Of particular interest is the fact that she is the largest democracy in the world and that she is committed to the goal of over-all development within a democratic political framework. Against heavy odds India has managed to maintain a balance between the goals of political democracy and socioeconomic develpoment. India's prospects of modernization are perhaps among the highest in Asia. Should India fail in her peaceful revolution, the consequences might well affect adversely the prospects of stability and peace in Asia, if not in the world.

Though the diversity, complexity, and size of the country preclude easy generalization, it may perhaps be safely claimed that the future of India is inextricably bound up with the destiny of the millions in her villages. About 70 per cent of India's population lives in villages, though there has been a steady migration of population from the rural to the urban areas. For the first time in the country's long history the rural population has been given an opportunity to influence national policies through the new political order inaugurated after independence. As an essential part of this political revolution, a strategy of total socioeconomic change through planning, legislation, and large-scale persuasion has been launched. The combined effect of these policies on village society and life has been profound and far-reaching.

II

In the last two decades, a number of studies have appeared on the changes that are taking place in village India. Though we need many more such studies in order to acquire a deeper and more comprehensive understanding of the nature, content, and direction of such changes, perhaps the time is now ripe for an interim appraisal and stocktaking of the situation. These studies have generally established the need for two approaches: first, the need for analyzing social change in terms of multiple factors rather than in terms of any single factor; second, the need to correlate micro-anthropological studies with macro-sociological analysis. On the one hand, we need intensive field studies of village life, but, on the other hand, we also need to link up such studies in order to map the morphology and content of social change in wider terms.

The study of Indian village society is significant on many levels. For the policy-makers and planners, it is an indispensable guide. It is being increasingly realized[1] that planning strategy is a total strategy, not a narrow economic one, and that it needs to take into account the social and cultural parameters which determine the practicality of planning. For the social scientist, it offers intellectual challenges and the opportunity to test basic conceptual perspectives. The variety and complexity of social institutions, their interconnections, their internal as well as intergroup dynamics, and the processes of change that affect the internal structure as well as the dynamics of intergroup relationships are all problems that provide material for social scientists. They offer not only intellectual stimulation and satisfaction but also opportunities to rethink some of the crucial conceptual tools of social science, including perhaps the nature of human social behavior itself.

A brief but by no means exhaustive list of key areas for study would include caste, family, kinship, economy, polity, language, ecology, technology, and culture of the village. In such a study, the emphasis has to shift from the structural and static concern to a keener sense of the dynamism and change-orientation of the system.

In the past, and for obvious historical reasons, Indian students of village society tended to operate within the methodological and conceptual framework of British structural functionalism. Village society offered a convenient focus for such an approach. It was regarded as a simple, homogeneous society, in which structural problems were of primary importance and functions were relatively less emphasized. This resulted in a somewhat lopsided concern with structural continuity at the cost of structural change. The static structural models were determined less by the empirical data than by a priori Indological perspectives. Whether deliberately or not, the values taken over from Indological literature were built into such models. A classic instance of this tendency was the attempt to explain the jāti data in terms of the varna model. The empirical departures from the varna model tended to be not so much explained as explained away.

The concept of Sanskritization which has been widely used in discussions of social change and social mobility in India may be viewed as an offshoot of such structuralism. Essentially, the concept involved a prejudice in favor of the classical varna model. But recent studies of

[1] See A. K. Hanson, The Process of Planning: A Study of India's Five-Year Plans, 1950-1964 (London, Oxford University Press, 1966).

rural social change, including those in this volume, though they have not wholly denied the need for such a concept, have clearly established the limited explanatory value of the concept. In his study of Chanukhera, a village in eastern Uttar Pradesh, Singh pleads for a more sophisticated conceptual tool in analyzing social change. He emphasizes, for instance, the need for the concept of levels, which would account more satisfactorily for the structural dilemmas raised by social change. This is also Gough's point when she prefers the notion of structural change to the notion of positional change.

In my study of Shivapur,[2] I was constantly struck by the discrepancy between the picture offered in the classical Indological literature and the actual conditions prevalent in the villege. In other words, an adequate sociological picture of the Indian village will have to be firmly grounded in micro-studies of the village.

III

A more flexible and realistic methodology would involve not only a willingness to use a variety of concepts, or approaches, but also a willingness to relate the study of rural social change to the economic, political, and demographic aspects of the phenomena of change. There is, therefore, a clear need to place the process of social change in a multidimensional matrix. Berreman's paper here, for example, builds up a complex model of cultural drift on a multicentered basis. He uses a wide variety of factors such as geography, language, social organization, economy, and religion. Mencher emphasizes the need to distinguish between the ritualistic and economic aspects of caste behavior. Moreover, practically all the papers here relate social change in the village to political processes at different levels—the village *panchāyat*, the state and national legislatures.

Not only is social change multidimensional, but it is also related to the wider processes beyond the village world. The changes in Nāmahaḷḷi recorded by Beals, for instance, cannot be explained without reference to the impact of the nearby urban center, and even beyond to the world society. Elder's Rājpur undergoes changes in occupational structure under the impact of competitive technology introduced by forces outside

---

[2] K. Ishwaran, *Tradition and Economy in Village India* (London, Routledge and Kegan Paul, 1966) and *Shivapur: A South Indian Village* (London, Routledge and Kegan Paul, 1968).

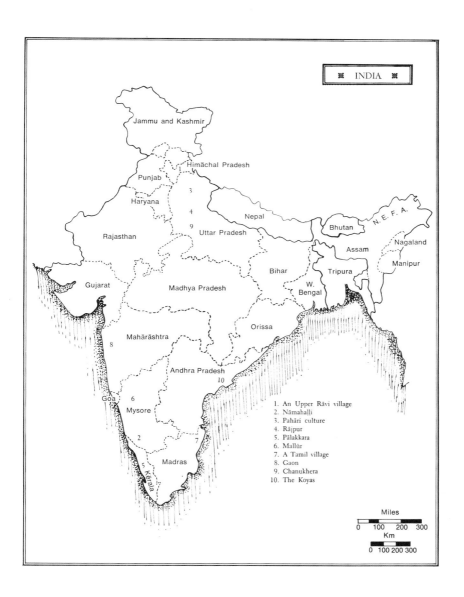

Jammu and Kashmir

Himāchal Pradesh

Punjab

Haryana

Rajasthan

3

4

9

Uttar Pradesh

Nepal

Bhutan

N.E.F.A.

Assam

Nagaland

Manipur

Gujarat

Madhya Pradesh

Bihar

W. Bengal

Tripura

Mahārāshtra

Orissa

8

Andhra Pradesh

Goa

6

Mysore

2

10

7

5

Madras

Kerala

1. An Upper Rāvi village
2. Nāmahaḷḷi
3. Pahāri culture
4. Rājpur
5. Pālakkara
6. Mallūr
7. A Tamil village
8. Gaon
9. Chanukhera
10. The Koyas

Miles

0 100 200 300

Km

0 100 200 300

the village. In fact, Gough takes an explicit stand on the issue when she argues that village studies are meaningful only "within a framework of knowledge and theory about what is happening to the larger society—in this case, to Kērala: beyond that to India, and beyond that still, to the relations between former colonies and both new and old power-centers in the Western and Communist worlds." In other words, it is not only necessary to compare, analyze, and collate empirical evidence in order to arrive at models of social change, but it is equally important to realize that each field study of a village cannot be understood except as part of a complex system of coordinates.

A more serious conceptual difficulty in interpreting social change in rural India relates to the question of modernization. It seems clear now that the social changes in village India cannot be interpreted in terms of a simple tradition-modernity model. This model assumes a sharp polarity between what are posited as traditional and modern society.[3] Further, it is assumed that change must proceed toward a single model of modernity. The model of modernity turns out to be an idealization and abstraction of the social, economic, and political processes that took place in Europe in the eighteenth and nineteenth centuries.[4] Broadly speaking, these are subsumed under the rubric of industrialization and what Bendix calls democratization. It is also agreed that the change from traditional order to the modern order presupposes a destruction of the traditional order. In other words, the model of change assumes (1) a sharp dichotomy between the traditional and modern orders, including the notion of mutual exclusiveness, and (2) the change from the one to the other predicted in terms of a historically deterministic pattern, that is, it must take place in a certain predetermined sequence.

The model has been challenged in recent studies.[5] The result has been a fairly fundamental reorientation of the concept of social change. As Bendix has argued, the change from traditional order to the modern is neither automatic nor unilinear.[6] It also involves the possibility of a breakdown in the process of modernization.[7] A crucial strategy in

---

[3] Joseph R. Gusfield, "Tradition and Modernity: Misplaced Polarities in the Study of Social Change," *American Journal of Sociology* (1966), pp. 351-62.

[4] Reinhard Bendix, *Nation-Building and Citizenship* (New York, John Wiley, 1964).

[5] For example, by Gusfield, Bendix, and Eisenstadt.

[6] Reinhard Bendix, "Tradition and Modernity Reconsidered," *Comparative Studies in Society and History,* IX, No. 3 (April, 1967), 313-46.

[7] S. N. Eisenstadt, *Modernization: Protest and Change* (Englewood Cliffs, N.J., Prentice-Hall, 1966).

meeting the danger of such a breakdown is the institutionalization of change. It is here that the inadequacy of the assumption that modernization should involve a destruction of the traditional institutions becomes apparent. I propose that any strategy of modernization should emphasize the change-potential of traditional institutions. If this is granted, it is possible to analyze social change in respect of traditional institutions like the caste, the family, kinship, etc., in a more consistent way. These institutions are not always, and not necessarily, hostile to the process of modernization, and one must be constantly on one's guard against any naïve assumption that whatever is traditional is *ipso facto* hostile to change. Mencher's paper illustrates what I have in mind. Her study of a village in Madras State shows that the caste institution has adopted new roles in response to new socioeconomic and political conditions, and that it is not necessarily in conflict with a continued emphasis on orthodoxy in ritual and family matters. By using considerable historical material she maintains that caste is being transformed into something other than what it was in the eighteenth and nineteenth centuries. In short, I am pleading for a model of change from which the built-in prejudice of evolutionary determinism and disguised ethnocentrism are eliminated. Such a model would go far in dissolving too sharp a polarity between caste and class, or urban and rural, or continuity and change. It would also mean that, when there is a breakdown of modernization, there is no automatic reversion to the premodern system. Even revivalism cannot be interpreted as a simple return to the old order.

IV

The model of social change proposed here involves a fundamental revision of certain stereotype notions of village India. It has been held that village society has not changed and does not show any positive desire for change. But this has never been true in the past, and is certainly not true of the present. We have sufficient historical evidence to indicate that caste structure, occupational structure, and the economic and political relationships of rural India have been undergoing constant change.[8] In the pre-British period, such changes came about in response to changes in demographic or ecological conditions. Under the British

---

[8] See Dharma Kumār, *Land and Caste in South India* (Cambridge, Cambridge University Press, 1965).

rule, there were changes in social mobility, in the economic system, and in the general style of life itself. But since independence, the rate of change and its scope have gone up dramatically, and its direction and content have taken a revolutionary turn. All the papers in this volume testify to the existence of a number of processes of change at different levels.

Before offering alternative explanations of the nature of such change, we might take as our point of departure a brief examination of some of the influential concepts used currently in explaining, interpreting, and evaluating social change. There have been three crucial concepts, namely, Sanskritization, dominant caste, and westernization. In my view, these concepts are inadequate for explanatory purposes. They have seldom been rigorously defined or consistently applied.

Sanskritization, in many ways the most important of the concepts, has proved to be the most unsatisfactory. It is too static, and therefore basically inadequate to cope with processes of rapid and complex change. It is too much tied to the varṇa model. Even if the charge that it is Brāhmanocentric can be partially met by making its institutional referent more inclusive, say, by admitting other models than the Brāhman, such as the Lingāyat, the Kshatriya, tribalization, etc., it still remains tied to one aspect of social mobility, that is, ritual escalation. This is because it still holds rigidly to the varṇa model of a pure, closed hierarchical social order. While Sanskritization might account for certain kinds of upward social mobility, it cannot account for any social movement outside this order. In the end, the positive and constructive aspects of movements for change have been played down. In particular, their aspiration to re-order social and cultural values in a new pattern has been insufficiently recognized. The protest[9] aspect of ritual escalation has been ignored because of the tendency to cast all ritual escalation in terms of a simple imitation model. It can be argued that imitation was primarily a protest against the injunction that a certain ritual behavior was the special prerogative of a particular group. The egalitarian implications of such protest cannot be entirely explained by the imitation model of ritual escalation. In view of the arguments so far advanced, there seems to be a good case for seeking more complex models of social change in contemporary India.

[9] See Eisenstadt, *Modernization*, for the implication of the term.

V

The second, and related, concept usually invoked to explain the process of social change has been the concept of the dominant caste. The social changes that are taking place are regarded as changes that have favored the dominant caste groups in Indian society. But this concept is essentially related to the varṇa model of vertical heirarchy.

However, the social realities in the village rarely, if ever, approximate to the dominant caste situation. If one observes village society, one finds that people start with the assumption that their own caste occupies a central position, and then count the other caste groups hierarchically to either side of their central position. In such a situation, there can be no stable or unanimous picture of hierarchy. People certainly do not use any varna model in reckoning their position. In Shivapur[10] I found that the social system of the village cannot be explained in terms of a dominant caste.

The dominant caste under the varṇa model is regarded as the watchdog of the pluralistic culture of the village. It has been argued that the dominant caste controls the process of social change by determining which group moves and to what extent it Sanskritzes itself. Perhaps such a role was played to some extent by the upper castes in pre-British India. But a clearer and more cogent historical picture of the process has yet to be constructed. In the absence of such a composite picture it would be difficult and misleading to generalize about the past. But so far as the colonial and postcolonial periods are concerned, it is clear that the upper castes have not been able to control the direction of social change by preventing the lower castes from westernizing themselves. They have certainly not stopped them in their efforts to acquire education, government employment, new styles of dressing, or even a sense of superiority. There is adequate evidence that the lower castes enjoy social and occupational mobility through educational or economic change.[11]

The dominant caste concept has frequently been used to explain the Indian political process at various levels. It has been argued[12] that democ-

---

[10] See my *Tradition and Economy in Village India*.

[11] See, for instance, Mencher's paper in this volume. She points out that the low-caste Paraiyans have been trying to improve their status economically.

[12] See, for instance, V. M. Sirsikar, *Political Behaviour in India* (Bombay, Manaktala, 1965) and also M. N. Srinivas, *Social Change in Modern India* (Berkeley, University of California Press, 1966), p. 153.

racy strengthens the dominant caste since numerical superiority is the foundation of electoral success. But as against this, it can be argued that the dominant caste seldom presents a unified front. It is split along more than one line. There are personal conflicts between ambitious leaders that break up the unity of the caste support. There are party interests, regional interests, and local factional pulls that constantly undermine the strength of a caste, even if it might command numerical majority. Sometimes, better organizational skills or economic and educational advantages can give certain groups disproportionate political influence or else mere numerical strength.

However, seldom do we encounter a clear-cut case of numerical dominance in an absolute sense. What we get is a situation in which no group is numerically dominant. This leads to the need for an intricate arrangement of political alliances. In my study of Mallūr, I have elaborated the argument that a realistic political model for Indian politics at the village level would be what I have called a coalition model. Since no caste group finds itself in a position to do without the support of other groups it is compelled to seek alliances on the basis of pragmatic bargains. Perhaps the coalition model could be applied to the political process at other levels as well.[13] Even a minority group can play a decisive role in tilting the precarious political balance in the direction favorable to it.

As a concept, the dominant caste suffers from imprecision. Since dominance can be viewed in terms of multiple factors such as numerical strength, economic power, and ritual status, it cannot be used effectively in analyzing sociological data unless a composite quantitative scale combining the different factors is constructed. So far, this has not been done. Therefore, both the conceptual and the empirical inadequacy of the dominant caste model should warrant at best a cautious and limited use of it.

Further, there is also need to realize that not merely the notion of the dominant caste but the political role of caste itself has been applied indiscriminately in the interpretation of Indian politics. All the arguments against the usefulness of the dominant caste concept remain valid against a purely caste-oriented interpretation of Indian politics. At best,

[13] See, for instance, Myron Weiner, *Party-Building in a New Nation* (Chicago, University of Chicago Press, 1967). The Congress Party is here seen as successful in terms of its ability to forge alliances between groups.

caste is one among the many factors that go into the fascinating calculus of politics. Language, regionalism, ideology, party loyalty, economic interests, and personal conflicts complicate the Indian political process. It is seldom noticed, for example, that Indian national politics cannot be explained easily in terms of caste. Other factors in a shifting pattern of bargain alliances better explain the political process at the national level. The political parties may be seen as mechanisms that facilitate the formation of such patterns of alliance.

VI

As for the concept of westernization, it can be contested on the main ground that it is a narrower term than modernization. While it is true that historically the modernization process was initiated under the impact of the West, it certainly is not true that it has continued to be a unilinear movement toward a merely Western model. Moreover, even the idea of a single westernization model is a heroic abstraction of a number of historical processes that have shown considerable local and regional variations in the modernization of Western society itself.

In so far as the values and ideals of modernization are concerned, whatever their historical origins, they have become so diffused globally and, what is important, have been adapted to such a variety of local conditions that the term "modernization" appears to be preferable to speaking of westernization. It may of course be argued that there are many ways of being modernized, and that westernization is after all one of them. By the same token, India can experience her own unique pattern of modernization.

Bendix[14] has suggested that, in this sense, all development remains partial development in relation to the ideal of modernization. It would be possible to draw up a list of crucial goals in such an ideal—such as equality, rationality, freedom, and progress—and then allow for a great variety of pattern-formation in the interrelationship between these goals. The changing social scene in India might be interpreted in terms of efforts to realize such goals, but through processes and mechanisms conditioned by a distinctively Indian content.

[14] *Nation-Building and Citizenship*, p. 9. See also the unpublished paper "Partial Modernization" presented by Dietrich Rueschemeyer at a conference on Partial Modernization at the University of Toronto in March, 1966.

VII

The papers presented in this volume display a remarkable thematic unity. They tackle common problems, articulate similar concerns, utilize the same kinds of methodological tools, and arrive at a broad consensus with regard to their interpretation of social, economic, and political processes.

Their temporal framework also brings these studies into a common focus. They all deal with the developments that have taken place in the post-independence years. However, this narrowing of the time perspective has not meant any loss of historical depth. The general criticism of the structural-functional approach and the systems approach that they ignore the historical dimension cannot be made against these studies. Apart from the emphasis on the element of time that derives from an emphasis on process, the papers consciously bring out the historical setting of the situations they have analyzed in terms of empirical data. In the case of Mencher, such a dimension is provided by relevant references to eighteenth- and nineteenth-century demographic movements. In Gough's paper, the historical framework is considerably elaborated in terms of three distinct historical phases—the feudal, the colonial-capitalist, and the democratic, state-sponsored. In Tyler's paper we even have an attempt to offer a conjectural history of the Koya society prior to 1808. On the whole, the papers maintain a balance between chronological sweep and chronological close-up.

They all record the processes of change in the areas of their study, and offer interpretations of the changes in terms of multicausal models. They avoid naïve explanations in terms of any single factor, such as caste, and they constantly keep in sight the complex interconnection between the different aspects of change. For instance, they take into account such diverse factors as language, caste, religion, technology, education, demographic changes, and the political-bureaucratic system. Some of them explicitly mention the term "modernization," as does Beals's paper on Nāmahaḷḷi, but all are trying to relate changes to such a process. Yet the kind of modernization they assume is no simple model. In fact, what they grope toward is a pattern of *partial modernization* in which traditional institutions are modified in terms of their structure or function, but seldom totally rejected. They also emphasize that the traditional and the modern components of the process of change have no single, uniform pattern of mutual relationship. But they all insist that the process of change usually utilizes the traditional elements in society without totally destroying them.

The papers also demonstrate what is perhaps the most revolutionary aspect of India's changing rural world—the systematic and institutional involvement of the remote rural populations in the larger national political or ideological processes. They also illustrate the impact of the technological and economic forces that impinge on village society from outside. An important phenomenon that they call attention to is the ability of the rural society to meet the challenge of change, and its ability to accommodate such change without suffering institutional disruption. Indeed, the traditional order appears to have been, though not always, the main mechanism through which the shock of change has been absorbed and constructively accommodated.

As implied in these studies, village society, then, is neither chaotically fragmented by the impact of modernization nor has it totally rejected such an impact. This would mean that rural society, by and large, has accepted the challenge of change, and that it has been undergoing a quiet revolution. Not to notice its ability to retain part of its heritage is to miss the essence of the changes occurring in village India.

VIII

All the contributors to this volume document, analyze, and interpret social change in different parts of rural India. There is complete agreement in their findings with regard to the fact of change. On the basis of their studies, it is possible to answer certain theoretical questions about social change in Indian villages, the answers to which are offered here not only as a contribution to the theoretical understanding of the nature, content, direction, and mechanism of such change, but also as a basis on which more effective and realistic socioeconomic planning can be done in India. The officially sponsored surveys are usually quantitative, and they seldom succeed in getting behind a mass of figures and tables to come to grips with the realities of social processes at the village level. Moreover, they are often conducted with the help of investigators whose technical skill is rarely up to the required specifications. More often than not, they are shelved away in stacks in offices and allowed to accumulate dust while nobody really bothers about them. This volume is specifically offered to help the planners locate the channels of social change and the barriers to change, so that they might formulate policies effectively geared to the sociological realities of Indian village life.

The crucial theoretical issues can be framed as follows: What is the nature of social change? Which areas of village society are undergoing change? What is the content and goal of such change? What are the channels of social change? What are the intrinsic and extrinsic sources of social change? What are the prospects for future change?

The first question regarding the nature of social change is, in fact, a comprehensive question, and it cannot really be answered unless the other issues are settled. Therefore, we may postpone consideration of a broad, conceptual model of social change until we have answered the other questions. If village society is changing, then what light do the papers here throw on the areas of change? No important area of social existence seems to have escaped the process of change. Beals reports that there was change in village organizational techniques, as manifested in the organization and operation of new types of institutions like the chit fund, the team, and the club. He also records change in the networks of communication. Berreman notes the changes in speech, ritual practice, dress, technology, and in the general culture of the people. Elders and Newell both record that the *jajmāni* system has weakened, but they also admit that it still has strength.

Gough notes that religious and ideological changes can find political expression; both the Īzhavas and Harijans have abandoned the Sanskritization process in preference to political activism through communication. Elder finds that ideological motivation on the part of the *kām karnewālā* caste of Chamārs has prompted them to give up the polluting profession of sweeping. Economic changes are noted by Gough, Mencher, and Singh. These relate not merely to institutions (Gough) but also to motivation (Mencher). The aspiration to economic improvement is underlined in most of the studies. There is also increased politicization of groups such as the Pālakkara Īzhavas and Harijans, the Gaddi caste of Himāchal Pradesh, the Bālutādars of Mahārāshtra, and the Rajputs of Chanukhera. My study of Mallūr shows changes in the economic system and material culture, and considerable politicization.

However, this picture of change must be balanced somewhat against the fact that certain aspects have proved to be less receptive to change in certain areas. Beals notes that increasing urbanization does not totally eliminate the rural element in Nāmahaḷḷi. Elder points out that the occupational changes in Rājpur leave unaffected certain core jajmāni groups like Brāhmans, Naīs (barbers), and Bhangis (sweepers). Mencher distinguishes between the relative persistence of the ritualistic aspect of caste and its changing economic role. Newell argues that while there is change in the means of social change, there is no change in its direction. Orenstein's Gaon modifies the *bālutā* system but does not abandon it. Singh sees a great deal of persistence in the pollution-purity norms, rituals, endogamy, kinship ties, and the jajmāni system. He also emphasizes the continuity of the core values of the Hindu world. In short, the traditional system has not been destroyed but it has either acquired new functions or modified its structure to some extent.

The answer to the question "What is the nature of social change?" is that it is a multifactored, multidimensional, and multimotivated process. While the emerging pattern clearly moves away from older processes like ritual escalation, it also retains to a considerable degree some traditional elements. Of course, the specific relationship between the two components differs from area to area, and the only generalization one can offer is that the traditional and the modern coexist. I propose to designate this as a model of an *Indian pattern of modernization*. Its paradigm is adaptive change and evolutionary absorption of the challenge of change. The traditional system is not destroyed, but, as Mencher suggests, it becomes an important channel of change.

The channels or the agents of social change are also equally multivariant. In Nāmahaḷḷi, the bearers of change are the young factory employees, and the process of change is multicentered. It involves traditional networks of communication within the caste and the family, though it also employs modern communication networks like the factory and the office. Berreman offers a complex mechanism of change, which he calls "cultural drift." It involves a condition of isolation in which a subgroup of culture develops along independent lines. This process of divergent or differential cultural change is supposed to involve variation, selection, and transmission, but in a context of relative isolation. Elder emphasizes impersonal channels like technology or demography but he draws attention to the efforts of the sweepers (Bhangis) to seek change consciously in response to an egalitarian ideology. In Gough's Pālakkara, the agents of change are not the upper castes but the lower-caste groups of Izhavas and Harijans motivated by the modern ideal of equality. In this case we have the interesting example of a change initially attempted through the traditional channel of Sanskritization being given up in favor of the modern political channel of election and ideological mobilization. In Mencher's village in Madras, the channel of change is traditional since caste is used as a means of promoting modernized ideals such as economic improvement or educational advancement. The low-caste Paraiyans articulate their aspirations to improved economic status through the channel of caste solidarity. This process has also meant, even if indirectly, a movement toward equality of social status. In the case of Newell's Himāchal Pradesh, we see new channels of change—the bureaucracy and the political party. Both these new channels have connections reaching beyond the village. In Orenstein's Gaon, too, the government officials and the political party constitute important channels of change. The need to utilize the new channels of change undermined the traditional leadership of the Rajput caste in the village. In Chanukhera the upper-caste groups of Rajputs and Brāhmans are the bearers of technological innovation. They have been responsible for the introduction of tractors and fertilizers. Contrary to the view that conflicts in the village lead to negative consequences, we find that in this village in eastern Uttar Pradesh conflict has been the mechanism through which social change has occurred. Singh notes three such conflicts: the Brāhmans versus the landlords, the tenants versus the landlords, and the ex-tenants versus the ex-landlords. In the case of the Koyas, we find no effective internal channels of social change. In Mallūr, the channels of change are primarily internal, though internally initiated changes gain additional impulse from external agencies like the market economy or the bureaucracy.

Even this brief listing of the channels of changed mapped in these papers shows their variety and complexity. Change can be seen to be channeled through both traditional and modern mechanisms. What is common are the goals that are sought through these channels. These common goals are, as we have noted, related to such processes of modernization as equality, a rational-secular world view, freedom, and material progress.

Finally, we may analyze the causes of social change as revealed here. They fall into two broad categories—extrinsic and intrinsic causes. They can also be classified on the basis of their content—technological, economic, religious, demographic, political, and ideological. But as a matter of fact, such a separation of the causes is valid only for theoretical purposes, for in concrete situations they intermesh with each other considerably. In particular, the process of social change cannot be explained exclusively in terms of either internal or external factors. It is when they reinforce each other that we have the best conditions for effective change. This is a lesson that needs to be recognized by planners because otherwise they may fail to tap the change-potential in the villages.

The source of change may be a factory in a nearby urban area, with which the village may have established multiple relationships—economic, social, and political. This is the situation in Nāmahalli, but as Beals takes care to note, modernization is not an automatic result of good jobs available in the factory. It involves the traditional communication networks as well. The external source of change cannot become effective without some cooperation from the traditional order.

In the case of Berremen's lower Himalayan village, the cause of change is external. The rapid post-independence assimilation of the area into the general national political system and the conesquent weakening of geographical isolation produce changes in the direction of emulating the plains people in the style of life. But this process is also related to the process of status emulation already at work.

Gough explains social change in terms of (1) changing relations in the society's subsistence base and (2) its changing relations with the wider society. Under (1), which can be stimulated by both internal and external causes, she would include technological and demographic changes. Under (2), she would include relations with the national or local governments or other prominent centers of power. Admitting that the first set of conditions involves a Marxist emphasis upon changes in the organization of production, she qualifies her economic determinism by recognizing the equal primacy of noneconomic factors like political processes or legislation or ideological inspiration, emanating from outside. However, change is not regarded as an entirely externally oriented development, for she notices that changes take place partly within the existing value system. In other words, internal factors have a positive role to play in the process of change.

Elder mentions three causes: competitive technology, increase in population, and ideological motivation. Of these, the first is clearly external, and the third is partly external and partly internal. No matter where an ideology comes from, it cannot be an effective element in the process of change unless it is accepted by the people. Elder further stipulates that change cannot become effective unless it is seen to be economically acceptable. Mencher also emphasizes socioeconomic factors. Newell notes the impact of factors like land hunger, sex distribution, and geographical location. Orenstein points out the importance of technological and ideological factors.

While external factors like technological innovations, demographic changes, geographical or natural conditions, ideological motivation, and ideological urges are emphasized variously as causes of change, there appears to be a consensus with regard to the importance of the ultravillage political processes and the bureaucracy as external factors. In other words, there seems to be substantial agreement that the introduction and operation of the political contribution of democracy at all levels—from the village panchāyat to the national government—has been one of the most important sources of social change. Not only does democracy release processes of social change, but the programs of socioeconomic development initiated by the government also strengthen the process of social change. Some observers have tended to see the two factors as distinct or even mutually hostile. But the studies here show that they usually tend to support each other in bringing about change.

A factor which has not been adequately recognized but which is of crucial significance in the effective channeling of change is the internally generated change-potential of village society. These studies show that village society is dynamic enough to accept change and responsive enough to assess it without serious institutional dislocations. This aspect is perhaps brought out most clearly in the case of Mallūr, though it seems to have been assumed in the study of other villages.

IX

If the papers gathered here are any indication of the future, the modernization process has a sound start. But it has not meant an abrupt breach with tradition. It has, on the contrary, meant a process of social change in which the traditional institutions have been peacefully modified to usher in a new life of hope for the villager.

It is, of course, arguable that the quiet revolution that has been slowly transforming the Indian countryside has yet to consolidate its gains, and that the outcome of the struggle to establish a new egalitarian order is as yet uncertain. But if the revolution fails it would mean more than the failure of a national experiment. In the context of an explosive Asian and world situation, it would mean a potential threat to the peace and stability of the Asian world. But that is only one of the possibilities. This volume is offered as an effort on the part of social scientists to avert such an eventuality by providing some understanding of the processes of social change that are at work in village India.

S. N. EISENSTADT

Prologue: Some Remarks on Patterns of Change in Traditional and Modern India

I

THIS COLLECTION OF PAPERS is of great value from two points of view. First, it presents very variegated and interesting materials on processes of change in modern—mostly contemporary—India. Second, it enables us to reevaluate the relations between patterns of change in traditional and modern India.

The various essays presented here constitute part of the recent upsurge of research on social change in modern India which has brought out, more and more, the necessity of looking at this change from a broad historical perspective.[1] Many of these studies tend to stress aspects of continuity between the process of change in traditional and more modern settings. However, the materials presented here also point out—perhaps to a somewhat greater degree than other recent research on India—some of the major points of discontinuity between "traditional" and "modern" settings and processes of change. In this way they tend, on the one hand, to belie the assertion—sometimes made in recent works on tradition and modernity in general and in those on India in particular[2]—

S. N. Eisenstadt is Professor of Sociology and was Dean in 1967-69 of the Eliezer Kaplan School of Economics and Social Sciences at the Hebrew University of Jerusalem. Parts of the research on which this paper is based were supported by a grant from the Wenner-Gren Foundation for Anthropological Research.

[1] See the pioneering work of Milton Singer, ed., *Traditional India: Structure and Change* (Philadelphia, American Folklore Society, 1959); M. Singer and B. Cohn, eds., *Structure and Change in Indian Society* (Chicago, Aldine Publishing Co., 1968); and also M. N. Srinivas, *Social Change in Modern India* (Berkeley, University of California Press, 1966).

[2] See, for instance, J. C. Heesterman, "Tradition in Modern India," *Bijdragem tot de Taal-, Land- en Volkenkunde*, Deel 119 (1963), pp. 237-53, and to some extent also Joseph R. Gusfield, "Tradition and Modernity: Misplaced Polarities in the Study of Social Change," *American Journal of Sociology* (1966), pp. 351-62.

that the distinction between traditional and modern social or cultural orders is meaningless. At the same time, they help us very much to pinpoint and clarify the nature of this distinction.[3]

II

The materials presented in these essays attest to the very great variety of processes and patterns of change in modern and traditional India alike—a variety which is closely connected with the great heterogeneity of that complex social and cultural entity which has been called India. Thus, for instance, the paper by Berreman analyzes patterns of change in cultural patterns and customs in Pahārī culture, whose social and cultural organization seems to differ greatly from the "usual" caste system of India. Most of the other papers provide very illuminating material on the heterogeneity of the very organization of castes in different regions in India. They indicate—in line with much other research—that the most important of these differences are the number of castes living together in any region or locality, the identity of the dominant caste, the relative economic, political, or social standing of different castes, and the details of the *jajmāni* relation among different castes to the (traditional) center of political power. They also show that these differences necessarily greatly affect the response of the various localities and castes to the processes of change in general and to "modern" changes in particular. Thus, for instance, Mencher reports that some of the castes tend to use the new opportunities opened up by the processes of change in order to bolster up their economic position as landowners while others use these opportunities in order to enable their children to attain new educational facilities through which they may be able to obtain various governmental positions.

It seems that the variable response to situations of change is due not only to the general characteristics of any given group in the broad, India-wide hierarchy of castes but also to a combination of some such general characteristics with various local circumstances and traditions—the latter being probably of somewhat greater importance than the former. Moreover, whatever evidence can be found in the papers presented here, as

[3] See, in greater detail, my review of several recent works dealing with this problem, entitled "Some New Looks at the Problem of Relations between Traditional Societies and Modernization," *Economic Development and Cultural Change,* Vol. XVI (April, 1968).

well as in other research reports, indicates that a similar, even if not identical, pattern of selective response to change has existed in historical, "traditional" settings. There, too, different caste groups in different localities also reacted selectively to situations of change and to the problems and opportunities arising in them—and quite often castes which were similar or parallel in terms of some India-wide ideology or hierarchy (if it is at all possible to make such countrywide comparisons) might have reacted differently in different localities. Thus in one place a Vaishya caste might opt for political or administrative channels of advancement while in another locality a somewhat similar caste might opt for economic, commercial, industrial, or rural (landownership) opportunities.

The great variety of responses to change, rooted as it is in the great heterogeneity of India—a heterogeneity compounded several times over by the existence of "tribal" groups, on the one hand, and by the overlay of Muslim culture since the Moghul conquest, on the other hand—necessarily raises the question as to whether it is unique to India or to be found in other "traditional" societies and cultures.

It is, of course, obvious that many of these variations, such as those between tribal and settled groups, among different localities or cultural groups, can be found in many other traditional societies—be it China, Indonesia, or any large-scale Muslim or Christian society. And yet, it seems that this heterogeneity of sociocultural patterns, and especially of responses to change, is more pronounced in India than in many other traditional societies.

In India this variety went beyond merely local variability in that it affected the very core of Indian civilization or tradition—the caste system—in its ideological and structural aspects alike. At the same time, paradoxically, the core of Indian tradition seems to have shown a far greater resilience or continuity than many another Great Traditional Civilization. No traditional political center, be it Chinese or any of the Indonesian or Muslim centers; no other Great Religion—Islam, Buddhism, or Confucianism—evinced such great continuity in the face of such seemingly great heterogeneity in its core.

This combination of heterogeneity in the core of the tradition with a continuity of identity can be best seen in the pattern of changes and in the modes of response to them that have developed in traditional India.

Traditional Indian society and civilization were indeed undergoing continuous processes of change. These changes were mostly in various local patterns and customs, in dynasties, in the geographical scope of principalities, in the relative spread of different religions, or in the settlement of tribal groups. But simultaneously there also took place in Indian history more far-reaching changes: changes in the levels of social, economic, and religious differentiation; changes giving rise to new types of economic or political organization based on wider political orientations (as in the Kingdom of Ashoka) as well as to new levels of religious organization—most fully manifest in the spread of Buddhism or Jainism.

These processes of change were, of course, of different scope, dimension, and import. But they all impinged, to some degree, on the existing patterns of social life and cultural traditions, undermining and threatening the social and psychological security of the members, while at the same time opening up before them social and cultural horizons and vistas of participation in new institutional and cultural orders.

In this way they created many new problems for Indian society, its elites, and its members; they always called for some reorganization of the individual's perceptual field, patterns of behavior, and social participation, and of the relevant organization, institutional, and symbolic frameworks.

The reactions of Indian civilization, of the major social and cultural groups in India, to these various changes were characterized throughout its history by a relatively great variety of responses, with what may be called the "adaptive" response being the most predominant. By "adaptive" is meant that type of response to change which is characterized mainly by a great readiness on the part of the members of the traditional group to undertake new tasks, to participate in various new groups, through the development of a high degree of internal differentiation and diversification of roles and tasks and by an increasing incorporation of such new roles within these various groups.

It was this type of response to situations of change that was the most predominant throughout Indian history. True enough, other types of response—such as resistance to change or militant neotraditionalism—could also be found very often in India, but on the whole they became predominant only in rare cases.

Perhaps the most important mechanism of this pattern of adaptation to change—which is fully documented in the various chapters of this volume—has been the great multiplicity of different reference orientations of structural channels of advancement that tended to develop in Indian society. Srinivas and many others have shown us that at least two types of such mobility can be discerned.[4] One is what may be called "simple" mobility in which different caste groups attempt to improve their relative—mostly local—positions in the economic and political spheres. The other is the so-called process of Sanskritization, that is, the process by which different caste groups try to improve their standing according to the central value system by attempting to assimilate in their styles of life various aspects of Brāhman culture, thus hoping to attain higher legitimate standing in the ritual field.

The papers presented here illustrate abundantly that with regard to both these types of mobility the number of ideal reference points or norms and of structural channels of advancement have been very numerous. They included a very great variety of both economic and political channels of legitimate access to positions or symbols of higher standing.

The existence of such a great variety of legitimate channels of access contrasts very sharply with the situation in other traditional societies— for instance, with the relative homogeneity of the bureaucratic literati channel in China or of court service in many patrimonial Southeast Asian societies. Indeed, it can be postulated that it is this variety of channels of access that enabled most of the active group in India to use the existing traditional symbols to find answers—within the realms of the existing social and cultural order—to new problems and situations.

How then can these characteristics of heterogeneity and patterns of response to change be explained? And what light do they throw on the relations between processes of change in traditional and modern India?

III

It seems that the root of the explanation of this paradox of continuity of cultural identity in face of great heterogeneity, or variety, as well as of the predominance of the adaptive response in situations of change in the very core of Indian tradition, can be found, first, in the structure of centers of Indian society and civilization, and second, in some of the major aspects of the contents of the Indian value system and of its structural repercussions; that is, in the nature of the Brāhmanic value system and especially of the structure of the caste system.

From the point of view of the structure of centers the most impor-

[4] See Srinivas, *Social Change in Modern India*, especially chapters 1 and 3.

tant aspect of Indian civilization is that it has been the only great historical civilization which throughout the march of history maintained its cultural identity without being tied to any given political framework. This is true not only of the last centuries of Muslim and later English rule but even of the period before that. Although there did develop in India small and large states and semi-imperial centers, there did not develop any single state with which the cultural tradition was identified. The basic religious and cultural orientations, the specific identity of Indian civilization, were not necessarily tied with any particular political or imperial framework.

The core of Indian identity was the Brāhmanic system of values, with its emphasis on the conception of parallelism between cosmic and social purity and pollution and on the manifestation of this parallelism in the ritual and social spheres. It was this Brāhmanic ideology that can be said to have constituted the major center of Indian civilization, with the various political units serving mostly as secondary and—except later under the Moghul and British rules—rather discontinuous centers.

But although this value system constituted the central focus of Indian identity, it was not organized as a homogeneous, unified center. It was constituted in a series of networks and many organizational-ritual subcenters in the form of temples, sects, etc.[5]

On the other hand, the various political centers, although themselves organizationally more compact, were not continuous nor did they serve as major foci of Indian cultural identity.

Thus, we find in India, in comparison with other great traditional civilizations, an almost unique situation in that whatever political centers tended to develop were usually partial and relatively "weak" in terms of the major orientations of the cultural systems and the commitments they could command thereby.[6]

The second aspect of Indian society which is of great importance for our analysis is closely related to the place of the political system in the system of stratification and to the internal cohesion of broader social groups and strata. The essential fact here is the very high degree of au-

[5] See McKim Marriott, "Changing Channels of Cultural Transmission in Indian Civilization," in V. F. Ray, ed., Intermediate Societies (Seattle, American Ethnological Society, 1959).

[6] See on this, in greater detail and in a comparative setting, S. N. Eisenstadt, "Transformation of Social, Political and Cultural Orders in Modernization," American Sociological Review, Vol. XXX (October, 1965).

tonomy evinced by these groups in terms of their internal identity. Parallel to the relative independence of the cultural traditions from the political center, the whole complex of castes, villages, and the various networks of cultural communication were also to a very high degree autonomous and self-regulating in terms of their own cultural and social identity, but with limited recourse to the political center or centers.

This was also to no small degree related to the discrepancy between the ideal Brāhmanic ideology of cultural and social order and the concrete patterns of social organizations. In theory, as is well known, the different caste categories or units were defined as countrywide and therefore in principle also engendered a countrywide caste consciousness and organization.

In reality, however, there did not exist such a unified countrywide hierarchy and caste organization—just as there did not exist the close functions, positions, ritual standing, and use of resources that was assumed in the official ideology. (Curiously enough, it was probably only the British who, by incorporating caste classification into their census, gave the sharpest push to the establishment of some such unified hierarchy.)

True enough, the Brāhmanic ideology and system of worship was in a sense India-wide, and served, as we have already indicated above, as a focus for the over-all basic cultural identity of the society. Moreover, among the same Brāhman groups—as well as among other, especially higher, castes—there did also develop to some—even if limited—degree wider social contacts. But on the whole the basis of caste organization and interrelation was local. In practice there were hundreds—if not thousands—of caste organizations organized locally, in villages, regions, and principalities.

The ideal of the caste division of labor, focused on countrywide ritual order, could not be applied on this regional or local level. With regard to the use of both political power and money, there developed, on this level, a great variety of activities which could not be bound by the ritual caste prescriptions. First of all, there was no full correspondence between the various occupational positions and caste categories. The number of the former was very great and was becoming more diversified. This very diversification often tended to create somewhat independent hierarchies of status which could undermine the status of local groups of Brāhmans and serve as starting points for the attainment of new caste status, often changing the existing caste order in general and the inter-relations and mutual obligations between different castes in particular.

The relations between the Brāhmans and the political powers bring out even more the limits of the pure ideological pattern in which the political order was subservient to the ritual. While this remained true on the ideological level, yet the concrete dependence of Brāhmans or the rulers for the upholding of their relative status was very great.[7] In many, if not most cases, it was up to the rulers to define the relative ritual standing of various caste groups. Hence they were able both to exert better "prices" from the Brāhmans and also to change to some degree the actual conditions of access to the upper ritual and other positions, thus weakening to some extent the closed styles of life and the segregation of different status (caste) groups.

The multiplicity of centers and networks, the dissociation between the religious or "ethnic" (Indian) and political centers, and the discrepancy between the ideal and the actual patterns of cultural and social organization tend to explain the multiplicity of legitimate channels of social mobility and access to higher positions in India and the predominance of the adaptive mode of response in situations of change.

But throughout the "traditional" period in Indian history this adaptability was kept definitely within the premises of the tradition, both in terms of preserving the basic relative evaluation of different dimensions of human existence (cosmic, ritual, political, economic, etc.) and in terms of keeping up the continuity of the collective identity in relation to this tradition.[8]

IV

To what extent do the changes which have taken place in India in modern and contemporary times and which are so fully reported and documented in the various papers in this volume conform to the "historical" pattern of change in Indian society?

The first impression that one may receive from these materials is that of an overwhelming continuity, if not outright identity, between the

[7] See B. S. Cohn, "Political Systems in Eighteenth Century India: The Banaras Region," *Journal of the American Oriental Society,* Vol. LXXXII, No. 3 (July-September, 1962); L. Dumont, "The Conception of Kingship in Ancient India," *Contributions to Indian Sociology,* Vol. VI (1962); and the latter's more general analysis of the Indian caste system, *Homo Hierarchicus* (Paris, Gallimard, 1967).

[8] See Dumont, *Homo Hierarchicus.*

patterns of change. Almost all the papers tell us of different changes in the relative standing of different caste groups, and about the different opportunities that they seize on in the situation of change. They tell us of the changes in the fortunes of these groups—changes greatly influenced by the structural placement of the groups in the new situations on the one hand, and by their own traditional values and orientations on the other. They tell us also about the development of conflicts centering on the distribution of goods and authority in the respective caste settings. In all this, it seems as if there is no qualitative difference with regard to more traditional patterns of conflict and change.[9]

There are, of course, many differences in the nature of the new types of opportunities which developed with the onset of modern periods. Thus entirely new types of opportunities developed in India in all the major institutional spheres; in the manifold changes in the agrarian structure; in the development of new modern educational frameworks and opportunities; in the concomitant development of new channels of occupational mobility; and lastly in the development of new cultural orientations.

But in themselves these new types of organizational or institutional frameworks do not necessarily entail an entirely new type of social and cultural order.

Moreover, the general pattern of adjustment to change—that of a high level of adaptability—seems to be very similar to one that we found in the traditional setting.

This relatively high level of adaptability was evident in the readiness of the various local and caste groups to incorporte new modern goals, to undertake new tasks which were developing in the new settings, and to use resources at their disposal both for obtaining access to such new roles and tasks and for the maximization of their performance of such roles. This could be seen in the economic-occupational, educational, administrative, and political spheres alike. In all these spheres there was a great degree of what may be called "openness" toward new structural possibilities and new goals.

These adaptations were not, of course, always peaceful or smooth. They were often connected with very sharp changes in the internal property, power, and "class" arrangements, with the development of new

[9] See Cohn, "Political Systems in Eighteenth Century India"; Singer and Cohn, *Structure and Change in Indian Society*.

groups such as the zamindāri, and with the growth of new types of inter-group conflicts. But somehow, at least in the first phases of these develop-ments, there seemed also to develop, both on the local and on the more central level, some regular mechanisms which were able to cope with these problems.

The adaptability of the Indian traditional "periphery" to the forces of modernization was perhaps even more evident in the fact that the various "traditional" groupings tended also to reorganize and to develop new kinds of goals and more differentiated frameworks and integrative mechanisms. Of special interest here is the fact that the process of change and mobility among caste groups developed in the more traditional direc-tion as well as into new, more differentiated, and modern directions.[10]

Side by side with the traditional patterns of mobility and structural change there also developed a new pattern in which the older types of caste groups gave way to new, broader, more differentiated, and more flexible networks of caste association, focusing mostly on new types of economic, professional, and political activities, assuming a great variety of new organizational patterns, and often, although not always, creating new "cross-cuttings" between the political, social, and economic hierarchies of status.[11]

It is with regard to most of these responses to change that a relatively great continuity between the traditional and the modern settings is to be found, although already here—in the development of new "modern" types of mobility and caste organizations—some elements of discon-tinuity can be discerned.

And, indeed, a closer look at the materials presented below indicates that this impression of continuity between the patterns of historical, traditional, and modern change is to no small degree one-sided. This is probably due to the nature of the studies themselves. Most of them—like most other field-work reports—focus on one locality or "caste" and on its adjustment to the new "modern" setting. Hence we find in them a great emphasis on the modes of response of different local or caste groups to the impingement of forces or processes of change on the groups—and it is indeed within this aspect of situations of change that a relatively great degree of continuity is to be found between the patterns of change in traditional and modern settings.

---

[10] See, for instance, the papers by Alan Beals and K. Ishwaran in this volume.
[11] See especially the papers by Singh and Gough in this volume.

But such continuity does not necessarily exist in the nature of the forces of change which impinge on these communities—forces which, although they are indeed very heavily stressed in the analysis of these papers, are in a sense kept in the background.

What, then, are these new, specifically modern forces of change, and what is the nature of the new type of problems which these forces create?

Two closely interconnected aspects or processes of change stand out. One is the expansion, together with these processes of change, of the very scope of the field of social and symbolic participation of the different local groups and communities beyond the given locality or region.

Something of this kind must also have taken place in several instances of change in traditional India, especially in those changes which were connected with a growing differentiation and universalization of the political or religious structures. There also, some new wider societal frameworks with more encompassing centers and communities developed in several cases. But there seem to be some crucial differences between such changes in a traditional and a modern setting, as reported here. The most important differences concerned the scope and the bases of these new communities—or, rather, of the new community. Its scope has become India-wide not only in an "ethnic" or ritual sense but also in a territorial sense, and its base is predominantly political.

The most important structural implication of the differences between the patterns of modern and traditional change in India can perhaps best be seen in the differences that developed in the two periods in the nature of the various links between the centers and the periphery. In the modern setting, many of the older types of links—such as the various religious centers and networks—have become greatly weakened; and more direct links between the new (mostly political) center and the broader frameworks on the one hand, and many of the peripheral groups on the other, are being created.

The participation of various caste, territorial, or kinship groups in the broad cultural, "national" community tends to become more and more direct, less and less mediated by traditional, ideological and structural links, and based on a new type of organization.

The new links between the center and the periphery are not only more "direct" than the "traditional" ones. Their organizational and territorial scope is much wider; they are often parts of new, countrywide organizations (like political parties or trade unions). Moreover, such territoriality tends to become a major autonomous basis of social organization, greatly weakening the importance of many of the traditional kinship, caste, and ritual bases of organization. Ishwaran's case study of the transplantation of a Mysore village provides one of the most interesting illustrations of this process.

The various papers presented here, and especially those of Gough, Orenstein, and Singh, point out clearly how the very formation of the new center and political ideology has influenced the directions of caste mobility and orientations, and how it has opened up entirely new types of activities, very often in what has been called—by Gough, Singh, and others—the direction of "class" activities.[12]

It is this new type of relation between the various local units and the broader and societal frameworks and centers that has created crises for many of the caste group, whose services are no longer needed because of competitive market forces, as reported by Elder, Ishwaran, and Tyler; this may be perhaps even more important and crucial from the point of view of our discussion for the older type of political and community leadership as reported by Orenstein.

This expansion of the scope of the community is closely related to the second major aspect of change in contemporary India, which can be denoted as specifically modern and which is greatly discontinuous from the patterns of traditional change—an aspect which is illustrated in most of the papers presented here (see especially the paper by Singh)— namely, that the major single and most overwhelming source of change in contemporary India has been the creation of a new centralized polity with a specifically modern ideology of political participation.

The first stages of this new polity were shaped by the British. They created the administrative, political, and legal center, and implanted the first seeds of modern political ideology. This ideology was then taken over, transformed, and greatly expanded by the Congress movement and the Congress government into full-fledged premises of political modernity, as manifested in the development of a broader political unity, of a conception of active participation of the periphery in the formation of the political centers, and in the acceptance of the structural and symbolic "openness" of these centers.

12 See on this also André Béteille, *Caste, Class and Power: Changing Patterns of Stratification in a Tanjore Village* (Berkeley, University of California Press, 1965).

It was this breakthrough to modernity that provided the framework for an entirely new type of change in Indian history. First of all, this breakthrough denoted a restructuring or reordering of some of the basic dimensions of the Indian sociocultural order. It gave rise to a tendency, if not of total merging and unification, then at least to some degree of closer mutual interconnection of cultural and political centers, and to the "upgrading" of the importance of the political dimension of human existence in general, and of the political centers in particular.

Second, and closely related to the former, was the attempt to re-define the nature of India's collective identity not only in cultural or ritual-cosmic but also in political terms, in terms of a common political center and order.

This attempt at the redefinition of the collective identity of Indian civilization has generated—through the creation of a general new atmosphere of political equality and through a series of policy measures[13]—a series of far-reaching changes and a totally transformed situation.

Through these the new political-ideological order and center became not only relatively autonomous with regard to the older, ritual one, but also an independent major force in generating far-reaching changes in the sociocultural order. This has been, of course, most clearly evident in the whole legislation abolishing the special legal privileges—or disabilities —of castes in general, and the disabilities of untouchability in particular.

True enough, this legislation has not always been effective or successful. It certainly did not succeed in eroding the traditional loyalties or always in improving the lot of many of the lower groups and castes— although in many cases it did so. But even in those cases where its major effect was to open up new and better opportunities for the upper groups and castes, its over-all effect on Indian society and culture was very far-reaching.

It has undermined the ultimate legitimation of the caste order in terms of a cosmic ritual hierarchy which is reflected in the political and secular spheres and which orders and regulates those spheres. The whole conception of the caste order has changed from, to use Gallanter's terms, a sacred to a sectarian or associational view.[14] The older, sacral mode

---

[13] See on this, in great detail, G. Rosen, *Democracy and Economic Change in India* (Berkeley, University of California Press, 1966).

[14] See Marc Gallanter, "The Religious Aspects of Caste: A Legal View," in D. E. Smith, ed., *South Asian Politics and Religion* (Princeton, Princeton University Press, 1966), pp. 277-311.

which was predominant in the traditional setting has become at most one variant within the whole gamut of various conceptions and organizations of caste which have developed in the modern situation.

More specifically, as a result of the breaking down of this mode, the basic relations between the ritual and the political or "secular" order have become to a large degree reversed. A group's relative standing within the caste order—the material, organizational, and motivational resources which the position of any group in the traditional order gave it—has become the means for the attainment of various "secular" goals, such as differential standing within the new sociopolitical spheres. These "secular" goals have in their turn acquired more and more autonomous legitimation of their own. Thus, the "secular," "mundane" political and economic frameworks and resources, instead of being avenues of access to ultimate participation in the ritual sphere have become autonomous and even predominant goals and cultural orientations.

Moreover, as we have seen, attempts have been made to define the collective identity of India in such terms. Even when the attempts to create new binding secular symbols may seem to have failed and given rise to new cleavages and problems—as in the case of regional and linguistic areas—the very protest has been already couched in such political and secular terms, even if the "contents" of these protests may seem to be "traditional."[15]

V

It would, however, be wrong to assume that the difference between patterns of traditional and modern changes in India can be seen only on the level of the central frameworks and of the new types of opportunities opened up by these frameworks—and not on the levels of response of the various local and traditional groups.

A closer look at the evidence presented in the various papers in this volume does indeed indicate that new modes of response to the impact of change on the "local," peripheral level have also developed and that most of them are closely related to the changes in the "basic" nature of the caste system which have been analyzed above. Perhaps the most important of these changes has been the extension of the caste organization beyond the single locality and region into translocal, regional, or even national frameworks. Closely related to this change is the nature

[15] See on this especially Kathleen Gough's paper in this volume.

of the goals of such organizations, which have become more and more oriented to political and economic goals, thus accepting the new reference goals and orientations—including the goals of economic development and advancement—set out by the political system as the bases of their own activities.

This has necessarily meant, first, a change from the hierarchical and horizontal to a vertical mode of such organization of caste activities and, then, to a greater emphasis on regional intercaste relations as against local intracaste relations.

Second, it has meant a basic change in the nature of intercaste relations. These, instead of being defined as before, as, for instance, in the jajmāni system, in terms of mutual "unconditionalities" of services and obligations, have become defined increasingly in terms of either freer competition in the open markets or a struggle over the access to the new political centers. It is through such access that the new types of "unconditional" rewards (for example, the right of access to education) can be obtained; they can no longer be obtained to the same degree as before through the more direct interrelations between different local groups and castes—at most with the local ruler as intermediary.

This has necessarily also given rise to an increase and intensification of the level of conflicts between various groups—be they caste groups or regional groups—to the development of new types of such groups or especially so-called class groupings and political parties, and the possibility of a great polarization and politicization of such conflicts on regional and even countrywide levels—a polarization and politicization to no small degree due to the development of a common political and ideological center and frame of reference which did not exist before.

WILLIAM H. NEWELL

An Upper Rāvi Village:
The Process of Social Change
in Himāchal Pradesh

I

ONE OF THE MOST DIFFICULT problems in studying social change in society is to isolate the particular unit of study and the particular period of time which will form the base reference. In India this problem is especially difficult because the enormous size of the country and the wide variations among the customs of different villages and different castes make it impossible very often to determine whether change is "natural" to the social system involved or whether it is the beginning of a change in the structure of the social system itself. Until the beginning of World War II, the general pattern of Indian sociology was to divide India into two main groups, urban and rural, and then to isolate the rural into villages, which were regarded as differing, depending on their cultural background and the extent to which they were near cities that "undermined" the rural village pattern.

In more recent times, however, this oversimplified and possibly untrue picture of Indian society has been affected by two tendencies. The first tendency is the recognition that the Indian village was never "self-contained" but always depended on neighboring villages and areas for essential services. These services were sometimes religious, in the sense that one had to travel to certain sacred centers for pilgrimages or to disperse the *pinds* of one's parents. Sometimes the services were economic in the sense that goods often passed from centers of production over very

William H. Newell is Associate Professor of Anthropology at the University of Sydney. He was formerly Professor of Anthropology and Sociology at the International Christian University, Tokyo.

wide areas even in pre-British times. Sometimes exchanges were deliberately encouraged by the caste system so that no village could provide all the artisans required and specialized castes undertook services over a wide area. Endogamy destroyed the self-sufficiency of the small village in the same way that the prohibition of family sexual relations, according to Lévi-Strauss, destroyed the continuity of the family.

The second tendency was the recognition that Indian cities were not special Western or foreign importations whose urbanizing influences were gradually undermining Indian rural society but rather just as much parts of the total Indian culture as rural India. The special problem of Indian urban society was not that the cities were cities without caste but rather that what was most fundamental in defining caste in the rural setting, namely endogamy, was perhaps not the most fundamental feature of caste in the urban situation. Although insufficient research has as yet been undertaken in the Indian urban environment, I think it is becoming clear that caste does not "disappear" once one goes to the city; instead it tries to adjust itself to the needs of the new environment, for example, by becoming identified with particular social or political groups.

The general process of social change in India since the introduction of railways has been one of giving more opportunities to strong features of the Indian social system to become stronger. Subcaste panchāyats can now extend their control over a wider area. The principle of "one man, one vote" makes those castes with more people more powerful in political matters. Famous centers of pilgrimage can now number their visitors in millions instead of in thousands as formerly. Manufactured goods can now be made relatively cheaply and distributed over a wide area so that the relationships between producer and consumer which formerly took place in the village include many more people and the basic personal relationship is transferred from jajmān and kāmin (servant) in the village to manufacturer and wholesaler and thence to retailer in the city. The anthropologist sees the weakening of ties between jajmān and kāmin. He does not see the nature of the relationship between wholesaler, manufacturer, and retailer. Is this relationship a truly "economic" one without any social aspect or do questions of caste, residence, and place of origin play any part in the chain? I know of no study in India on this subject, but in Japan the patterns of manufacturing and distribution are profoundly influenced by the Japanese *oyabun-kobun* relationship.[1] I would be surprised if there were not a traditional Indian fashion of economic relationship at the upper level of industry to replace the breakdown of jajmāni economic relations in the village.

Thus it is possible that social change in India is more apparent than real. There is only a shift in the *areas* of change. From the point of view of the whole of Indian society, total change would be less than any particular part of it. Thus the question of the unit involved is important.

In 1952 and 1953 I was fortunate enough to undertake fieldwork along the upper reaches of the Rāvi River in the Brahmaur *tahsil* of Chamba State, now part of Himāchal Pradesh. The highest village in the area is the village of Kugti at a height of about 10,000 feet above mean sea level. From Kugti to Chamba city, the capital of the district, is a distance of about 50 miles. Chamba is at a height of about 2,000 feet. The valley along the side of the river can be divided into three main ecological divisions. In the lower section from Chamba to Ulansa, a distance of about 13 miles, it rarely snows, the farmers live on their land all the year round, and communication with Chamba is easy, since a bus regularly covers the route when the road has not been washed away temporarily by floods.

In the middle section from Ulansa to the Upper Brahmaur Valley, a distance of about 20 miles, the ground is covered with snow for about two months a year and communication with Chamba is difficult. In former times one had to cross a high pass near Chhatrari by foot but within the last ten years a jeepable road has been built, although the normal means of communication is still by foot. After passing over the Chhatrari pass the river divides into three sections coming from the direction of Holi, Brahmaur, and Tundah. All three river valleys have the same ecological pattern but the majority of the population live along the Budl Nadl, the river coming from Brahmaur. Brahmaur is at a height of 7,000 feet.

The third section is the part of the Budl Nadl between the Upper Brahmaur Valley and Kugti. The road between Kugti and Brahmaur

---

[1] These are traditional relations between superior and inferior known as "father-son" relationships. They have been extensively studied by Japanese sociologists. See, in English, John William Bennett and Iwao Ishino, *Paternalism in the Japanese Economy* (Minneapolis, University of Minnesota Press, 1963).

is often impassable owing to floods, snow covers the ground for about four months a year, and, during the winter, it is usually impossible to travel between Kugti and other parts of the district.

The whole valley thus shows a gradual change in ecological conditions from Chamba city at the bottom to Kugti at the top. The bottom section grows a small amount of rice, maize, and wheat but the upper and middle sections grow only maize and wheat plus other high-level crops.

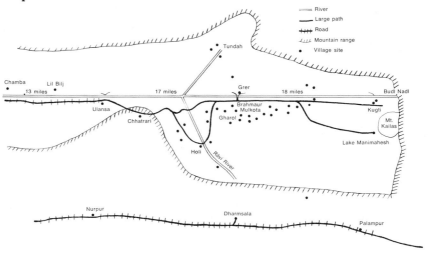

Diagrammatic Map of Brahmaur *Tahsil* and Surrounding Territories

At the present time the two upper sections are part of Brahmaur tahsil and the lower section is administered directly by Chamba city. In former times, however, the whole of the valley was administered as a unit. There are few historical records before the ninth century, but in 920 the capital of the state was transferred from Chamba to Brahmaur, which was then the center of an independent kingdom. In 1330 the capital was transferred back to Chamba although it appeared that the Raja of Chamba ruled only the Upper Rāvi River at that time. After various conquests by surrounding territories and reconquests by the Chambalis, at the end of the eighteenth century the state acquired its present shape, a territory about fifty miles in diameter surrounded by high hills and bounded by Kashmir, the Kulu Valley, the Kangra Valley, and the Punjab. Although the state consisted of a union of five nationalities, Tibetan, Brahmauri, Punjabi, Panguli, and Chambali, the Brahmauris were always regarded as the backbone of the state; at his coronation the Raja was dressed in Brahmauri clothing on the first day. Thus the valley was basically a political unit from the earliest times.

The valley was also a religious unit. Along the whole course of the river are various shrines dedicated to Triloknath Dev, a Brahmauri culture hero. At the annual festival to the god Shiva at Lake Manimahesh, delegates from Lil Bilj (near Chamba), Holi, Brahmaur, Tundah, and Kugti bring their local gods to pay their respects to Shiva. In the center of the territory is Mt. Kailas, which has never been climbed, on which Shiva is supposed to reside. The whole territory is sometimes known as Shivbhumi, the land of Shiva. The valley is also an economic unit, connected by the one road. The inhabitants of the middle section have very close ties with the inhabitants of the Kangra Valley on the other side of the Dhaula Dhar range. For the months of the year when snow lies on the ground the majority of the villagers used to emigrate en masse to the Kangra Valley and beyond. Many villages on the Kangra side also formerly belonged to the Gaddi caste, and at one period the Raja of Brahmaur claimed part of Nurpur in the Kangra Valley as being within his territory. Moreover, at the present time many of the inhabitants of the Brahmaur tahsil also own land in Dharmsala. During the winter those Gaddis who own sheep and goats often pass over the ranges to graze them in the Kangra Valley. The passes over the Dhaula Dhar are not all impassable even during the winter, and in terms of communication it is as easy for the inhabitants of Brahmaur and Holi to reach the Kangra Valley as to reach Chamba. Thus while the inhabitants of the lower section are almost entirely Chamba-oriented, the upper sections are administratively connected with Chamba but have most of their personal relations outside the valley in Kangra.

The special interest of the Upper Rāvi River as an area for studying the process of social change lies in the fact of its comparative isolation until modern times, its economic and religious unity, and the recent systematic attempt by officials from other areas under instruction from the central government at Delhi to deliberately induce a process of change in the valley by means of new schools, increased spending on public works, and the Community Development Program. As I hope to show, there are two processes at work. First, a slow and steady change has been proceeding for several hundred years in which the dominant position of the Gaddi caste has been gradually undermined. The results of this change can be observed if one compares the present situation in the lower part of the valley with the Brahmaur and Kugti areas. Second, there was a deliberate change in the power structure of the village when the organs of change were transferred from the traditional institutions of the area to newly created bureaucratic organs operating through civil servants responsible to government departments with headquarters outside the area. The question which arises is whether this second change in power structure has the effect of changing the direction of the social change itself or whether it is accelerating a tendency already present. These two changes cannot, however, be studied in isolation from a third factor, the rapid increase in population density, which was creating such excessive strains in the social system even before the postwar systematic development policy that it was considered doubtful whether the valley could solve its problems without outside assistance.

I now propose to describe the social system of the valley with a view to showing how it is necessary to regard the whole of the valley as a social system, formerly largely independent of the larger Indian society but now gradually losing its distinctive social features. Some of my information has been derived from the 1961 census, and since such information is available to me for the Brahmaur tahsil only, it is to this tahsil that I will mainly confine my comments. The 1961 census was the first census ever carried out in this area using the village as a basis. By a village I mean a residential unit territorially separate from surrounding units and with its own land nearby. Since the overwhelming majority of the residents are farmers, and since, until recently, there was no alternative means of obtaining a livelihood in the valley, there is practically no occupational differentiation.

Within the total area of the Brahmaur tahsil in the 1961 census there were 105 nucleated settlements with an average of 43 households (sharing one *chula*, or cooking stove) and 36 houses to each settlement. I will henceforth call each settlement a village even though it may consist of only one house. The total population of the tahsil at this time was 14,105 males and 11,250 females, making a total of 25,625. The number of households per village was as follows:

Households per Village	Number of Villages	Households per Village	Number of Villages
1- 5	5	51- 55	4
6-10	10	56- 60	5
11-15	5	61- 65	3
16-20	6	66- 70	2
21-25	5	71- 75	2
26-30	9	76- 80	0
31-35	6	81- 85	2
36-40	10	86- 90	4
41-45	3	91- 95	2
46-50	5	96-100	1
		100+	8

Note: The 8 villages of 100+ households consisted of villages of 102, 104 (2), 112, 117, 125 (2), and 148 households. The total number of villages comes to less than 105, since some single houses were included in larger villages by the census.

The largest village is Brahmaur, the second largest is Mulkota (about half a mile from Brahmaur), and the third largest is Gharol, which is on a flat ridge joining the Budl Nadl to the Upper Rāvi. If one combines the figures for Upper and Lower Kugti (and they are less than a quarter of a mile apart), then Kugti has 132 households. The size of villages increases evenly with no marked discontinuity.

Let us take a cross section of the valley at Brahmaur. At the top would be the region of perpetual snow; then below this would be spring grazing land or forests planted by the Chamba Forest Administration; then the area of crops and villages; then rough scrub used for local grazing of sheep and goats; and below this an almost precipitous drop of several hundred feet to the river. It is possible to see people clearly in a village at the same level on the opposite side of the river, yet it might take several hours to reach them by climbing down to the base of the river and up the other side of the valley. The distribution of villages from the higher crop area downwards consists mostly of small villages containing from one to fifteen households; then larger villages; then smaller villages again just above the rough scrub. This is a general pattern over the whole Brahmaur area and shows that the number of households in a village is determined by the amount of arable land surrounding the village, since most arable land is found halfway up the valley. If this were not the case, one would expect a random distribution of the size of villages at every level dependent on natural increase.

Over the whole valley the proportion of women to men is 82 per cent, yet if we work out the sex ratio of villages in proportion to the size of villages we have the following uneven distribution. (I regard the sex distribution as being uneven where there are fewer women than men by 5 per cent.)

Out of 31 villages with up to 25 households, 24 villages have an even sex distribution.

Out of 32 villages between 26 and 50 households, only 12 have an even sex distribution.

Out of 16 villages between 51 and 75 households, only 5 have an even sex distribution.

Out of 17 villages with over 75 households, only 3 have an even sex distribution.

It is thus clear that, as the villages become larger, the proportion of women to men becomes less. This may be due either to women emigrating from larger villages without the corresponding entrance of wives, or to men in smaller villages emigrating. In Kugti, according to the national census, there is one female to every two males. Since the 1961 census was the first census ever undertaken on a nucleated settlement basis, it is impossible to obtain earlier figures for comparison. However, it is clear that there is a difference between smaller and larger villages in terms of (a) position in the valley and (b) sex ratio. It is also significant that between 1952 and 1962 no new villages were formed, although the population almost doubled in size between 1931 and 1962. But the distribution of the relative size of villages remained almost the same in the two periods as measured by household size. This conclusion is based on a discussion with villagers in different villages plus a private census that I carried out myself in three villages. The pressure on the land is very great, since most of the land is too steep or uncultivable. In 1960, assuming the cultivated area in the tahsil as 17.37 square miles, the pressure of population would be 1,508 people per cultivated square mile. It is clear that there is acute land hunger. During the period of snow, the majority of the villagers emigrate to the Punjab plains for casual work.

In my opinion there is a connection between the three factors, of land hunger, sex distribution, and size and position of the village. Both in former times and now, the larger villages occupied the better land in the center of the valley slopes. These slopes are now occupied mostly by those castes which were regarded as the first settlers in the valley, namely, Gaddis and Sipis. The worse positions were occupied by later settlers, Brāhmans and low castes such as Riaras or Hallis. As severe land hunger first occurred in the center villages (since new land on the edges had already been occupied by new villages), daughters started to emigrate down the valley but were unable to be replaced by wives coming up the valley (which would mean coming from better areas to worse) nor by a sufficient number of women from the smaller villages along the edge of the valley. But men are not able to emigrate permanently with their sisters because there is no work which they can undertake; so they remain in the villages. Thus an uneven sex distribution occurs. In Kugti, a very distant place and one difficult to get to, the sex distribution is very uneven. In Grer village, a village suffering from acute land division, there are considerably more men than women even though it may be regarded as a medium village, whereas another village of the same household grouping but with more land had a higher proportion of women. Thus shortage of women is to some extent a measure of poverty.

The marriage pattern of the area is roughly as follows:

(1) Women of Kugti marry inside Kugti or into the Brahmaur area.

(2) Women of the Brahmaur area tend to marry into Holi, Dharmsala, or Chhatrari.

(3) Women of the Holi area tend to marry into that area, into Dharmsala, and into Brahmaur.

(4) No women from the Brahmaur-Holi-Kugti area will marry into the Tundah area and never into the Lil Bilj area below the valley near Chamba.

(5) Tundah women seem to marry into Tundar or into Lil Bilj.

Although it is difficult to document, it is clear that women marry down the valley in the order Kugti, Brahmaur/Holi, Kangra. They do not marry below Ulansa, although there are a few isolated marriages to Brahmauri emigrants in Chamba city itself.

In what I have to say subsequently, my generalizations must be placed against a background of acute land hunger, marriage of women for the most part down the valley, and lack of opportunity for men to find a measure of livelihood. Moreover, for several hundred years the Gaddi caste traditionally held a dominating position among the other castes of the valley and in the state, a position which rested upon their possession of the best land and in undertaking the occupation with the highest status, soldiering.

II

Residents of the Brahmaur district were members of an elementary family, an exogamous unit larger than the family (the gotra) a village, and an endogamous unit which I will call a caste. The head of the family had the basic responsibility of administering the land on behalf of his elementary family. His right to do so was derived from his gotra membership and was inherited within the gotra. The basic ownership of the soil rested with the Raja but the right to use the land passed by inheritance from father to sons. In the absence of sons it passed to brothers. In the absence of brothers or sons it passed to other members of the gotra. In 1952, land could not be bought or sold, but land which belonged to a gotra with no living members was auctioned by the Raja to members of the same village. Thus "owners" only had the right to usufruct. A gotra was an ultimate land distributing group and (with certain exceptions) was also an exogamous unit, the members of which were not allowed to marry among themselves. The members of a gotra in different villages never met together, but within a village the gotra members regarded themselves as kinsmen. There was no method by which members of a family could change or lose their gotra membership. In marriage the wife retained a sort of residual membership. In the rare cases of loss of caste, the offending member still retained his gotra membership and any rights to land which accompanied it.

CASTE RELATIONS IN BRAHMAUR

In contrast to the exogamous gotra, there was an endogamous unit, the caste. In the valley of Brahmaur there were four traditional castes divided into upper and lower. The upper castes consisted of the Brāhmans and the Gaddis, the lower castes consisted of the Sipis, Riaras, and Hallis. The rough proportion of caste members was 80 per cent Gaddi, 10 per cent Brāhman, 3 per cent Sipi, and 2 per cent low castes. In the central area of Brahmaur each caste was strictly endogamous and intermarriage was absolutely forbidden. When I visited the area first in 1952, each caste ate separately at public feasts and would only eat food cooked by the same or a higher caste. According to a retired Gaddi *likhnara* (head-man), at the turn of the century at public festivals, although intermar-riage was forbidden, Brāhmans and Gaddis would often eat together in the same line in order of seniority or age but not of caste. Only the lower castes ate absolutely separately.

When pressed for an answer the Gaddis would often state that they were Rajput, Thakur, or Rana as well as being Gaddi. According to tra-dition, many of the Gaddis fled from the Punjab plains at the time of the Aurangzeb persecution and took up service with the Raja of Chamba as soldiers, for which they received an annual grant of land. Although they came from different higher castes, in the course of time they lost their caste individuality and married anyone of the other three former castes. The Gaddis thus consider themselves an isogamous union of a group of higher castes. They wear distinctive clothing of a round hat and woolen cloak, but their special caste symbol is a woolen rope (*dhora*) which they wrap around their waists. It was formerly used for rescuing sheep and goats from crevasses in the mountains. Brāhmans and Sipis who come from this area also often wear the same clothing but, in a technical sense, the term Gaddi is a caste name and only those of the caste should wear the uniform. Since Sipis and Brāhmans today till the soil and are eco-nomically similar to Gaddis, they all tend to wear the same clothing.

CASTE RELATIONS IN THE UPPER VALLEY

Lower Kugti consists almost entirely of Brāhmans, while Upper Kugti consists of half Brāhmans and half Gaddis. The two castes freely eat with each other and (with the exception of a small group of *pujāris* at the state shrine) freely intermarry. The child takes its caste from the father.[2] In justification of their practice they have two arguments. (1) Since the population of the two villages is only about 500, it is difficult for each caste to marry within itself without breaking the rules of marriage. (2) "Brāhmans and Gaddis carry out the same occupations and do the same work and are indistinguishable in character. Therefore why should they not marry each other?" (I should mention here that none of Kugti Brāh-mans are *purohits* [family priests]; a priest from a village one day's journey

---

[2] See my article "Inter-Caste Marriage in Kugti Village," *Man* (April, 1963), pp. 55-56, note 59.

away serves the whole village). If a child from Kugti goes to Brahmaur to visit his relatives (for many Kugti women marry down the valley to Brahmaur), he will eat only with relatives of his father. The offspring of such mixed Kugti marriages seem to be in no special disrepute if they visit Brahmaur; in fact, the secretary of the local tahsil panchāyat was one such Brāhman with a Kugti Gaddi mother.

CASTE RELATIONS IN THE LOWER VALLEY

In Ulansa where the valley widens out, thirteen miles from Chamba at the end of the newly opened bus road, the local village gives signs of being formerly Gaddi. The head of the largest house has a Gaddi-type loom in his basement and the house style is a mixture of Punjabi plains building and Gaddi foundations. The caste composition of the village of about twenty-five households is, in order, Rajput, Rana, Halli. On a rise some half-mile away is another village entirely Brāhman in composition. Although I did not have time for a detailed examination of the village marriage pattern, it was clear that these three groups were absolutely endogamous. Moreover I discovered that no member of the Rana or Rajput caste would ever dream of marrying one another or anyone from the Gaddi villages up the river. They were quite aware that there were many Rajput families among the Gaddi castes, but, as the head of the leading house explained to me, "They were really Gaddi, whatever other caste they might formerly have been. According to the census inquiry, Rajputs were one of the top castes in Hinduism and this was the most distinguished caste of which to be a member. Gaddi is not a recognized caste." Yet by various indications in the village and also inquiry in some of the higher villages, it was clear that at one time this was an area dominated by Gaddis. Moreover, the gotra name of the Rajput family was a common one also found among the Rajput Gaddis of the higher valley.

Further down the valley again was the community of Lil Bilj. Although living in isolated houses on their own fields and not even in the small nucleated settlements typical of Brahmaur, some of the inhabitants still wore pieces of Gaddi clothing but of a coarser and cruder style than the hillmen. They still sent a delegation periodically to Lake Manimahesh to worship Shiva at the festival. However, as far as I could tell they did not seem to have the local Gaddi lineages (als) and it was clear that, in so far as they could be considered "Gaddi" by the surrounding inhabitants, they were despised as a low caste. Here the best thing to be was an ordinary upper-caste Chambali wearing ordinary Chambali clothes. The Lil Bilj Gaddis as a group had failed to assert their upper-caste status and had sunk to a low-caste position.

It is thus clear that at one time "Gaddiland" stretched along the whole distance of the Rāvi from Chamba up to Kugti. The special features of the "Gaddi way of life" were a common religious attitude and a common allegiance to the national cult objects, Lake Manimahesh and the worship of Shiva on Mt. Kailas. Gaddis were distinguished from other people by a distinctive clothing and way of life. Yet at the same time the inhabitants of the valley were deeply Hindu and carried out orthodox Sanskritic ritual practices with Brāhman priests responsible for their performance. Since the land was all owned by the Raja, who was basically Gaddi in outlook (for he depended on their ability at fighting to protect his kingdom), there was no opportunity for the development of a special class of landlord owners who controlled their followers by owning the land on which they worked. Thus caste specialization did not proliferate. Surplus land was allocated to new settlers rather than to old residents to employ nonfamily members as laborers (kāmin).[3] As numbers increased, new villages were founded, largely named after the original founder. Early in this century all the cultivable land became used and yet the population continued to increase. The right to use land became inherited instead of being a reward for military services (as Chamba depended for its protection on the British government). This change in the function of the land users from a military to an agricultural citizenry began to separate the castes again. The change started from the bottom of the valley where the land was more plentiful. Where the land users were successful in increasing the productivity of the fields, castes became differentiated, with the higher castes acquiring more land. Where the land users were not successful in increasing productivity because the increase of population was greater than the land available for use, the Gaddis sank as

---

[3] It is also possible that a hundred years ago the value system of the Gaddis was oriented against agriculture, that land was of little value and prestige derived only from hunting. One of the older residents of Goshen village told me a story that the raja took back part of the land of his grandfather because it was not cultivated for three years. The owner was a brilliant hunter and said he did not want the land. A bow and arrow takes an important part in certain rituals connected with *rites de passage*.

a group, lost their dominant position in the area, and failed to assert their Rana or Rajput origins. The most marked division between those Gaddis who wished to keep the old way of life and those who reasserted their former Rajput or Rana status took place below Ulansa. Hence the Brahmauri Gaddis refused to intermarry with those from Lil Bilj, who in fact had lost their dominance over the society, a dominance still retained by the Brahmauri Gaddis. That in Brahmaur the Gaddis until 1900 were still the basic pattern on which the surrounding castes wished to model their way of life was shown by the fact that the Brāhmans dressed in Gaddi clothes, that up to 1900 in Brahmaur and up to the present day in Kugti both castes ate together, and that up to 1950 such government offices as were available for local residents in Brahmaur were predominantly held by Gaddis. The Brāhmans tended to support local interests rather than to seek special advantages for themselves as a caste. The Brāhmans and Sipis, being in a substantial minority and having no special economic power by which they could claim special privileges separately from the Gaddis, tended to follow the lead of the dominant caste. Yet, that caste differences were becoming more important even before the changes described in the next section were introduced by the Indian government can be seen by comparing the more equalitarian attitude of the Kugti villagers with the Brahmauris; and by comparing the more equalitarian attitude of the Brahmauris with the area below Ulansa.

III

When I first visited the area in 1952, the Indian government had not interfered with the traditional system of the valley. No settlement had even been undertaken and hardly any development or external deliberate interference with local customs had taken place.[4] When I returned in 1962, I found a number of important changes which I will briefly list in order of importance.

(1) The agricultural land had been surveyed and patwāris (who were non-Gaddi) had been appointed to register all land changes. In other words, land allocation had been taken out of the hands of the gotras in the villages and transferred to a bureaucratic agency.

(2) Private ownership of land was recognized and land could be bought and sold.

(3) Women could inherit. It was possible for a man with an only

---

[4] One exception to this was the renunciation by the Raja of the right to settle village accusations of witchcraft by divination. This right was abolished about 1860.

daughter to have her husband come to live in the village and take over the man's property on his death to the neglect of his brothers and their sons. This struck the valley as so unfair that they petitioned the government not to introduce the law, but without avail.

(4) Panchāyats were set up for each patwāri circle and elections were instituted. This immediately resulted in big villages organizing themselves against groups of small villages in order to gain government advantages. The secretary of each panchāyat could recommend to the government villagers for certain privileges, such as cutting trees at a concession rate. He could also obtain jobs for certain villagers in road building. The selection of panchāyat president and secretary thus became very important to the villagers.

(5) A substantial development policy was instituted. The two most immediately beneficial processes were the establishment of numbers of new schools and the employment of local people in road building.

(6) A much larger number of government officials entered the area as advisers on cooperatives and block development schemes. Many of these schemes were totally unsuccessful but all these government employees required servants or other local people as assistants, and they constantly insisted on the superiority of their way of life over the local people and showed it by having a higher standard of consumption and behavior which they regarded as being a model for the Gaddis to copy. They also had the power to let contracts and distribute money to those whom they regarded as being most able to use it. These were of course not necessarily those who were most important in the traditional valley system.

It is against the introduction of these changes that one can understand the background of the panchāyat election at Brahmaur for the position of president in 1962. The villages which made up the grām panchāyat circle in Brahmaur consisted of Mulkota (dominant caste, Gaddi), Bari (Brāhman), Sechuin (Gaddi), Brahmaur (all castes but mostly Brāhman), Goshen (Gaddi), Seri (Brāhman), Kris (Sipi), Goa (Gaddi). Castewise, Gaddis were most numerous, Brāhmans were second, and the lower castes were third. The elections for president were as follows:

| Lakshman Das | Gaddi | 331 votes (94 female) |
| Banshidar | Brāhman | 151 votes (81 female) |

Of the 331 votes for the Gaddi candidate, only three votes were cast by Brāhmans who were the wives of certain Brahmaur shopkeepers; their husbands voted for the Brāhman candidate, thus keeping in with their customers. No Gaddis voted for the Brāhman candidate, although many Gaddis abstained from voting. A third Gaddi candidate stood from Mulkota but he withdrew his candidature on the day before the election. The Brāhman candidates were almost entirely from Bari village and Brahmaur. The Seri Brāhmans (who have close relations with the Gaddis inasmuch as they are nearly all purohits and are descended from a famous rajguru family) suddenly arranged a death anniversary celebration at the time of the elections since they felt that even with their votes the Brāhman candidate would be defeated and they did not wish to antagonize the Gaddis. Thus they had an excuse for not attending the voting.

This modern separation into Gaddi, Brāhman, and Scheduled Castes in the political sphere is a long stretch from the situation described by my old likhnara informant where all the castes were so closely in sympathy with each other that they all ate in one long line and where a Gaddi likhnara could have a Brāhman char (assistant headman) to assist him.

What is it which has precipitated this caste distinction? When I visited the valley in 1952 I often attended weddings and other celebrations in which I ate goat meat and drank a very mild form of intoxicant known as sur made locally from roots. At these parties I noticed numbers of Brāhmans as well as Gaddis. In 1962, however, I found a strong campaign instigated by the government officials and eagerly taken up by local Brāhmans with government contracts against the un-Sanskritic practices of drinking beer and eating goat meat. What surprised me the most, however, was that some of the very Brāhmans with whom I had drunk in 1952 now claimed that they were completely teetotal and superior to the common Gaddis who never knew any better. The Gaddis naturally resented this Brāhman change in attitude and, moreover, realized that, unless they kept control of such organs of local government as the panchāyat, the Brāhmans would try to force the views of the government officials on them under the excuse that it would improve their way of life.

In traditional Brahmaur, the religious and political system was closely integrated. The Raja was not only the head of state; he was also the religious leader even to the extent of granting the sacred thread to lower castes. The moral standards of all castes in the community were similar.

There was a close connection between one's position in the political hierarchy and the extent to which one conformed to the same value system as was found in the valley generally.

With the introduction of a source of wealth outside the traditional agriculture—government money—and the introduction of a group of officials not holding to the local value system and able to dispense this money, those castes who were able to assert their independence from the Gaddis started to do so by adopting the new value system, especially as those Brāhmans and others who opposed *sur* drinking and certain alleged un-Sanskritic practices such as *sudonoj* (the sending of a wife to her husband's home one year after marriage) were able the more easily to obtain employment with government agencies. Thus Brāhmans began to be treated with some suspicion by the majority of Gaddis as hypocrites, people who ten years ago were supporting or at least tolerating Gaddi behavior and who now claimed to be superior.

Since the Gaddis were more deeply involved in the former social system in the valley than other castes, it is not surprising that they have taken longer to realize that their overwhelming superiority in numbers may also give them an advantage in the new system of voting. Individually a higher proportion of Brāhmans and Sipis have entered both primary and middle schools in order to obtain an education sufficient to fit them for the eventual position of government servant or schoolteacher. The more successful of them will probably not return to the valley. As a group, the Gaddis could, if they remain united, always control the majority of the votes in elections. There have been three elections to the assembly at Simla since adult suffrage has been introduced. In the first election, only about 600 voters participated from the Brahmaur tahsil, practically all male. The candidate who was returned was a rich Hindu merchant from Chamba city who had commercial interests in the valley. He was known to be very critical of the Gaddis, whom he regarded as being only suitable for menial tasks. At the second election, the number of voters in the area greatly increased and there were two candidates, the sitting member and the son of a former Gaddi likhnara, who was employed as a schoolteacher. It was well known that both candidates used considerable funds which were paid out in direct bribes and neither candidate at that time was very highly respected by the voters. At the third election the Gaddi schoolteacher tried to obtain the Congress Party nomination but failed, allegedly on the grounds that he would not be successful. The congress committee thought it better to support the incumbent Hindu candidate, although it was known that he was losing his support gradually. The Gaddi schoolteacher then offered his candidacy to the Swatantra Party, which was unorganized in Himāchal Pradesh, and was accepted. In a close fight, the Gaddi candidate was returned. One feature which influenced the voters was that the Congress Hindu sitting member constantly betrayed the interests of the valley in the eyes of the Gaddis by supporting a law favoring prohibition in the area. There are now a number of excise officers in the Brahmaur area who receive "tips" from dissatisfied Gaddis and raid the homes of villagers in which stills are alleged to be hidden. When I interviewed the sitting Gaddi schoolteacher member, he told me that in his first election he did not see the issues clearly and thought that his election depended only on the money he spent, but that at the next election he intended to make his platform that of Gaddi nationalism. He realized that to pay money to people to vote for him was not likely to be a successful way of ultimately becoming elected. There are a number of Gaddis who are opposed to this candidate because of his alleged "proud" attitude, but the Gaddis are now learning their lesson that if they remain united they are more likely to be successful than if they allow their personal differences to intrude. Considering the overwhelming superiority of the Congress Party in the Himāchal assembly, in the long run it is better for the representative of a minority group like the Gaddis to make deals within the Congress Party in the assembly rather than to stay outside in proud isolation.

It thus appears that if the Gaddis can remain united as a group and can vote collectively in elections they may recover some degree of their dominance in the valley which they lost by not understanding the nature of the new political system as rapidly as the minority castes.

IV

The value of this study from the point of view of the analysis of social change is that, since the valley is a comparatively large unit and yet to some extent isolated by difficult communications from Indian society in general, it is possible to identify change over a long period of time. Moreover since the whole valley is entirely Hindu, with ritual practices which are much closer to traditional Sanskritic practices than are found in the Punjab, for example, we do not have a fundamental clash in religious values to contend with in our model, as would be the case if, say, Gaddis were Muslim.

It is clear that the processes making for change in the valley have been continuing over a long period of time. These processes can be summarized as follows: caste differentiation; a change of economy with emphasis increasingly on agriculture and a higher standard of living until the gains become wiped out by excessive population increase; improved communications; and a breakdown of the form of obligation to the state from that of personal service to bureaucratic administration.

In the part of the valley below Ulansa these changes took place in the main before the 1900s; in the central part of the valley the changes were continuing up to about the 1930s when the rapid population increase wiped out the possibility of the valley forming its own independent social system, so that women started increasingly to marry outside the valley. In the Kugti area there has also been a population increase with agriculture unable to absorb the surplus. Thus women have tended to marry outside to better areas instead of marrying within Kugti. From 1955 on, the new Indian government has undertaken a substantial development program which undermined the traditional value system of the valley but provided opportunities for enterprising residents to become socially mobile in the wider Indian society. This, however, will only continue to be a successful policy provided the new economic opportunities continue.

One must make a distinction between the direction of change and the means by which change comes about. The direction of change in the valley is the same as previously. Brahmaur is becoming more like Ulansa with increasing caste differentiation and Kugti is becoming more like Brahmaur with increasing prejudice against Brāhmans and Rajput Gaddis marrying each other. If economic and social opportunities continue to improve, occupational differentiation will also increase. But the means by which change is coming about is different from previously. The increased amount of money or productivity in the valley is not the result of the activities of the villagers themselves but the result of a bureaucratic machinery controlled from outside the valley. The way in which the money is allocated is determined by rules and systems of values over which the local villagers have very little control. It is possible that, as the Gaddis understand more and more clearly the method by which the government operates through an elective parliamentary system, they will be able to control the bureaucratic system to some extent. But the basic relationship for the purpose of development is now between the valley members and the government, whereas formerly it was between the dominant caste and the other castes. Whereas relationships between castes are permanent life relationships between those in adjoining villages, bureaucratic rules imply standardized procedures but temporary personal relations. The pattern for change is therefore different; the direction is the same.[5]

[5] For a more detailed description of the Gaddi social and political system see my Report on the Castes and Scheduled Tribes of Himāchal Pradesh, Volume XX, Part VB, *Census of India*, 1961 (Simla, Government of India Press, 1967).

ALAN R. BEALS

Nāmahaḷḷi, 1953-1966:
Urban Influence and Change
in Southern Mysore

BETWEEN 1877 AND 1953, Nāmahaḷḷi,[1] a village twenty miles from Bangalore in South India, was affected by a variety of urban, industrial, and Western influences.[2] These influences consisted of six basic factors: (1) the expansion of centralized authority at the expense of local and traditional authority; (2) the expansion and improvement of transportation, communication, and trade; (3) the development of nearby urban centers; (4) the introduction of European-style systems of education and welfare; (5) variation in regional and local population; and (6) changes in the accessibility of the worldwide and urban cash economies. Although the first four variables listed were closely correlated, both population and participation in the cash economies have varied independently. When there have been low agricultural prices, increasing population, and/or a lack of opportunity to sell goods or services in the city, there has been a tendency for processes of modernization to come to a halt and for the village to revert to its more traditional (or at least less urban) subsistence and barter economy.

Alan R. Beals is Professor of Anthropology at the University of California at Riverside.

[1] Field trips to Nāmahaḷḷi (anglicized to "Namhalli" in previous publications) were made between March, 1952, and August, 1953, under a fellowship from the Social Science Research Council; in January, 1960, under a National Science Foundation Research Grant; and from March to July, 1966, under a fellowship from the American Institute of Indian Studies. Nāmahaḷḷi is a pseudonym adopted in order to spare the village's literate and urbanized people from any embarrassment that might occur as a result of errors of fact or misinterpretations. Scholars with bibliographic interests will find the correct name of the village published in an obvious place.

[2] Alan R. Beals, "Interplay among Factors of Change in a Mysore Village," in McKim Marriott, ed., *Village India: Studies in the Little Community* (Chicago, University of Chicago Press, 1955), pp. 78-101.

In 1952 and 1953, rising population, a shrinkage of opportunity following the end of World War II, and a serious crop failure produced a crisis. This crisis[3] led to the emergence of pervasive factionalism and an abrupt decline in the effectiveness of traditional methods of settling disputes and organizing cooperative projects. The crisis came to a head in August, 1952, when there was a near riot between two factions and the police were called in. Following this there was a virtual cessation of cooperative activities. In the economic sphere, things seemed to be as unpromising as they were in the social sphere. The village grazing lands had been practically ruined. Too many acres had been under intensive agriculture and there was inadequate cow dung to maintain fertility. Almost all of the trees surrounding village fields and watercourses had been cut down for firewood. Children born during World War II were coming of age and there seemed to be no place for them either in the village or in the city. Because by 1953 government development programs had had little impact, there seemed every likelihood that in the future things would get worse, not better.

THE NEW PROSPERITY

In the period just before World War I and again in the 1930s, prosperity meant that almost every family grew enough food for the year with something left over for one or two changes of clothing, some cooking vessels, and a pilgrimage or wedding ceremony. The new prosperity, appearing unexpectedly after 1954, meant that a family member held a salaried factory job with a good union and a good pension plan. Failing this, prosperity meant the possession of an acre or two of garden land which could be devoted to grapes, tomatoes, flowers, vegetables, or some other garden or orchard crop for which prices could not be controlled by importing grain from the United States.

In 1953, although a number of people had left the village to take jobs in government or industry, the only salaried residents were schoolteachers. One man who held a salaried industrial job moved out in 1953, leaving his young son to operate the family farm as best he could. A few people from the village were in the habit of waiting at the gates of the telephone factory seven miles away in the hope of gaining temporary

[3] Summarized in Alan R. Beals and Bernard J. Siegel, *Divisiveness and Social Conflict: An Anthropological Approach* (Stanford, Stanford University Press, 1966).

employment. By 1960 thirteen residents of the village were permanently employed in the telephone factory and seven in other industrial jobs. In 1966, twenty-one residents were working in the telephone factory, seven in a newly constructed glass factory, and seven in other industrial jobs. The number of schoolteachers residing in the village remained constant at a figure between seven and ten. There was also an increase in the number of persons employed in handloom weaving, blacksmithing, goldsmithing, and tailoring. In 1966, one barber had moved to the city and the other had a shop in a large nearby village. The washerman had moved away to take employment in a laundry doing contract work for an aircraft factory. By that time a number of people had electric irons and the village lost none of its newly acquired urban sartorial polish. Without going into precise detail it can be concluded that the period 1953 to 1966 was one of movement into an expanded ecological niche provided by enlarging opportunities for participation in the urban economy. Almost every household contained one or more salaried workers. Of the new opportunities, the most important was that provided by the commuter bus carrying its daily load of workers to the telephone factory seven miles away.

The expanded agricultural economy of the village, although less visible, was probably as important a new factor as the industrial employment. With a growing labor shortage, marginal lands were returned to forest through the planting of casuarina trees destined ultimately for the cooking stoves of Bangalore. The village milk industry was thriving. With a good well and adequate quantities of chemical manure there seemed to be almost no limit to the profit that a family could make gardening. Some families had abandoned other forms of agriculture almost entirely to grow one food crop and two cash crops yearly on their garden land. Finally, the market price of land in Nāmahaḻḻi increased tenfold between 1953 and 1966.

The depth of the new prosperity can be measured in terms of the reactions of the village to the partial crop failure of 1952-53 (the agricultural year begins in March or April) and to the total crop failures of 1877-78 and 1964-66. In 1877 possibly 30 per cent of the population died of starvation; in 1952 there were relatively few deaths but there was a substantial increase in the number of divorces, suicides, murders, thefts, and conflicts. In 1966, despite virtually complete crop failure, there were no complaints about theft and no indications of other difficulties. At least five new wells were constructed during the dry weather; both wells for drinking water were cleaned out; and, after a false start, the village was able to participate in a school lunch program made possible by gifts of American grain and powdered milk. The failure of the millet and rice crops and the loss even of trees in garden lands caused sorrow and regret but did not create a crisis.

The new prosperity is outwardly visible in contrast to traditional times when wealth was carefully hidden against the coming of thieves or rapacious government officials. Houses have been enlarged, plastered, equipped with chimneys, roofed with machine-made tiles, and furnished with chairs, tables, elevated cooking stoves, and elaborate wooden bedsteads. The grain storage jar has been supplemented with rows of cans storing spices and minor grains. Wristwatches, clocks, bicycles, and radios are commonplace. The village stays up after dark to read by the electric light or to listen to the radio and the village gets up at 4 A.M. to the buzzing of the alarm clocks of the factory workers who also go from house to house waking each other up with loud knockings and shouts. Almost everyone has trousers, coats, shoes with socks, umbrellas, and underwear. Sick people and those who miss the last bus from town travel in taxis. Tea, coffee, and soda pop are regularly consumed and the village store stocks canned goods, flashlight batteries, and a hundred other items, many of which cannot be found in provincial towns having twenty times the population of Nāmahaḷḷi. Between 1877 and 1954, Nāmahaḷḷi flirted with urban life; after 1954 it became a junior partner in the affluent society of the city. Nāmahaḷḷi's ability to grasp the fruits of its new partnership with the city depended upon the capacity of the village to organize its activities. This involved much more than the application of traditional methods to new problems. There was a complete remodeling of the social structure of the village to conform to needs for rapid change and adjustment. When a city is built next door to a village, the village is likely to prosper in one way or another. At the same time, adjustments to urban life may be traumatic and painful. In Nāmahaḷḷi the traditional ways of reaching consensus and getting things done could not survive the moral and economic confusion of a rapidly changing situation. Following the crisis of 1952-53, new ways of organizing the life of the village were found.

CHANGES IN VILLAGE ORGANIZATION

Since 1900 the organization of the village has been based upon a committee of elders drawn from all of the major castes including the otherwise excluded and lowest ranking Ādi Karnātak jāti (untouchable caste). Decisions of the committee were necessarily unanimous. If the elders decided that there should be a particular ceremony, that a particular person should be expelled from the village, or that each household should contribute labor for the digging of a well for drinking water, each household obeyed. If any person or household refused to abide by the decisions of the elders or refused to participate, the cooperative activity automatically ceased until arbitration had been completed and agreement reached. There were no precedents for calling in outside help and it was considered improper to appeal either to civil or criminal authorities without the consent of the elders. At times the authority of the elders was flouted, but up to 1950 or 1951 it had always been possible to work out appropriate adjustments, so that except for a few wily "court birds," the council of elders remained the chief source of law and authority. The crisis of 1952, along with various preliminary disputes in which the local leadership proved helpless, was a final demonstration of the inadequacy of the traditional system in dealing with those prepared to appeal to external sources of law and authority. While the traditional social organization was encountering resistances which it could not overcome, the first vestiges of the new organization were beginning to develop.

The source of the new forms of organization was a group of boys and young men who referred to themselves as the "educated class." It was this group which originally encouraged the ethnographic study of the village. In 1951 members of this group, with the help of an outsider who later became a paid field assistant, had attempted to form a Young Farmers' Club. The formation of the club was vigorously resisted by the village elders, who said there was no need for such an institution and that nobody wanted to have a "president" ordering everybody around. The "educated class" contented itself with the establishment of a volleyball team. During the village-wide conflicts of 1952-53, two volleyball teams came into being. Later, the volleyball equipment was stolen. This casual attitude toward organizational property may stem from the fact that the head of a joint family has virtually unrestricted rights to sell or dispose of property. The belief of leaders and treasurers that these rights also extended to the property and funds of traditional organizations such as drama companies and of new organizations such as clubs and teams has always been a source of difficulty, although there seem to have been no problems with drama companies until they began to charge admission.

In 1953, with some assistance from the ethnographer, the members of the educated class established a library, the Berkeley Union Reading Room. The founder-president of the reading room obtained employment as a research assistant with another ethnographer in another village. During his absence books, furniture, and funds disappeared. The educated class lacked the organizational skills and skilled organizers required to make a Western-type organization function. After 1954, the number of middle school and high school graduates in the village increased progressively. These young men moved into factory jobs and government positions as schoolteachers, clerks, or medical assistants. In many cases, their jobs carried the young men outside the village; still, the numerical strength of the educated class continued to increase.

There also developed a powerful informal organization built around workers who commuted daily to the telephone factory. These workers possessed access to excellent free medical and legal care and had available to them the organizational resources of what seems to be a model labor union in a benevolently operated factory. Because jobs in the telephone factory permit workers to live in or close to the village, supervise their landed properties, and live in their own houses, telephone factory jobs are considered most desirable by schoolboys and their parents. The factory employees control access to those jobs and the means of seeing that those who fail to behave properly fail to obtain jobs or lose them if they have them. Factory workers possess reserves of cash and can obtain loans from their pension fund. The emergence of conflict within the group of factory workers is controlled by company and union officials who investigate complaints and nip potential conflicts in the bud. The factory workers have youth, power, health, economic security, and cash. Many of them also have, perhaps owing to a series of remarkable village primary-school teachers, a strong sense of morality and public responsibility. The factory workers are strongly organized; they have no enemies; everyone, including the village elders, is nice to them.

This pattern of informal organization, although it has some caste-like and classlike overtones, is something new. Traditionally the village was smaller than it is now and many of the formal organizations were run in a relatively informal way. Nevertheless, except for small inter-caste peer groups (perhaps more common in small multicaste villages than in large), group membership was a formal matter centering upon such things as birth, wealth, and family size. Factional alliances, based upon mutual enmities as much as anything else, probably existed from a relatively early period, yet such alliances derived from malfunctions of the traditional formal organizations and many of the hostilities upon which they were based stemmed from divisions within jātis and families or conflict between jātis. The status group and peer group formed by the telephone factory workers is relatively stable and is as concerned with the regulation of conflict as with the carrying on of conflict.

The existence of a large, informally organized set of factory workers within a village does not set the stage for any wholesale movement of the village into the urban world. The factory worker group must be articulated with the social structure of the community. Such articulation has involved the introduction and development of additional new forms of organization.

THE CHIT FUND

In 1956 two of the elders, one of whom was a factory worker, formed the first chit fund in the village. To form a chit fund, a group of members each contribute ten rupees or so to make up a sum of be-tween 150 and 200 rupees. This sum is then auctioned to the person willing to pay the largest amount of interest for the privilege of borrowing the money for one month. Outsiders must be vouched for by a share-holder. Proceeds of the monthly auction, often as much as 20 per cent, may be divided among the membership or invested in worthy causes.

Previous to the formation of the chit fund, there had been no successful cooperative activities since 1952 except for two or three in-stances of unity in the face of a shocking happening or an outside threat. In 1953, when an unwilling wife jumped into a well, the village united in forcing her husband and his family to send her home. Late in 1953 and again in 1954, strange noises at the roadside (three-quarters of a mile from the village) caused the entire male population to seize knives and staves and set out in pursuit of imaginary thieves. Such incidents appear not to have taken place before or since, suggesting that a need for unity may be sufficient to create its own outside threats. In 1954 a drama was organized for the benefit of the Berkeley Union Reading Room and everyone in the village attended except for the former village headman who had been replaced early in 1954. The proceeds from the drama were stolen.

The chit fund of 1956 was also boycotted by the former headman. Early in 1957 the new headman organized a procession of bullocks in connection with an annual ceremony. The successful procession involved little cooperation since people merely had to decorate their own bullocks and lead them through the village. Later the same year, a group of schoolboys collected funds to celebrate a festival in honor of Rama. Although the festival had not previously been an important event, the ceremony was carried out successfully and representatives of every household accepted consecrated food when it was distributed. More functional cooperation centering upon the fixing of wages for laborers, the exchange of labor at sowing time among household heads, the repairing of plows, and the holding of family ceremonials had probably started considerably before this formal acceptance of the end of the conflict. A chit fund was soon started to perpetuate the festival of Rama.

In 1958 an image of the village deity around whom the previous conflict had centered was brought from a neighboring village and the previously conflictive ceremony was carried out again. Everyone participated and accepted consecrated food. A chit fund was started to repair the village temple and restore the images which had been stolen. Incidentally, information concerning the robbery of the village temple was collected in 1960. In 1966 everyone denied that the village temple had been robbed and said that it was another less important temple.

By 1960 there were chit funds for everything. The Rama chit fund contained 100 rupees, the village god chit fund had 200 rupees. Chit funds for other gods reached nearly three hundred rupees. There was a 200 rupee chit fund to pay for a trip to Madras and there were several profit-making funds.

The chit fund made it possible to hold ceremonies and carry out other necessary village functions without relying upon unanimous consent. The carrying out of community activities now rested upon a small group of public-spirited citizens, drawn largely from the "educated class." Tradition-minded citizens could participate or not as they chose. The choice of religious ceremonies for the early demonstration of the new method of organization suggests a desire to do things to which nobody could object. Another important accomplishment of the chit fund was less overt. It consisted of making available to the farmers of the village sources of ready credit. Even though 20 per cent per month is high interest, the borrower can certainly write off a considerable part of it to good will. He can also recover a part of the interest later by using his profits, which would be considerable if he used his chit fund borrowings to purchase chemical fertilizer or improved seed, to buy shares in commercial chit funds. The chit fund, together with money borrowed directly from the wealthier factory workers, provides a bridge between the factory group and the farmer group, and although direct evidence is hard to come by, it seems to have been the means by which the village agricultural economy has been modernized.

One of the more puzzling aspects of chit fund operations is that only one of the funds, a fund organized by the members of a single jāti, has encountered difficulties as a result of embezzlement or failure to return auctioned funds. The chit fund offers a prospect of continuing availability of credit, perhaps thereby stimulating a desire to maintain a good credit rating. Chit fund loans are written up as personal on-demand loans from the president of the fund and the legal papers may be frightening to most people. Finally, the organizers of the chit funds include telephone factory workers, and the chit fund is regarded as a creation of the factory world. Nobody wants to risk offending the factory workers, particularly individual workers. Punishments administered by the factory workers are not always crude and physical, but may include such delicate maneuvers as refusing to lend money, refusing to repair radios or help with wiring jobs, refusing to help in the filling out of petitions, and refusing to provide information about how to get jobs.

THE CLUB PATTERN

In addition to chit funds and despite the inevitable failures, the leaders of the "educated class" continue to experiment with Western-type teams and clubs. Although the life of these teams and clubs is never very long, the life of such organizations in more industrialized nations may also be relatively brief. This does not always mean that the organization has failed in its purposes. Following the death of the Berkeley

Union Reading Room, a group of young men founded a new reading room to which each contributed a magazine subscription. The new reading room lasted for several years. The volleyball team was resurrected after 1960 and then interest shifted to the more nationalistic game of kabbadi. Later, the kabbadi team was broken up. A wrestling team was formed and drew great strength from the fact that a wrestling club had existed in the 1920s. Although the wrestling team was beginning to dissolve in 1966, its aim was to train village young men so they could join their factory wrestling team and take exciting tours of India, hardly a traditional goal.

About 1961 a new schoolteacher from a village some forty or fifty miles away was appointed to the primary school. The new teacher was very popular with the factory workers and the "educated class" and every day a group of boys and young men took walks together, prepared snacks, gossiped and otherwise amused each other. The school, a one-room mud-brick building built before 1910, showed signs of imminent collapse. The schoolteacher attempted to get the building repaired, but found that all government funds were committed to the building of new schools. An alternative way of tapping government funds would be to establish a Young Farmers' Club in the village. Forty persons joined the club, providing a monthly subscription of ten rupees, enough to permit the opening of yet another chit fund. Club members also organized a lottery which made a gross profit of 400 rupees of which half was for prizes, fifty rupees to buy school supplies for the poor, and the remainder for the club. Members of the Young Farmers' Club and some nonmembers as well reconstructed the village resthouse to serve as an office. Members dug drainage pits to keep used bathwater from puddling in the village streets, cleaned up around the village wells, repaired roads, and built a shelter for bus passengers at the village gate.

The "village level worker," a minor government official in charge of village development, appears to have expressed great pleasure at this activity and to have poured government funds into the village. Free fertilizer was given to farmers taking up the so-called Japanese method of paddy cultivation. Two people obtained loans to dig irrigation wells. The tālūka board president (a tālūka is an administrative unit usually containing two or three hundred villages) visited the village and told the Young Farmers' Club to invite the state planning minister to visit. They did so and he came, but before he could provide the new school and the well repairs demanded by the membership he was defeated in an election. Later the village received a new school building, but as late as 1966 no repairs had been made to the old school building, which still continued in use.

In 1965, two defeated candidates for the offices of president and secretary of the Young Farmers' Club accused the victors of receiving a grant from the National Extension Scheme and keeping the money for themselves. The rumor was widely believed and most of the membership of the club quit to join a dramatic group started by the disaffected candidates. The club ceased to function, the schoolteacher who founded it was transferred to a village near his home, and the village level worker stopped coming. Although Nāmahaḷḷi's struggles with the new style of organization are plainly not over, there has been a steady increase in the effectiveness of the organizations founded by members of the "educated class." When things do get done in the village it is now largely through such organizational efforts as were involved in the Young Farmers' Club.

The village council, in so far as it is a village institution, continues to exist but the elders rarely engage directly in political activity and seem to prefer a kind of elder statesman role. They arrange to contribute money to projects, but they rarely propose activities or engage directly in their supervision. The formal, government-sponsored village council has largely been replaced by a joint council which combines Nāmahaḷḷi with a larger neighboring village. This fact is bitterly resented in Nāmahaḷḷi, which recently blocked a proposal that would have provided drinking water for the larger village but not for Nāmahaḷḷi. The proposal was blocked by means of a direct appeal to a minister. Nāmahaḷḷi also came into conflict with the larger village over the question of installing street lights. From Nāmahaḷḷi's standpoint, the new "democratic" village self-government program is an arbitrary government institution imposed from above and serving to encourage the exploitation of small villages by larger villages. Despite this continuation of the long-term tendency for state and national governments to impose new forms of social and political organization upon the village, Nāmahaḷḷi has been able to resist relegation to hamlet status and has recovered its ability to take action as a unit. Organizationally this has been accomplished through chit funds and through a variety of short-lived clubs and teams. Informally it has been accomplished through the development of an "educated class" dominated by the workers of the telephone factory.

NETWORKS AND COMMUNICATION

In addition to the above-noted means of controlling matters within the village, Nāmahaḷḷi has become increasingly articulated with regional and urban social and political structures. The most important ties remain those of kinship and village affiliation. Over the years the structure of these relationships has gradually changed. In the early years, both migration and intermarriage were confined to a relatively small geographical area. Today, through its schoolteachers, minor government servants, and, above all, marital migration, Nāmahaḷḷi has members living in literally hundreds of villages. People living in the city attempt to arrange marriages with people in Nāmahaḷḷi because country people have the reputation of working harder and because dairy products, grain, and vegetables can often be obtained cheaply from country cousins. People living in isolated rural areas value contacts with Nāmahaḷḷi or similarly situated villages because such contacts give them a direct access to the city and to factory jobs. As people in Nāmahaḷḷi become educated and move out to join factory colonies or to accept posts in distant towns and villages, poor relations from the Telagu-speaking regions to the east move in to take jobs as farm laborers and eventually to place their sons in factory jobs. In 1966 the village seemed to be filled with strangers, many of whom were unable to speak the local language, yet the population remained relatively constant in the neighborhood of 600.

In addition to English, Kannada, and Telagu, factory workers from Nāmahaḷḷi find themselves speaking Tamil, Malayalam, and Hindi. The long tradition of polylingualism in the Bangalore area may be an important factor in the integration of Bangalore's factory work forces, which often include supervisory personnel coming from Europe or North India and laborers coming from Madras, Kerala, or Andhra. Active participation in the social organization of the factory permits citizens of Nāmahaḷḷi to develop networks of friendship and influence outside of traditional fields of interaction. What cannot be accomplished through caste and kinship networks available to members of the village can certainly be accomplished through the use of networks belonging to fellow workers in the factory.

If someone from Nāmahaḷḷi wishes to spend the night in Bangalore, he can stay with relatives in the suburb of Ulsur or he can sleep on the roof above a room rented by a Nāmahaḷḷi man who works at the machine-tool factory. One night in 1966 when the ethnographer was stranded in Bangalore, he was picked up by some "relatives" who lived four miles south of Nāmahaḷḷi. The "relatives" bargained for a taxi at a reduced rate and then insisted on riding the taxi all the way to Nāmahaḷḷi to make sure that the ethnographer was not cheated. People in Nāmahaḷḷi have favorite taxis run by relatives or financed by telephone company employees. For each government office, there is a proper person to see, a person who will be glad to hear about his relatives in the village and only too delighted to help out a friend of theirs. Such and such a sub-inspector of police is a "very nice man." Such and such a restaurant is "better than any other" even if you have to walk two miles to get there. The farmer who goes into town and buys a secondhand wristwatch without consulting his friends at the telephone factory is ridiculed as a bad businessman.

Although networks are often used to personal advantage or to gain influence, they also serve to transmit information and to make it possible to secure things that would be otherwise unavailable. At the bus stand in a nearby town, a farmer from Nāmahaḷḷi heard some travelers talking about the possibility of growing wheat. He decided to try growing wheat himself, but when he asked the agricultural officer, it turned out there was no wheat available. The farmer went to the city to the botanical garden, found no wheat, saw a new kind of fruit tree, and purchased it. He obtained wheat seed from relatives living in a distant town and experimented. In three months he had a good yield and made an excellent profit. Through radios, newspapers, magazines, and personal contacts, there is a constant access to information and to influence.

The movement of Nāmahaḷḷi's citizens into jobs as schoolteachers and government and factory workers has given the village a kind of brokerage function. Nāmahaḷḷi's role in providing jobs and advice to kinsmen in other villages has already been noted. In addition, people from Nāmahaḷḷi—and presumably from other similarly situated villages— being neither peasants nor fully urban men, are in a position to bridge the gap between tender-handed urban-reared government officials and hard-handed rural people. People from Nāmahaḷḷi have toured much of Mysore State in such roles as "mosquito inspector," birth control campaigner, projector operator for traveling cinemas, ethnographic research assistant, cigarette salesman, primary schoolteacher, bus conductor, smuggler, and rural development worker. All of these roles represent points of contact between the city and the country.

CONCLUSION

The period 1950 to 1955 appears to have been a low point in the development of the village. During those years, severe economic difficulties and pervasive conflict made it almost impossible to carry out organized activities. Later the village improved its economic position and made significant and effective changes in the traditional pattern of village organization. These changes involved the introduction of new forms such as the chit fund and the team or club; they involved the construction of larger and wider networks of interaction between Nāmahaḷḷi and other organizations and groups, as well as the emergence of the village as a kind of broker between the urban and rural sectors.

Nāmahaḷḷi has not been urbanized in the sense that it has ceased to be rural. It is still a small rural village. It has been urbanized in the sense that many of its people work in factories, keep unusual hours, and generally involve themselves in noise, bustle, and social interaction. People living in Nāmahaḷḷi, particularly the factory workers, are more than urban; they are urbane. They devote themselves to learning and to the making of friends and the influencing of people. Traditional Nāmahaḷḷi believed in training each person for the job he was to do and maintaining established social groups and established patterns of interaction. Modern Nāmahaḷḷi believes in "lifelong learning," and in the massive extension and interlinking of social groups. In modern Nāmahaḷḷi upward mobility is standard and is achieved through education. In traditional Nāmahaḷḷi upward mobility was practically irrelevant. To the extent it existed it meant more grain in the storage jar, not any change in style of living, diet, medical care, occupation, or prestige.

The changes in attitude toward the urban life came about because, after years of waiting, people in the village were made junior partners in the urban affluent society. People can now try and buy new ideas, new things, and new techniques. The knowledge and information which makes all of this newness possible is diffused through a variety of networks. For example, participation in the chit fund required the combination of knowledge gained in the school with knowledge gained in the factory. The Young Farmers' Club involved a combination of school knowledge with information supplied by the government's development program. Wheat, one of many new crops in the village, was introduced as a result of the combining of information derived from bus-stand gossip, the development program, and relatives who had grown wheat, to say nothing of the botanical garden founded in the eighteenth century by Citizen Tipu Sultān. In 1952 and 1953, people in Nāmahaḷḷi were quite skeptical concerning the location of the United States; they doubted that the world was round and they doubted that it was dark in California when it was light in India. In 1960, they said, "You were right after all, because when our factory manager called New York on the telephone it was dark there."

The model of diffusion taking place in terms of traits or complexes moving linearly along simple geographical routes does not fit the situation in Nāmahaḷḷi. Newer and more complicated models which involve the spreading of ideas from urban elites to rural proletariats are equally insufficient. Traits and complexes appear to diffuse in bits and pieces which are put together by the recipients; these bits and pieces come from a variety of sources. The urban elite in Bangalore does not form a very tightly knit group; the intellectual, political, and industrial elites in particular seem related to each other relatively weakly. The information supplied by these elites does not come from a point source. For example, knowledge of the radio and of radio repair diffuses not from the urban elite but from factory worker to factory worker. In particular, knowledge of radio repair seems to have spread horizontally from European factory workers to Nāmahaḷḷi's factory workers: "A man at the factory showed me how to do it."

There seem to be in the village small information-sharing groups centered upon family and peer group. These groups may extend beyond the village, although it seems plain that there cannot be intensive interaction between people who are in different places most of the time. Members of these information-sharing groups establish individual networks within their fields of social interaction, particularly within caste and family and within the factory or office. Information and influence derived from these networks may then be pooled. As information derived from superiors and inferiors (children are always "debriefed" when they come home from school) and from friends and neighbors is collected and pooled, the bits and pieces are fitted together, there are consultations, and appropriate action is taken.

The village itself, along with other urban fringe villages, plays a significant role in the diffusion of information and the formation of networks. The village is attached to the city by all sorts of occupational, political, and kinship networks, but it is attached to the rural area primarily by means of traditional kinship networks. Facing east, Nāmahaḷḷi is rural; facing west it is urban. The fringe villages seem to be very much like the center part of a funnel. On one side their networks widen out into the city; on the other side they flatten down almost to a linear geographic pattern.

Reading the history of Nāmahaḷḷi at a superficial level, it almost seems as if all that is needed for modernization is an abundance of high-paying factory jobs. Certainly economic success, expressed as better pay and better living conditions, is an appealing feature of urbanization. Granted the seductiveness of high wages and good pension plans, the modernization of the village as a whole could not have taken place without strong modification of its social structure. Traditional small communities seem to rely upon total cooperation and consensus in getting things done, whereas urban-influenced communities rely upon public-spiritedness, partial cooperation, and an absence of strong disagreement. Formal voluntary organizations such as chit funds, teams, or clubs make it possible for individuals to pursue independent courses of mobility and still contribute to the community. Finally, neither good jobs nor good organizations make modernization inevitable; this is accomplished through the involvement of the village in multifarious and complicated channels of communication and networks of interaction.

GERALD D. BERREMAN

Pahāri Culture:
Diversity and Change in
the Lower Himalayas

THE LOWER HIMALAYA MOUNTAINS between western Kashmir and eastern Nepal are populated by peoples sharing common and distinct cultural, linguistic, and historical traditions.[1] Therefore, this is clearly a "culture area" within the usual meaning of that term.[2] The populations of this area, collectively termed *Pahāri* (of the mountains), comprise a variety of subgroups which share basic cultural patterns but show local differences in such features as dialect, ceremonial forms, deities worshiped, house styles, dress and ornamentation, range of castes, and rules of marriage. These variations are often extremely limited in distribution so that it is possible for one acquainted with a region to identify readily the particular valley or ridge from which a person comes by his speech or dress. It is not difficult to pass through two or more such areas in a day's trek. This highly localized cultural diversity is especially striking to one acquainted with the people of the plains to the south.

Gerald D. Berreman is Professor of Anthropology at the University of California at Berkeley.

[1] This paper is a revised and expanded version of an earlier publication, "Cultural Variability and Drift in the Himalayan Hills," *American Anthropologist*, LXII (1960), 774-94, which was based upon research supported by a Ford Foundation fellowship during fifteen months of 1957-58. The research process has been described in a short monograph, "Behind Many Masks: Ethnography and Impression Management in a Himalayan Village," Society for Applied Anthropology, Monograph No. 4 (Ithaca, New York, 1962) (also in Bobbs-Merrill Reprint Series in the Social Sciences, Reprint A-393). The substantive results of the research were reported in book form in *Hindus of the Himalayas* (Berkeley, University of California Press, 1963). The author wishes to thank John J. Gumperz for his helpful comments on the earlier version of this paper.

[2] Cf. Gerald D. Berreman, "Peoples and Cultures of the Himalayas," *Asian Survey*, III (1963), 289-304.

A second impressive feature, at least in the subarea to be reported here, is the relative cultural homogeneity across caste lines within a particular locality in the hills. A stranger's caste affiliation is difficult to determine, even by someone of his own area, except by direct inquiry or by observing him in his traditional occupation or in his social relations with others known to him. While there are cultural differences among Pahāri castes, they are less pervasive and less conspicuous than the differences reported among plains castes.

In this account, the facts supporting these generalizations will be briefly described. Then an attempt will be made to analyze and explain them in terms of common conditions and processes. In so doing some further light may be thrown upon change and stability in village India. Special attention will be focused on the concepts of cultural drift and culture area, their relationship to one another, and their relevance to an understanding of Indian society and culture.

The research reported here was carried out in and about the village of Sirkanda situated in the lower Himalaya mountains of North India, about one hundred fifty miles north and slightly east of Delhi and within a day's hike of the well-known hill station, Mussoorie.[3] Sirkanda is large for a hill village, containing some 384 residents, half of whom live all or most of the time in outlying cattle sheds or field houses and half of whom live in the village proper. The people of Sirkanda are speakers of a subdialect of the Central Pahāri language or dialect group. They live on the western border of the area in which that language is spoken, next to Jāunsar Bāwar where begins the Western Pahāri language.[4] They are also on the western border of the former princely state (now district) of Tehri Garhwāl. They spend most of their lives within the four air-mile radius of Sirkanda that comprises the three parallel spurs of hills known as Bhatbair (sheep's den) containing less than 5,000 people in 60 villages and settlements. Their lands, their relatives, and the people with whom they deal for goods and services are nearly all found within this area.

---

[3] The author has, in addition to the areas reported here, some familiarity with other parts of Tehri Garhwāl to the east and with Jāunsar Bāwar and the Punjab hills as far west as Simla.

[4] There are roughly 3,200,000 speakers of Western and Central Pahāri. Eastern Pahāri, better known as Nepali, is spoken only in Nepal.

PAHĀRI CULTURE AREA

The narrow crescent comprising the lower Himalayas qualifies as a culture area as well as any area could, other than an isolated island. It is sharply defined culturally and geographically. Its people are considered by themselves and by others to be ethnically distinct. They are known collectively as Pahāri. They acknowledge this appellation, distinguishing other Indians from themselves as *Desi* (of the country) and the Tibeto-Burmese mountain people as *Bhotiya*. High-caste Pahāris—those who claim Brāhman and Rajput status—are dominant numerically and economically. They have long been known as *Khasa* or *Khasiya* and are thought by many scholars to be descendants of Aryan-speaking immigrants from Central Asia.[5] The Pahāri service castes, widely and loosely referred to as *Dom*, are generally said to be descendants of pre-Aryan indigenes.[6] The Pahāri population has been supplemented by occasional immigrants from the plains, for the mountains have long been a place of refuge from political persecution and individual troubles.

Pahāris are physically indistinguishable from other residents of North India, and they speak an Indo-Aryan language closely related to that of Rājasthan.[7] They are not tribal people in any conventional sense of that term. Rather, they are hill-dwelling Hindus who, though undoubtedly rustic by the standards of their plains-dwelling countrymen, share much of the tradition of North Indian village Hindu culture.

Pahāris are effectively isolated from close contact with non-Pahāris. To the north are the high Himalayas inhabited only in pockets by the racially, linguistically, and culturally distinct Bhotiyas with whom contacts have been limited.[8] At the foot of the mountains, to the south, lie two uninhabited and uninviting strips of land, the *bhabar* (barren and rocky) and below that the *tarai* (low, swampy, and malarial). Beyond

---

[5] George A. Grierson, *Linguistic Survey of India* (Calcutta, Superintendent of Government Printing, 1916), Vol. IX, Part IV, p. 7.

[6] H. G. Walton, *Dehra Dun, a Gazetteer* (District Gazetteers of the United Provinces of Agra and Oudh I) (Allahabad, Government Press, 1911), p. 97.

[7] Grierson, *Linguistic Survey of India*, p. 2.

[8] There has been considerably more contact in Nepal and in the Kali River valley immediately west of Nepal (constituting its western border). What is said here applies more substantially to the Western and Central Pahāri areas west of the Kali River valley.

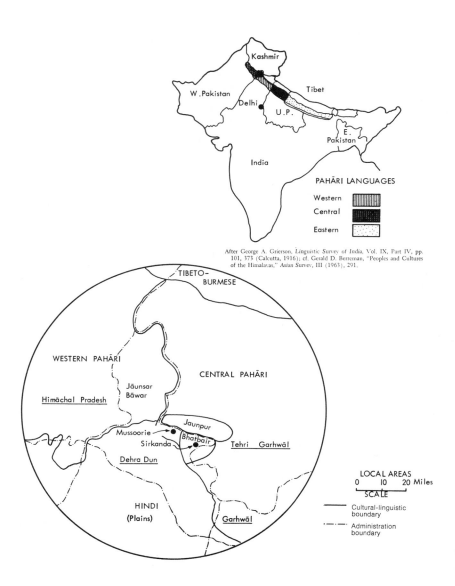

PAHĀRI LANGUAGES

Western
Central
Eastern

After George A. Grierson, *Linguistic Survey of India*, Vol. IX, Part IV, pp. 101, 373 (Calcutta, 1916); cf. Gerald D. Berreman, "Peoples and Cultures of the Himalayas," *Asian Survey*, III (1963), 291.

TIBETO-BURMESE

WESTERN PAHĀRI

CENTRAL PAHĀRI

Jāunsar Bāwar

Himāchal Pradesh

Jaunpur

Mussoorie
Sirkanda
Bhatbair
Tehri Garhwāl

Dehra Dun

HINDI
(Plains)

Garhwāl

LOCAL AREAS
0   10   20 Miles
SCALE

———— Cultural-linguistic boundary
—·—·— Administration boundary

Fig. 1. Pahāri Language Distribution, with Detail of Area Studied

these are the plains from which some and perhaps ultimately all Pahāris once came, but whose people have long been in infrequent and unintensive contact with the hill regions.

The distinctiveness of the Pahāris as a group is suggested by the fact that they share a common and distinctive linguistic stock. They also share a number of other cultural features which distinguish them from the rest of the North Indian culture area and specifically from the plains-dwellers adjacent to them. These features, like their language, are not entirely unique or divorced from those of the rest of North India, but are divergent forms grounded in a common heritage. In emphasizing differences, care must be taken not to ignore the numerous and basic similiarities common to Pahāris and other North Indians. Differences are, however, the primary subject of this analysis. Among distinguishing Pahāri characteristics are:

(1) A somewhat distinctive caste structure wherein there is a major division between the dominant high or twice-born castes ("big castes" in local parlance) made up of Brāhmans and Rajputs, and the "untouchable" (achut) low or "small" castes. The former are the landowning agriculturalists; the latter comprise all of the service castes (blacksmiths, carpenters, weavers, musicians, shoemakers, and others), collectively termed Dom, and make up only about 10 per cent of the population in any area. While there is hierarchical caste ranking within each of these two major categories, it is of significance primarily to those within that category. From across the high-low caste pollution barrier, it appears insignificant. The range of castes found in the hills is smaller than in the plains. Conspicuous by their absence are indigenous Vaishya (merchants) and Shudra (clean caste artisans). On the other hand, occupational variability within castes is considerable in the hills.[9]

(2) A number of rules pertaining to marriage which would be unacceptable to many plains groups and especially to those of high caste. These include bride-price marriage with no necessity for a Sanskritic marriage ceremony, polyandry in some areas, levirate, divorce by mutual consent, remarriage of widows and divorcees, toleration of intercaste marriage within the high- or low-caste group. There is also a good deal of postmarital sexual freedom and sanctioned relations of brothers with one another's wives. Marriage is universally prohibited only among own and mother's sibs, and village exogamy is not everywhere the rule.

[9] Berreman, *Hindus of the Himalayas*, pp. 70 f.

(3) No seclusion of women and freer participation of women in more aspects of life than on the plains, including their participation in singing and dancing at festivals. Relatively free informal contact between the sexes is usual.

(4) A number of religious and ritual features such as absence of the requirement for a Sanskritic marriage ceremony and absence of the requirement for a sacred thread ceremony for high-caste boys, though such ceremonies are coming rapidly into vogue in some areas. Distinctive Pahāri marriage and death ceremonies are performed. There is a great reliance upon mediums and diviners and in some areas the Brāhman priest is relatively less important than on the plains.[10] Frequent and elaborate ritual purification and other religiously motivated acts common on the plains are less widespread in the hills. There are many distinctively Pahāri religious beliefs and forms of worship. Animal sacrifice is a part of most Pahāri ceremonies and buffalo sacrifice is found in some areas. Pahāris are widely known for their devotion to the Pāndavās of Mahābhārata fame and to Shiva. The unique and spectacular rope-sliding ceremony is performed in honor of the latter.[11]

(5) Distinctive folklore, songs, dances, and festivals.

(6) Consumption of meat and liquor by all castes.

(7) Greater flexibility of intercaste relations and freer intercaste interaction than on the plains. The caste hierarchy is important and caste status differences are actively enforced, but the rules allow considerably more contact and informal interaction than is usual in India.

(8) In addition to a nucleated settlement adjacent to a concentration of village lands, temporary-cum-permanent dwellings on widely scattered and often distant agricultural and grazing lands. These are thought of as part of the village even when other villages intervene.

(9) Terrace agriculture with primary dependence on millets, wheat, and barley. Soil productivity is maintained by systematic fertilization, crop rotation, and fallowing. Irrigable land is scarce but wherever possible is used for wet-rice cultivation.

10 Cf. Gerald D. Berreman, "Brāhmans and Shamans in Pahāri Religion," *Journal of Asian Studies*, XXIII (1964), 53-69. Also in Edward Harper, ed., *Religion in South Asia* (Seattle, University of Washington Press, 1964), pp. 53-69.

11 Gerald D. Berreman, "Himalayan Rope Sliding and Village Hinduism: An Analysis," *Southwestern Journal of Anthropology*, XVII (1961), 326-42.

(10) Dwellings of stone and timber, often with slate roofs; distinctive architecture of two stories with the lower floor as the barn and the upper floor as the living area, often with a large open veranda or porch at the upper level.

(11) A number of artifacts including lathe-turned wooden utensils, elaborately carved wooden porch columns, lintels, windows, etc.; virtual absence of pottery.

(12) Distinctive women's dress and ornamentation including full skirt, fitted jacket, and several types of gold and silver jewelry. Men's dress is not as distinctive and has rapidly become like that of men of the plains, but now includes a black or colored cap, a woolen blanket, and a cane as typical Pahāri accouterments.

This list is suggestive rather than exhaustive.[12] Some items may not be as widespread in the hills as others, especially in the area east of Garhwāl, for which there is little information. The list serves to make the point, however, that this area can for some purposes be considered a distinct culture area or subarea within the greater North Indian area. In view of its geographical and ecological isolation, its distinctiveness is not surprising; in view of its common heritage with the rest of North India, its basic similarity thereto is only what would be expected.

CULTURAL DIVERSITY IN THE PAHĀRI AREA

In the above description, the Pahāri area has been treated as though it were inhabited by a culturally homogeneous population. At one level of generalization this is true. At others it is not. Anyone who has trekked through these hills cannot but be struck by the cultural variation which appears from locality to locality even over relatively short distances.[13] This is not a unique characteristic; it is found in many parts of the world

---

[12] For more detailed discussion of each point, and for additional points, see Berreman, *Hindus of the Himalayas.*

[13] In citing examples of such variations in order to explain them, my own materials will be used. It is my impression from some observation and from the sparse literature on the area, however, that such variation is even more prominent in the Punjab hills west of the region reported here (cf. Collin Rosser, "A 'Hermit' Village in Kulu," in M. N. Srinivas, *India's Villages* [Calcutta, West Bengal Government Press, 1955], as an extreme case). This perhaps reflects a longer period of settlement there. Cultural variation in these hills is associated with political fragmentation. They have long been divided into many "kingdoms," or feudal estates, some extremely minute. The extent of these units very likely correlates to some degree with culture areas.

and especially where terrain makes for relative isolation of small groups, as in the hill areas of Assam, Burma, and the Philippines.[14] It is, however, a striking fact which deserves comment and explanation.

In the vicinity of Sirkanda cultural variation occurs at several levels. Jaunpur is an area just north and over a ridge from Sirkanda, accessible by a three- to six-hour trek on foot. It may be considered a subarea comparable, and in apposition, to Bhatbair. A woman of any village in Jaunpur can be easily distinguished from one of Bhatbair by the style of her ankle bracelets, her earrings, the color of her skirt, and the cut of her jacket. If one were to see her house, it too would show minor but distinctive differences of design. Slight differences of speech are reported by those on both sides of the ridge. The pool of household and village gods from which any particular village's pantheon is drawn in Jaunpur differs somewhat from that in Bhatbair. If one inquires about the Jaunpur area and its residents among Sirkanda villagers, one finds that, while they are not considered entirely alien, they are suspect. Most significantly, they are suspected of witchcraft, and this is given as a reason why marriages are arranged with them rarely and reluctantly. It is frequently pointed out by villagers that of five brides sent to that area, three died shortly of witchcraft despite careful advance inquiry into the condition of their prospective husbands' families. There has never been a witch in Sirkanda, villagers affirm; and only one currently exists in all of the villages of Bhatbair. She, significantly enough, lives in one of the most distant and peripheral villages of this area. Witches are alleged to be plentiful, however, in Jaunpur.

These are the kinds of cultural differences found between the residents of adjacent watersheds (i.e., subculture areas) who interact infrequently. Within each of these areas cultural differences are less but not entirely absent. Within Bhatbair, for example, there are some characteristic local differences in jewelry styles.

Across wider boundaries cultural differences increase. One style of large, colored beads worn by women from the area immediately beyond Jaunpur is considered mildly ludicrous in Sirkanda. A type of building used there is considered comical in that it is round instead of rectangular. A day's walk to the southeast lies a Pahāri area strange enough that lin-

---

14 Cf. E. R. Leach, *Political Systems of Highland Burma* (Cambridge, Mass., Harvard University Press, 1954), and Fred Eggan, "Some Aspects of Culture Change in the Northern Philippines," *American Anthropologist*, XLIII (1941), 11-18.

guistic differences become important though they present no great difficulty in communication. In response to inquiry as to the possibility of
marital arrangements being made in that area, the following story was
told about a man who went there to contract a marriage for his nephew:

In the alien village he overheard the brother of the prospective bride
make a statement to his mother which, in the dialect of that region,
meant "the buffalo is ready to be milked," but to the visitor it sounded
like "I am ready to have sexual intercourse." The mother replied,
"Then untie the calf," which in the visitor's dialect meant, "Then untie
your loincloth." Shocked and frightened to hear a man speak in this un-
seemly fashion to his mother and to receive such a reply from her, the
visitor ran out of the village, headed for home. The dismayed family
shouted after him "Stay, for tomorrow we will kill a goat to feast on,"
which only served to accelerate his departure, as in his dialect it meant,
"Stay, for tomorrow we will engage in sodomy." For such reasons exchange of brides is rare between areas with different dialects.

Sirkanda lies on the western edge of the Central Pahāri-speaking
area, as has been noted above. This linguistic boundary is a major one and
corresponds closely to other kinds of cultural differences, most notably
marriage rules. Jāunsar Bāwar is the area immediately to the northwest
where Western Pahāri is spoken. Polyandry is practiced extensively in
Jāunsar Bāwar and has been reported as prevalent here and there throughout the Western Pahāri-speaking area.[15] It is not practiced in or around
Sirkanda nor, so far as I am aware, is it found anywhere in the Central
and Eastern Pahāri areas. Therefore, the western limit of its distribution
corresponds closely with an important linguistic boundary and with the
several associated features such as dress, house-type, and worship, which
distinguish the culture of Jāunsar Bāwar from that of Tehri Garhwāl.

Sirkanda residents' first hand knowledge of Jāunsar Bāwar is almost
nil, but their ideas about it are not inhibited by this fact. Sirkanda informants aver that Jāunsar Bāwar is populated by people who not only
speak an alien, albeit Pahāri language, but who are immoral and many
of whom are witches or sorcerers. The country is infested with evil spirits,
and even the livestock there is unusually dangerous. It is an area best
avoided. That they have followed their own advice on this point accounts

---

[15] D. N. Majumdar, *The Fortunes of Primitive Tribes* (Lucknow, Universal Pub-
lishers, Ltd., 1944); Gerald D. Berreman, "Pahāri Polyandry: A Comparison,"
American Anthropologist, LXIV (1962), 60-75.

for the fact that they are only vaguely aware, if at all, of the less spectacular differences, such as those of architecture, dress, and worship, which obtain between their own culture and that of Jāunsar Bāwar.

The cultural differences which distinguish Jāunsar Bāwar from Tehri Garhwāl may most plausibly be accounted for by reference to historical factors: localized developments and outside contacts. It is not possible to explain such regional peculiarities as those of language, worship, or ornamentation by reference to advantages derived by their possessors. The same is apparently true of the distribution of polyandry. Its appearance has been attributed by observers to a variety of social, economic, and historical forces. But whether its distribution is a result of diffusion, indigenous development, or an earlier more widespread pattern, it seems clear that in these hills there is one basic pattern of family organization of which polyandry is a locally variant form, rather than two radically opposite and unrelated types of organization (polyandry and non-polyandry), as is often assumed to be the case.[16] The question then becomes one of why there is so much regional variation in the culture of the Himalayan hills.

ANALYSIS OF DIVERSITY

The most general characteristic of areas of common and distinct cultures is their isolation. The Pahāri area, as a whole, is isolated from neighboring areas by geographical and cultural-linguistic barriers greater than those which separate Pahāris from one another. Therefore, interaction among Pahāris is more frequent and intense than that between Pahāris and non-Pahāris. This is also the case with regard to relations within and among the various subareas that have been mentioned. Evidence for this isolation of area from area is abundant from the local level up to that of the entire hill region versus the plains.

Sirkanda villagers, for example, interact with one another more than with outsiders if for no other reason than that movement is slow and difficult in this terrain. Moreover, their contacts outside of the village are almost entirely within Bhatbair. Eighty per cent of all Sirkanda marriages have been contracted within this four-mile radius. Virtually all Sirkanda-owned and -cultivated lands are within this area, as are all the

---

[16] Cf. Berreman, "Pahāri Polyandry."

diviners and mediums consulted in times of trouble. Two important intermediate markets lie on the peripheries of Bhatbair. The most important annual fair for Sirkanda villagers is a local one. These constitute the kinds of attractions which take people away from their homes: attendance at marriages and other ceremonies involving kin and friends, visits to kin including affinal relatives, trips to tend property, consultations with diviners and mediums, marketing expeditions, attendance at the annual fair. Only trips to the larger urban centers of Dehra Dun or Mussoorie, each a day's journey away, regularly bring people out of Bhatbair. Such trips, for marketing and dealing with government officials, are made several times a year by most men and even more frequently by some. They do not, however, result in intense interaction with urbanites. They are usually brief and often uncomfortable sorties. No Sirkanda villager has friends or relatives with whom to stay or visit in either of these places—an indication of the lack of intimate contact. The night must be spent in a temple or in the shop of an indulgent merchant unless the villager can return to a Pahāri settlement before dark. If possible, trips are scheduled to make the latter alternative possible. There are adults in Sirkanda who have never been to a city.

When Pahāris do venture out to non-Pahāri areas, they feel conspicuous by their rusticity and distinctive dress, language, and behavior. They are sensitive to the fact that they may be objects of ridicule. They prefer to go in groups and to avoid association with non-Pahāris. When they attend a fair or market, they choose one where Pahāris will be numerous. As one young Sirkanda man commented in comparing distant Delhi, which he had visited, to Dehra Dun: "I like Dehra Dun because you can always see Pahāris around in the bazaar. In Delhi there were only plains people and they made fun of my Pahāri cap." Another commented: "Even if we spend 200 rupees on the finest cloth and have it made into the best clothes, we still look like hillbillies when we go to town." No Sirkanda family has contracted a marriage with a non-Pahāri except in two cases where women were "sold" by poor families who then lost contact with them.[17]

Not only do Pahāri villagers avoid intensive interaction with people in non-Pahāri areas; they also avoid such interaction with outsiders who

---

[17] In addition, a barber family of non-Pahāri origin but long resident in Sirkanda has sent some brides out to the nearby Dehra Dun valley in order to marry them within the caste.

come to the hills. A Pahāri village is a very closed system, as teachers, village level workers, and others who have dealt with such villages will readily testify.[18] The usual reaction to a stranger is to studiously avoid and ignore him. This accounts in part for the singular lack of success with which such governmental programs as community development, rural cooperatives, and even schooling have met in many Pahāri areas. The Sirkanda teacher, a Pahāri from a neighboring area to the east, complained after three months in the village that no one had invited him to a meal, brought him grain, or even inquired as to his home and family status. In a nearby village the teacher had been unable to establish a school despite a potential student body of over fifty pupils. Government forestry officers were warned to bring their own food, water, and bedrolls in this area, for the hospitality to strangers characteristic of plains people is lacking. Few outsiders succeed in establishing effective contact at all with villagers. As a result, alien customs and beliefs have long been slow to influence those of the Pahāris.

The Pahāri culture area is, therefore, largely isolated from the non-Pahāri area to the south. Contacts between the two are characteristically infrequent and unintensive, although there have been periods during which plainsmen have sought refuge in the mountains and have stayed to live. Also, of course, current contacts are increasing through schooling, radio, community development, and other governmental contacts, improved transport, and increased trade. The relative isolation of the mountain region finds its analogue, to a lesser degree, in lack of contacts among subareas within the Pahāri region. At one level, Tehri Garhwāl may be considered a culture area as distinct from Jāunsar Bāwar to the west. The distinction, as described above, is evidenced by a number of cultural differences prominent among which are language and marriage rules. Contact across this boundary is relatively slight. No Sirkanda villager has been to Jāunsar Bāwar, fifteen air-miles to the northwest, although people of the two areas occasionally meet and interact at markets or fairs, primarily in Mussoorie. Jāunsar Bāwar is considered to be a strange and dangerous land. Equally distant parts of Tehri Garhwāl to the east, however, are not strange at all. The latter is the ancestral home of Sirkanda villagers. Most have been there occasionally to visit kin or

---

[18] Cf. Berreman, "Behind Many Masks."

attend marriages and funerals. About 5 per cent of all marriages have been contracted in Tehri Garhwāl at distances comparable to that of Jāunsar Bāwar, which has furnished no marriage partners. Sirkanda lies on and near important trade routes between interior Tehri Garhwāl and the valley, so people from that area are not infrequent visitors. There is no occasion for Jāunsar Bāwar residents to pass by Sirkanda or vice versa. Interaction is, therefore, relatively frequent within Tehri Garhwāl, and very infrequent across into Jāunsar Bāwar. This is not to deny that there is a transitional zone, but only to assert that it is a relatively narrow one. This situation may reflect an earlier period of greater geographical isolation of the two areas. Sirkanda village has probably existed for no more than three hundred years. Prior to that its residents came from Tehri Garhwāl to the east and ultimately, perhaps, from Kumaon farther east. It is thus possible that the two populations, though of common origin, were isolated from one another for some time by an unpopulated area or one populated by peoples now gone or absorbed into other groups. If that is the case, contact between them has been reestablished relatively recently after the westward migration of people from Tehri Garhwāl.

On a more restricted local level, there are differences between nearby Jaunpur and Bhatbair, as cited above. Contacts are less between than within Jaunpur and Bhatbair, though contacts between these areas are more frequent and intense than those across the plains—Pahāri and Jāunsar Bāwar–Tehri Garhwāl boundaries. No land is owned in Jaunpur by Sirkanda people. No markets in Jaunpur are frequented by Sirkanda people, though common markets on the border are attended regularly by residents of both areas. No Jaunpur fairs or religious ceremonies or religious practitioners attract Sirkanda residents. Few marriages have been arranged across this boundary.[19] Visits to Jaunpur are limited to those among kin and to occasional visits by Jaunpur residents en route to the valley to do business.

Pahāris ascribe their localism to the terrain, and this is certainly a factor. A Sirkanda man remarked: "On the plains it is easy to travel and

[19] About 3 per cent of all Sirkanda marriages have been contracted in Jaunpur as compared to 80 per cent within Bhatbair. Such local isolation in marriage relations is not unique to Sirkanda or Bhatbair. D. N. Majumdar, "Demographic Structure in a Polyandrous Village," *The Eastern Anthropologist*, VIII (1955), 172, reports, for example, that in a village of Jāunsar Bāwar, 92 per cent of the Rajput marriages were contracted within 12 miles of the village.

they go great distances for brides. Here it is very difficult to get around so we have to find ours closer to our own village. It is as hard to go one mile here as it is to go five miles in the plains on foot, and many places there they can go by motor bus or at least by cart." Trail miles are at least double the air distances, and trails are generally rough and steep. Sixteen trail-miles is a day's journey and this is the round-trip distance within which 80 per cent of all Sirkanda marriages are contracted.

Terrain, then, is in part responsible for the isolation of group from group. Isolation means less frequent and less intense interaction or communication among groups. It means less opportunity for diffusion of goods and ideas. As a result, there is greater opportunity for development of locally variant cultural forms such as have been described above.

Equally important isolating factors are sociocultural ones. It might be asked, for example, why residents of Bhatbair and Jāunsar Bāwar are more like one another than those of either area are like their non-Pahāri neighbors to the south. It is a fact that Bhatbair residents go frequently to the non-Pahāri area and virtually never to Jāunsar Bāwar, although residents of the two areas meet occasionally and there is indirect contact through the transitional zone separating the two.

The obvious answer is that historically Pahāris have a common origin and cultural tradition which is distinct from that of the plains. Their common culture has been modified locally but not obliterated by the differential contacts and developments consequent upon their dispersion. Another factor is, however, that even infrequent or seemingly casual contacts among Pahāris may be more effective in accomplishing communication and diffusion than more frequent contacts between Pahāris and non-Pahāris. The reason is that Pahāris meet one another to a large extent on common cultural ground and on terms of equality. They understand one another not only in language but in total behavior patterns. They share common definitions of the situations in which they meet. Pahāri–non-Pahāri contacts always involved a lack of communication and understanding at many levels. Above all, the Pahāri feels himself to be at a disadvantage in terms of knowledge, sophistication, and prestige in such situations. Truly informal contact between the groups is almost impossible. They are simply too different. As a result Pahāris do not identify themselves as people who can learn or benefit from the ways of people of the plains. The traditional Pahāri attitude is expressed in their frequent comment: "That's all right for plains people, but it would never work here. The hills and hill people are different." This enables Pahāris to have frequent contacts with non-Pahāris without adopting many of their ways. Thus there are different kinds or qualities of contact with make frequency of contact alone an inadequate criterion of isolation and communication. Occasional intra-Pahāri contacts may serve to maintain a good deal more communication and hence cultural homogeneity than more frequent Pahāri–non-Pahāri contacts. It probably takes less intensive interaction to maintain common culture than to change it. Casual contacts may be more effective in maintaining cultural similarities among similar groups than in causing radically different groups to become similar.

Relative isolation, therefore, has allowed independent cultural developments in the hills vis-à-vis the plains and in Bhatbair vis-à-vis Jāunsar Bāwar. Isolation in the latter has been less extreme than in the former largely because of the quality of the contacts involved and the cultural context in which they have occurred. Before elaborating on the implications of isolation for culture change, its usefulness in understanding other features of Pahāri culture will be investigated in the hope of demonstrating its wider significance.

CROSS-CASTE CULTURAL HOMOGENEITY

There is striking—though by no means absolute—cultural homogeneity from caste to caste within the Pahāri locality in which the author worked. One finds, for example, that the high-caste Brāhmans and Rajputs have the same dietary habits as the untouchable blacksmiths and musicians. All worship the same gods in the same ways. All patronize the same diviners and mediums. All perform the same ceremonies. All wear the same clothing and ornamentation. Differences which exist are primarily those associated with differences in occupation and wealth, and those brought about by high-caste sanctions to maintain the caste hierarchy. In the latter category are prohibitions against low-caste worship in temples, former restrictions against landownership among low castes, and the like. It is my impression, without having engaged in intensive research on the subject, that there are very few caste-specific linguistic differences among indigenous Pahāri groups in the Bhatbair area, although

87

there are honorific forms required of low-caste people in greeting high-caste members.[20] This contrasts with the plains situation where cultural differences among castes of the same village community are prominent features and where such differences are reflected in language differences.[21]

This Pahāri feature—relative intercaste cultural homogeneity—seems to be unusual in the Indian context, but is not surprising when viewed in the same light as regional variability. It is, in fact, what would be expected as the obverse effect of the same factors which lead to regional variation in culture.

In Pahāri villages (at least in Tehri Garhwāl) low castes rarely make up more than 10 per cent of the total population. Often each low caste, or even each caste other than the dominant Rajput or Brāhman group, is represented by only a single family in those villages where it occurs at all. While each low caste will normally be represented within an area, each caste is not represented in every village. More importantly, there are not nearby and easily accessible villages in these rugged mountains. An arduous journey is often required for a minority-caste person just to see a caste fellow, and such journeys are not frequently made. If day-to-day social interaction is to occur at all for minority-caste people, it must occur across caste boundaries. Caste-fellows are simply too few and too inaccessible.[22] Within the Pahāri context such interaction is easily accomplished and is apparently the rule. For, while caste interaction is restricted

---

20 In the past fifteen years a few representatives of an alien shoemaker caste from the Punjab hills (Kangra) have come into this area where formerly there were no shoemakers. These people are western Pahāris, culturally and linguistically distinct from Bhatbair groups. They have not been allowed to settle in extant villages nor to interact freely or informally with other castes, but they are tolerated in the area as useful artisans. As aliens the shoemakers do not fit into the local culture nor the local caste hierarchy, so they are socially isolated. Their unclean occupation has contributed heavily to this isolation—they are considered uniquely defiling and untouchable by all local castes. The discussion in this article excludes this caste of unclean outsiders.

The one indigenous Muslim family of Bhatbair is, on the other hand, treated as any other indigenous low caste. The one family of barbers, brought from the neighboring plains at the founding of the village and now almost entirely assimilated, is also treated as an indigenous low caste. The barbers can marry into either of two local low castes and may become assimilated into one of these in time.

21 John J. Gumperz, "Dialect Differences and Social Stratification in a North Indian Village," American Anthropologist, LX (1958), 668-82.

22 Gumperz (ibid., p. 680) found in a plains village that among the least populous "middle castes" informal intercaste contact was more frequent than among the more populous high and low castes.

and these restrictions are enforced, the rules are relatively flexible and permissive in comparison to those common to the plains area.

In Sirkanda low-caste people cannot normally enter high-caste houses nor sit on the same cot nor eat with high-caste people. However, there are numerous opportunities for informal social interaction. Low-caste people can sit on the step or doorsill of high-caste houses. Since an open veranda serves as living room, they can participate quite fully in social situations without entering the house. On the other hand, it is not unusual for a low-caste man to be asked in to the veranda (never the kitchen) of such a house to share in a drinking party—an occasion when normal rules are relaxed. Informal drinking groups of men are often multicaste groups. Since high-caste people feel no compunction on entering a low-caste home, a drinking party may be held there. In addition, there are many caste-neutral places in the village where much informal social interaction takes place: shops, the places of work of artisans, the village water source, yards of houses, the fields and forests where people work, a large stone fortification left from some earlier era and now used as a place to sit and view the countryside. In these places people gather to talk without regard for caste. Children's playgroups are intercaste in composition, including the whole range of indigenous castes. Often men and/or women work in one another's company without caste distinctions. When cooperative labor is called for, as when a house beam is to be lifted, roof tile is to be transported, or rice is to be transplanted, caste is ignored in the composition of the group. The most notorious Bhatbair woman-selling gang of thirty years ago was made up of three men who worked in close concert sharing the risks and profits—a Brāhman, a Rajput, and an untouchable. The surviving Brāhman is now a respected elder and priest. When someone wishes to travel to another village, or more especially to a market or an urban area, he attempts to find a traveling companion, and caste is of little importance. Pahāris seek mutual support regardless of caste in the presence of strangers. All castes may and generally do attend or at least watch religious ceremonies carried out in the village except those held inside high-caste homes.

Ritual pollution does not pose the threat of inconvenience to high-caste Pahāris that it does to plains people. It occurs only as a result of such unlikely contacts as commensality, a contaminated pipe or water vessel, entrance of a low-caste person into a high-caste home and more especially into its kitchen. Such contamination is rare, so the need for purification is rare. Objects are occasionally contaminated, but individuals almost never are.

On the plains, by contrast, intercaste interaction is more limited, especially when status differences are great. There are often larger numbers of caste-fellows within a village or at least in neighboring and easily accessible settlements than is true in the hills. There are fewer opportunities for frequent and intensive intercaste contacts as a result of more stringent rules restricting such contacts. Pollution occurs more easily and entails more inconvenience for the high-caste plainsman. Informal contacts across the "pollution barrier" are few. Gumperz reports that even children's playgroups exclude touchable-untouchable contacts.[23] Consequently, most social interaction on the plains occurs within the caste or among closely similar castes, and this frequently involves interaction across village lines.

Thus, in the hills there is little opportunity for cultural differences to arise or to be maintained among castes simply because there is little intercaste isolation in any one locality. On the plains the situation is reversed; caste isolation is the rule and intercaste cultural differences, especially across the pollution barrier, result. Common culture, like common language, depends upon the interaction of those who share it. As Bloomfield has noted, "The most important differences of speech within a community are due to differences in *density of communication*."[24]

Frequency of contact alone, however, is not sufficient to determine degree of cultural homogeneity among castes or ethnic groups any more than it is among culture areas. Gumperz found that dialectal differences between castes in a plains village depended not on the number of intercaste contacts but on their form.[25] Work contacts (i.e., employer-employee relations) showed no correlation with linguistic differences. Informal friendship contacts seemed to be determinative. Mandelbaum reports that among the Todas, Badagas, Kotas, and Kurumbas of the Nilgiri Hills, "Although contact was frequent, social intercourse was confined to a fixed number of narrowly defined activities. Any intimate contact, of a kind which would allow members of one group to mingle freely with

---

[23] *Ibid.*, p. 679.
[24] Leonard Bloomfield, *Language* (New York, Henry Holt, 1933), p. 46.
[25] Gumperz, "Dialect Differences and Social Stratification in a North Indian Village," p. 681.

another, was stringently tabooed."[26] As a result, the groups remained culturally distinct. It has been widely observed that people emulate those whom they envy, not those they despise. Thus in India low castes often attempt to adopt attributes and behaviors of their social superiors while the reverse does not occur. In fact, it seems that this tendency to high status emulation can be prevented only by the application of sanctions which isolate the low castes and prohibit them from displaying characteristics inappropriate to their rank.

Obviously, then, the kind and intensity of interaction is important. It is in this respect, perhaps even more than in frequency, that Pahāri intercaste relations differ from those on the plains. Characteristically such contacts on the plains are formal, "contractual," restricted in scope and content, and are accompanied by a good deal of inhibition on both sides. Prohibitions against emulation of their superiors by low castes are strictly defined and sanctions are stringently applied. In contrast, in the Pahāri area intercaste contacts are more often informal, intensive, and extensive. There is relatively little concern about differential life styles of the various castes. Specific rules of interaction and privilege are enforced, but emulation is not regarded as particularly threatening. This is perhaps both cause and effect of the relative cultural similarity among Pahāri castes. Plains castes exclude one another from knowledge of, and participation in, their problems and ways of life, and the high prohibit imitation by the low. Pahāris exclude outsiders but are little concerned with concealing their affairs from local members of other castes or with restricting particular life styles to high castes alone. Pahāri castes are thus not closed social and cultural subgroups to the extent that plains castes tend to be.

The accompanying diagram (Fig. 2) may help make clear the contrasts in plains and Pahāri interaction patterns and hence cultural differentiation by caste and locality. In this diagram broken arrows indicate limited interaction, solid arrows indicate extensive and intensive, informal interaction. Interaction in the plains culture tends to be horizontal (i.e., within the caste and across local boundaries), while Pahāri interaction tends to be vertical (i.e., within the local area and across caste boundaries). These are consequently the directions of the primary diffusion of

[26] David G. Mandelbaum, "Culture Change among the Nilgiri Tribes," *American Anthropologist*, XLIII (1941), 20.

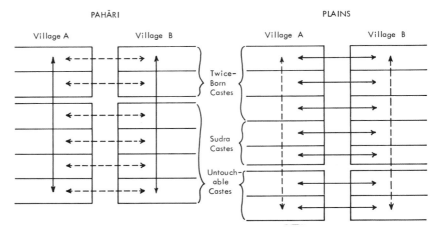

Fig. 2. Contrasting Interaction Patterns

ideas and behaviors, so that maximum cultural homogeneity occurs along the axes of the solid arrows. Not shown here is the fact that interaction within a local caste group (or perhaps even among different castes of similar status in a locality) is probably in all cases greater than that between castes or communities.

Isolation is a factor which sheds some light on another feature, namely, the greater regional distinctiveness evidenced in the dress and ornamentation of women as compared to men. Aside from language (which might well show some sexual difference too) the most sensitive indicator of regional affiliation in the hills is probably women's costume. A factor which contributes to this is the fact that women travel outside of their husbands' villages rarely except for occasional visits to their parents' villages. Men travel more widely and more frequently. Since women are relatively isolated from women of other localities, the women's subculture tends to be more localized than that of men. This seems to be true on the plains as well.

Thus, the degree of cultural difference found among the castes, areas, and perhaps even between the sexes, as reported here, varies directly with their degree of isolation from one another defined in terms of rate and quality of interaction and determined by social and physical accessibility. This is not to assert that social isolation, where it occurs, is always the causal factor. Cultural differences may bring about social isolation or vice versa. Moreover, the differences that have been cited here between caste and areal distinctiveness in the plains on the one hand and in the hills on the other are quanitative rather than qualitative. Isolation and interaction are relative matters which vary with frequency and intensity of contact among groups. There are culture areas on the plains as well as in the hills, but they tend to be larger in the former and perhaps their transition zones are more gradual. Similarly there are intercaste cultural differences in the hills, but they are less than on the plains.

STATUS EMULATION AND CHANGE

A prevalent and widely discussed type of socioeconomic change in India is Sanskritization or, in its more general form, status emulation.[27] This is the process mentioned above whereby members of a group—usually a caste or segment of a caste—express a claim for higher status than that previously accorded them by adopting behaviors and attributes associated with the status to which they aspire. The consequence is that symbols of high status diffuse downward and the apparent cultural differences in a community or region between the mobile castes and those they wish to emulate threaten to diminish. Accomplishment of this decrease in cultural diversity depends not so much on frequency and intensity of interaction as upon the opportunities for successful emulation. First, of course, an upwardly mobile group must perceive certain attributes and behaviors as status-relevant and hence worth emulating (or necessary to be emulated) as means to higher status. Generally this does not present a problem, for the crucial symbols of high status are well known and relatively superficial, so that little subtlety and even less intimacy are required for them to be perceived, identified, and imitated. Obstacles to successful emulation, therefore, do not come from lack of knowledge but from barriers to expression. The caste system depends for its existence upon maintenance of the hierarchy of sharply bounded groups. Those

[27] Cf. M. N. Srinivas, *Religion and Society among the Coorgs of South India* (Oxford, Clarendon Press, 1952), pp. 30 ff.; M. N. Srinivas, "A Note on Sanskritization and Westernization," *Far Eastern Quarterly*, XV (1956), 481-96; M. N. Srinivas, *Social Change in Modern India* (Berkeley, University of California Press, 1966), pp. 1-45.

groups at the top hold the power. That power is threatened by mobile groups. Those at the top therefore admit others to privileged positions only when forced to do so or when the traditional criteria of privilege become irrelevant to them (as when, in some modern urban contexts, they choose to seek status by secular means). Status emulation therefore requires courage in the attempt and power in the accomplishment—either that or indifference on the on the part of the emulated.

In the mountains, as in the plains, status emulation is employed as a mechanism for social mobility and results in a degree of downward diffusion of high-status attributes. In the mountains, however, emulation of high castes by low is not so significant as a source of change as in many regions in the plains. This may be due in part to the very homogeneity of Pahārī culture—there simply are not sufficient overt differences between cultures of high and low castes to make emulation an obvious route to upward mobility. More important may be the small numbers of low-caste people in any given locality and the relative isolation of each community. The opportunity to succeed in effective and successful emulation of powerful, decisively dominant high castes is simply lacking among those who might wish to make the attempt; the sanctions would be swift and formidable.

The primary manifestation of status emulation in the mountains is found not among upwardly mobile low castes but among all castes, high and low. They emulate not privileged members of their own society but members of plains society. Plains culture has become, for Pahārīs of many regions, a way of life worthy of emulation by all castes. Whether or not it is attempted in any particular region, and the degree to which it is attempted, seems to depend upon the extent to which there is contact with people of the plains. Such contact has increased rapidly since independence. The practitioners of plains culture have come into increasing contact with Pahārīs as administrative officials, teachers, community development workers, lawyers, military personnel, merchants, and in many other roles. They increasingly affect and even control the destinies of Pahārīs as national administration, education, and commerce increasingly penetrate the mountains. The opinions, judgments, and preferences of plainsmen become increasingly relevant to Pahārīs. Moreover, plains people are symbols of sophistication and often of affluence, resembling the admired personages of radio, film, and the other role-models characteristic of popular culture. Plains people therefore come to comprise an important positive reference group for Pahāris.[28] One finds Pahāris of all castes adopting ways of life which they assume to be characteristic of high-caste plainsmen. Elsewhere I have referred to this as "plainsward mobility."[29] It is manifest in speech, ritual, dress, technology, and many other spheres. It even (and expectably) leads to attemp's by high castes to distinguish themselves more sharply from low castes in their behavior and attributes, in imitation of plains practice. This pervasive trend toward plains emulation is an unambiguous instance of diffusion of the way of life of a dominant society to the members of a subordinate subcultural group. Specific changes to the plains model of behavior (e.g., vegetarianism, elimination of mixed dancing, abandonment of bride price) are often covertly resisted or disregarded by Pahāris even as they are given lip service, for many such changes are regarded as immediately undesirable or disadvantageous. The desire for acceptance by, and the esteem of, plains people, however, makes their adoption (or the appearance of their adoption) desirable as means to the long-run goal. The trend to plainsward mobility has become prominent only recently, not because contacts did not previously exist between the plains and the mountains, but because only with national sovereignty and with improved communication have plainsmen come to constitute an important positive reference group for Pahāris. Only recently have they been in a position to judge and to reward or deprive Pahāris by their approval or disapproval.

The trend toward emulation of the culture of the plains is likely to accelerate with the increase in direct contacts with plains people, through the influence of mass media and education, and, ultimately, as participation of Pahāris in the plains-oriented and -dominated national culture increases. If, as seems likely, that culture becomes increasingly secularized, Pahāris will doubtless follow the trend but, as in the case of upwardly mobile low castes in the plains, there will probably be some degree of lag on the part of plainswardly mobile Pahāris. They are likely for a time to seek acceptance by emulating traditional plains culture even as sophisticated plainsmen are shifting their energies and aspirations to nontraditional spheres. Eventually, though, they will doubtless follow

---

[28] Cf. Robert K. Merton, *Social Theory and Social Structure* (Glencoe, The Free Press, 1957), pp. 225-386; Gerald D. Berreman, "Aleut Reference Group Alienation, Mobility and Acculturation," *American Anthropologist*, LXVI (1964), 231-50

[29] Berreman, "Himalayan Rope Sliding and Village Hinduism," p. 338.

the national trend, whatever it may be, for increasingly effective communication and increasingly pervasive interaction seem destined to lead to a decrease in cultural diversity in the nation. The relative isolation of Pahāris from plains culture, of Pahāri communities from one another, and of plains castes from one another is bound to diminish and with it the cultural differences between the Pahāris and the plains people. Without social or physical isolation they will be incapable of remaining culturally disparate.

CULTURAL DRIFT

The importance of isolation to biological evolution has long been recognized and has been cited as the necessary mechanism for genetic drift.[30] Sapir noted its importance in dialectation or linguistic drift.[31] Redfield is among those who have commented that isolation is necessary for the development of any distinctive culture,[32] and from the beginning the idea has been implicit in the work of those who have used the concept of culture area.[33] But the relevance of isolation to cultural variability has not been made explicit.

Isolation is a necessary but not sufficient explanation for the origin and maintenance of cultural differences. A broader concept such as "cultural drift" (or perhaps "cultural divergence") gives promise of greater utility.[34] By this I mean a process exactly parallel to that of linguistic drift and analogous in many respects to genetic drift.[35] These

[30] Sewall Wright, "The Evolution of Dominance," *American Naturalist*, LXIII (1929), 560; William C. Boyd, *Genetics and the Races of Man* (Boston, Little, Brown and Company, 1950), p. 155.

[31] Edward Sapir, *Language* (New York, Harcourt, Brace and Company, 1921), p. 150 (Harvest ed., 1949).

[32] Robert Redfield, *The Folk Culture of Yucatan* (Chicago, University of Chicago Press, 1941), pp. 349 f.

[33] Clark Wissler, *The American Indian*, 3d ed. (New York, Oxford University Press, 1938); Alfred L. Kroeber, *Cultural and Natural Areas of Native North America* (University of California Publications in American Archaeology and Ethnology), XXXVIII (1939), 1-242.

[34] Cf. Melville J. Herskovits, *Man and His Works* (New York, Alfred A. Knopf, 1951), pp. 580 ff.; Fred Eggan, "Cultural Drift and Social Change," *Current Anthropology*, IV (1963), 347-55.

[35] A more accurate but more unwieldy term would be "sociocultural drift," since as used here "cultural drift" applies equally to social structural phenomena and cultural content. See Sapir, *Language*, pp. 147 ff., and Wright, "The Evolution of Dominance."

terms describe the process whereby subgroups diverge from the main stream of characteristics shared by the larger group of which they are a part—the "stock" or "cultural substratum"[36]—and develop along independent lines. Cultural drift may be described as the process of divergent or differential cultural change.

Cultural change, like genetic evolution, comes about as a result of *variation, selection,* and *transmission,* while drift or divergent change requires the additional condition of *isolation,* that is, relative lack of communication among the groups involved.

Variation—the occurrence of changes and alternatives–is a continuous and inevitable process in every culture. It results from various processes, the uniform psychological aspects of which Barnett has described as innovation.[37] Change or innovation is impelled especially but not exclusively by contact with alien ways of life, by the stresses resulting from new or changing physical and sociocultural integration.[38] Sources of variation which have led to Pahāri cultural distinctiveness have been sought by commentators in such diverse factors as climate, topography, the heritage from Indo-Aryan invaders and their indigenous predecessors, diffusion resulting from contacts with Tibetans and with people of the plains of North India, and specific historical events from ancient to modern times.

From among the range of variations available to the carriers of a culture there must be *selection.* This determines the direction of cultural change and drift. Selection in cultural change differs from the natural selection of biological evolution in an important way. In culture, selection depends ultimately upon the choices made by people in the context of their total social-cultural-physical environment, of which the value system is an important aspect.[39] Cultural selection may be pur-

[36] Marian W. Smith, "Culture Area and Culture Depth with Data from the Northwest Coast," in Sol Tax, ed., *Indian Tribes of Aboriginal America* (selected Papers of the 29th International Congress of Americanists) (Chicago, University of Chicago Press, 1952), p. 93.

[37] Homer Barnett, *Innovation: The Basis of Cultural Change* (New York, McGraw-Hill, 1953).

[38] Cf. Clifford Geertz, "Ritual and Social Change: A Javanese Example," *American Anthropologist,* LIX (1957), 32-54; Morris E. Opler, "Component, Assemblage, and Theme in Cultural Integration and Differentiation," *American Anthropologist,* LXI (1959), 955-64; and Evon Z. Vogt, "On the Concepts of Structure and Process in Cultural Anthropology," *American Anthropologist,* LXII (1960), 18-33.

[39] Cf. Vogt, "On the Concepts of Structure and Process in Cultural Anthropology," pp. 25 f.

poseful or not; conscious, as in the case of adoption of Sanskritic rituals by Pahāris, or unconscious, as in linguistic drift.[40] It bears no necessary relationship to survival advantage, nor does it emerge, as does biological survival advantage, from a vast, seemingly random range of actually and potentially occurring variations. Rather it results from an accumulation of human behaviors including choices. In both kinds of change selection occurs because the variations are too many for all to be transmitted, but the mechanisms by which selection is accomplished are quite different in culture and biology—a fact which the identity of terminology should not be allowed to conceal. An important difference between cultural and genetic drift (as distinguished from evolution or other kinds of change) is that genetic drift is usually defined as the result of chance variations in gene frequencies. If a selective advantage operates the change is, by definition, not drift. In cultural drift, as I am using the term, selection according to advantage, real or imagined, intentional or unintentional, is not ruled out and, in fact, plays an important role in determining the direction of the drift.

Transmission is, of course, necessary in order to pass on within the group the selected variants along with the rest of culture. It is achieved with varying degrees of efficiency through processes subsumed under such titles as socialization and enculturation.

For cultures to diverge from a common stock and become distinctive subcultures, some degree of isolation is required. Two groups are isolated from one another to the degree that contacts between their members are infrequent, restricted, superficial, formalized—in short, neither intensive nor extensive. Without isolation, interaction leads to common experience and consequent common culture. This is the crux of the argument of this paper. The Pahāri culture area and those smaller subareas within it have become distinct as a result of cultural drift in general and isolation in particular. Plains castes have become or have remained culturally distinct as a result of isolation from one another, while Pahāri castes have become or have remained culturally homogeneous because of their intimate contact with one another on the local level. Change can occur in the content of any culture, language, or

[40] Cf. Sapir, Language, p. 155.

biological race; differential change or drift can occur only in isolated subgroups.[41]

CULTURE AREAS

Isolation is rarely absolute. Degrees of isolation correlate with degrees of divergence or drift. Culture areas, therefore, exist only to the extent that there is effective isolation, lack of communication, among groups. The distinctness of a culture area or cultural group corresponds with the degree, duration, and kind of isolation of the people involved. Those who attempt to delimit such areas or groups are faced with the same taxonomic problem which faces the dialectologist and the population geneticist, that is, what kind or degree of difference is to be adjudged critical. Differences and similarities occur at many l els. Just as no two people speak exactly alike, so their patterns of behavior and belief differ. Roberts has demonstrated cultural differences even in adjacent and closely related households.[42] In discussing cultural affiliations of Sirkanda residents one could defend as valid their membership in any or all of the following "culture areas": North India, Pahāri, Central Pahāri, Garhwāl, Tehri Garhwāl, Bhatbair. Other culture areas could be delimited, including some crosscutting these. Groups peripheral to some of these areas might be located centrally in culture areas defined by different criteria.

Drift and diffusion are not uniform and culture elements are not rigidly linked to one another. Therefore the boundaries of distribution of various traits or patterns—the "isotraits," "isoelements," or "isopatterns" as they might be called—do not always coincide. They often have varying or even independent distributions. Here it has been shown that polyandry and Western Pahāri speech have a common eastern boundary in the Himalayan hills. Their distribution is not, however,

[41] "Now dialects arise not because of the mere fact of individual variation but because two or more groups of individuals have become sufficiently disconnected to drift apart, or independently, instead of together. So long as they keep strictly together, no amount of individual variation would lead to the formation of dialects." Sapir, *Language*, pp. 150-51.

[42] John M. Roberts, *Three Navaho Households: A Comparative Study in Small Group Culture* (Peabody Museum of Harvard University Papers, Vol. 40, No. 3) (Cambridge, Mass., Peabody Museum, 1951).

identical. Leach has reported cases where language and other aspects of culture have independent distributions.[43] Dialect geographers are familiar with nonconforming isoglosses. "Almost every feature of phonetics, lexicon, or grammar has its own area of prevalence—is bounded by its own isogloss."[44] Population geneticists meet the same problems with isogenes.[45]

The cultural geographer has to decide what elements are to be used, their relative weighting, and the number and degree of correspondences (i.e., bunching) of isoelements required to define a cultural or subcultural boundary. His choices will depend largely upon his purposes and will affect the precision with which the culture areas he designates can be delineated. The distinctness of culture areas depends both on the criteria used in determining them and on the conditions of isolation and contact among those to whom the criteria are applied. In some regions, such as the Himalayan hills, culture areas can be sharply and consistently differentiated, with narrow transition zones. In others, such as the plains of North India, they may be less sharply demarcated, with broad transition areas.

There can be no single correct way to define a culture area or cultural group. A broad definition might parallel that of the geneticists' definitions of race, e.g., "a population which differs significantly from other human populations in regard to the frequency of one or more of the genes it possesses."[46] Thus *culture area* might be defined as *the area inhabited by people or social groups who share more culture content (including social structure), or more of particular elements of culture content, with one another than with those outside of the area,* the amount and kind of common culture to be decided on the basis of the problem to be studied. A cultural group could be defined similarly without the

[43] Leach, *Political Systems of Highland Burma*, p. 48.
[44] Bloomfield, *Language*, p. 328. In determining culture areas the procedure followed by Wissler (*The American Indian*, pp. 219 ff.) and that used later in the trait distribution studies of Kroeber and his associates bore similarities to the procedures used by dialect geographers (cf. Raven I. McDavid, "The Dialects of American English." in W. Nelson Francis, *The Structure of American English* [New York, The Ronald Press Company, 1958], pp. 498 f.). Gumperz, "Speech Variation and the Study of Indian Civilization," *American Anthropologist,* LXIII (1961), 976-88, has discussed in detail problems of dialect geography and their relevance to culture areas and groups.
[45] Boyd, *Genetics and the Races of Man*, pp. 204, 226.
[46] *Ibid.,* p. 207.

areal criterion. Such a definition allows the flexibility to conceive of culture areas or groups at various levels of abstraction. It implies no judgment, for example, as to the relative validity of designating Bhatbair, Garhwāl, and North India as culture areas. Each is a relatively homogeneous culture area isolated from comparable areas.

Another complicating factor in determining culture areas and affinities lies in their variability through time.[47] Cultures are constantly changing at all levels; drift and diffusion are continuous processes. Kind and degree of isolation, sources of variation, criteria of selection, and methods of transmission are all subject to constant change with resultant changes in the distribution of traits and patterns. In Sirkanda the adoption of Brāhmanical or Sanskritic ceremonies is proceeding continuously in all castes at present. In this respect, the area is coming increasingly into the orbit of the plains culture area. Leach describes continual cultural variations in the population of the Kachin Hills of Burma.[48] A culture area is a static model which, like a photograph, picks one configuration out of a moving scene and immortalizes it. It must be recognized and treated as such.[49] However accurate the description may have been, the culture area has changed as soon as it has been observed.

There is also the problem of cultural variation among social groups within an area. Among plains castes in India, for example, there are significant cultural differences on different status levels within the same area, and various castes may form different culture areas. Drift and diffusion may occur at different rates and in different directions among various groups in a region. In this case a multidimensional model or a

[47] Cf. Julian H. Steward, *Theory of Culture Change* (Urbana, University of Illinois Press, 1955), pp. 82 f.

[48] Leach, *Political Systems of Highland Burma.*

[49] "Recently, a new interest in the culture area has developed, and with it an attempt to add a dynamic dimension and utilize its potentialities more carefully. Bennett [Wendell C. Bennett, "The Peruvian Co-Tradition," in *A Reappraisal of Peruvian Archaeology,* Memoirs of the Society for American Archaeology, Vol. XIII, No. 4 (1948)], working with Andean materials, introduced the concept of areal co-tradition, a taxonomic tool for classifying one of the ways culture areas develop through time." Douglas W. Schwartz, "Culture Area and Time Depth: The Four Worlds of the Havasupai," *American Anthropologist,* LXI (1959), 1060. See also Smith, "Culture Area and Culture Depth with Data from the Northwest Coast," and Robert W. Ehrich, "Culture Area and Culture History in the Mediterranean and the Middle East," in Saul S. Weinberg, ed., *The Aegean and the Near East: Studies Presented to Hetty Goldman* (Locust Valley, N.Y., J. J. Augustin, 1956).

series of overlays are required to depict cultural distributions simultaneously by areas and groups. This is also a problem in mapping dialectal and racial distributions. It makes especially necessary explicit description of the populations and the defining characteristics which have been used in setting up any culture area.

These complexities do not make the concept of culture area useless any more than they do the concepts of dialect or biological race. They do put them in proper perspective as abstract configurations drawn from a continuum of variations over time and space and among socially defined groups.

Finally, the use of culture traits or patterns to trace cultural drift, to define culture areas and groups, may be criticized on grounds that this obscures more important cultural wholes or leads to neglect of crucial information. This is a frequently recognized problem. Kroeber notes that his study of cultural areas in North America "deals with culture wholes, and not, except incidentally, with culture elements or 'traits,' nor with those associations of elements which are sometimes called 'culture complexes' but which constitute only a fraction of the entirety of any one culture."[50] Distributions of over-all configurations rather than of traits are the subject of interest in most culture area studies just as they are the ultimate referents in many linguistic and genetic distribution studies. Particular items are selected, in most cases, merely as convenient indicators of cultural (or linguistic or racial) similarities, differences, distributions, and changes which cannot with present techniques be adequately studied as wholes. It is therefore more generally a methodological problem than a conceptual one. Perhaps multivariant analysis or a scheme grouping cultural components into broad categories[51] will eventually enable us to study cultures as wholes, or at least take us farther in that direction. This would alleviate the distortions so common under present methodology. For the time being, however, the crude groupings which result from culture area studies are subject either to the limitations inherent in the study of a few elements or patterns selected from the universe of cultural data and divorced to some extent from their cultural context, or to the limitations inherent in the subjective comparison of total configurations. In the study of cultural distributions one has to

---

[50] Kroeber, *Cultural and Natural Areas of Native North America*, p. 2.
[51] Cf. Opler, "Component, Assemblage, and Theme in Cultural Integration and Differentiation."

choose the methodology which seems most feasible in terms of the data and most defensible in terms of the problem and these limitations.

CONCLUSION

Herskovits has noted that drift is a concept which "despite its usefulness for the study of culture, has been strangely neglected by most cultural anthropologists."[52] Eggan has demonstrated that the neglect has been relative rather than absolute, and has himself contributed to the rectification of that neglect.[53] This paper has been in part an effort toward enhancing the usefulness of the concept of drift as a descriptive and analytical device by defining its operation explicitly and by viewing it broadly in the context of cultural diversity and change. In order to do this an attempt has been made to relate the dynamic concepts of drift and change to the classificatory and generally static concept of culture area. The latter may be made more useful by viewing cultural variation not only as a problem in population movement and diffusion, but also as a result of the continuing process of cultural drift as defined here: of culture change in conditions of intergroup isolation with consequent divergence. Further research into the conditions and effects of isolation of varying kinds and degrees, the associated types and intensities of interaction, the sources of variation, the criteria and processes of selection, and the processes of transmission should increase the usefulness of such a model as cultural drift for the study of cultural change.

[52] Herskovits, Man and His Works, p. 582.
[53] Eggan, "Cultural Drift and Social Change."

JOSEPH W. ELDER

Rājpur:

Change in the Jajmāni System

of an Uttar Pradesh Village

THE VILLAGE OF RĀJPUR[1] lies less than 200 miles east of Delhi in the state of Uttar Pradesh. In location, family composition, farming practices, religious beliefs, and festivals it resembles such villages as the Wisers' Karimpur,[2] Marriott's Kishan Garhi,[3] Majumdar's Mohana,[4] Lewis's Rampur,[5] and Hitchcock and Minturn's Khalapur.[6] Like such villages, however, it also has its individual features, including its particular set of castes arranged in its own hierarchy. In 1957, when this study was in progress, Rājpur's population of 938 was divided into eleven castes—seven Hindu and four Muslim. The villagers generally agreed that these eleven castes could be arranged in a hierarchy of five ranks, with the Jāt landed farmers at the top and the Bhangi sweepers at the

Joseph W. Elder is Professor of Sociology and Indian Studies at the University of Wisconsin.

[1] Rājpur is a pseudonym for the village in which I lived from 1956 to 1958 with a Foreign Area Training Fellowship from the Ford Foundation. Although this paper provides no reason for concealing the identity of the village, a forthcoming book, in fact, does.

[2] William and Charlotte Wiser, *Behind Mud Walls* (New York, Richard R. Smith, 1930).

[3] McKim Marriott, "Little Communities in an Indigenous Civilization," in McKim Marriott, ed., *Village India: Studies in the Little Community* (Chicago, University of Chicago Press, 1955).

[4] D. N. Majumdar, *Caste and Communication in an Indian Village* (Bombay, Asia Publishing House, 1958).

[5] Oscar Lewis, *Village Life in Northern India* (Urbana, Ill., University of Illinois Press, 1958).

[6] John T. Hitchcock and Leigh Minturn, "The Rajputs of Khalapur, India," in Beatrice B. Whiting, ed., *Six Cultures: Studies in Child Rearing* (New York, John Wiley and Sons, 1963).

bottom. Although all castes owned some land in the village, the distribution was in no way proportional (see Table 1).

Table 1: Caste and Landownership in Rājpur

Caste	Rank	Persons	Per Cent of Total Population	Per Cent of Total Cultivated Land
Jāt (landed farmer)	1	149	16	33
Bhāgbān (vegetable grower)	2	76	8	5
Dhīmar (water carrier)	2	49	5	1
Kumhār (potter)	2	60	6	3
Dhunā (cotton carder)	3	32	3	2
Chamār (leatherworker)	4	332	35	18
Barhaī (carpenter, Muslim)	4	41	4	1
Lohār (blacksmith, Muslim)	4	8	1	2
Naī (barber, Muslim)	4	33	4	2
Tēli (oil presser, Muslim)	4	133	14	8
Bhangi (sweeper)	5	25	3	0
Total		938	99	75
Outsiders				23
				98

Even a cursory examination showed that Rājpur's eleven castes were bound together in an intricate web of economic relationships. Certain Chamār young men worked for monthly wages as field laborers for Jāt farmers; Muslims as well as Hindus cut sugar cane for any farmer—earning the leaves stripped off the cane to use as fodder; Barhaī carpenters regularly repaired the plows of particular Jāts in return for grain, while on the side they built bullock carts that they sold for cash; cotton carders worked strictly on job contract, as did the tailors; at the time of their weddings Bhangis went through the village from door to door collecting funds for their wedding celebrations; Bhāgbān vegetable growers carried their produce 1½ miles to the bazaar, where neighbors bought their vegetables and carried them back to Rājpur; the Brāhman priest collected a double armful of grain from every farmer at harvest time; when he performed special ceremonies he received additional cash, blankets, food, or clothing.

In 1936 William Wiser stated: "There is today within a North

Indian Hindu village community an interrelation of services which carries with it certain responsibilities and rights. These responsibilities and rights constitute the structure of the Hindu Jajmāni system."[7]

Even as he presented his detailed description of how the jajmāni system operated, Wiser noted that "distintegrating factors are at work today in Karimpur"[8] and added, "[The Hindu Jajmāni system] cannot withstand the competition of trade from the outside without making some radical adjustments in its own social organization."[9]

In 1957 in Rājpur it was clear that some "radical adjustments" had already been made and more were in the process of being made in its jajmāni system. The following account will (1) trace the outlines of Rājpur's jajmāni system as it was in 1957 and as it had been thirty years earlier in 1927 and (2) look for basic patterns that may explain changes in the jajmāni system in Rājpur as well as in other Indian villages.

RĀJPUR'S JAJMĀNI SYSTEM

A description of Rājpur's jajmāni system requires an examination of each caste in turn. Below are descriptions of the major economic relationships between Rājpur's castes, beginning with the Jāts at the top and extending to the Bhangis at the bottom.

JĀT (LANDED FARMER)

The Jāts were the wealthy, powerful farmers of the village. Although they constituted only 16 per cent of Rājpur's population, they owned 33 per cent of the cultivated land. They had built five of the seven brick, two-story houses, and the only tractor in Rājpur belonged to them. Their political power was reflected in the fact that six of the total seventeen members of the village council (panchāyat) were Jāts, including the pradhān and assistant pradhān (equivalent to chairman and vice-chairman). What records I uncovered suggested that in 1927 as well the Jāts had been the wealthiest, most powerful caste in the village. At that time the village had been within the tax-collecting domain of the Raja of Nīlganj, who in turn had commissioned one of the prominent Jāts to be

---

[7] William H. Wiser, The Hindu Jajmani System, new ed. (Lucknow, Lucknow Publishing House, 1959), p. 1. (First published in 1936.)
[8] Ibid., p. 117.
[9] Ibid., pp. 126-27.

village headman responsible for collecting Rājpur's land taxes. Such a position brought with it both wealth and power.

There appeared to have been little change between 1927 and 1957 in the way in which the Jāts fitted into the jajmāni system. During both periods they had constituted the backbone of the jajmāns—the receivers of services. They were the ones whose plows the carpenters repaired, whose hair the barbers cut, for whom the potters shaped pots and the priests performed ceremonies. And in return the Jāts reimbursed the kam karnewālās (the service performers) with grain, cloth, cooked food, and money. As we shall see, between 1927 and 1957 the Jāts were crucial in affecting the position of certain kām karnewālās. But their own position as jajmāns had undergone little change.

BHĀGBĀN (VEGETABLE GROWER)

Nearly all the castes in Rājpur engaged in agriculture, but the Bhāgbāns were the experts. Although they constituted 8 per cent of the village population while owning only 5 per cent of the land, they more than made up for their deficiency in landholdings by digging their own wells, irrigating their plots, growing vegetables, fruits, and grams rather than the more common sugar cane, wheat, and rice, fertilizing, weeding, and rotating their crops periodically.

The Bhāgbāns, like the Jāts, were less the providers of services than they were the receivers of services—from such people as barbers and oil pressers. They generally sold their fresh vegetables for cash in the open bazaar held 1½ miles away in Lālbārī Tuesday and Friday afternoons. There they set the prices of their eggplants, tomatoes, and cauliflower according to supply and demand. Their neighbors in Rājpur, if they wanted to buy vegetables from the Bhāgbāns, also had to walk the 1½ miles to the Lālbārī bazaar. Only in rare cases—for example, upon the arrival of some unexpected guest—could one go to a Bhāgbān's home in Rājpur to buy vegetables, and then there was always the difficult problem of setting a price. Both the Bhāgbāns and their customers seem to prefer to let the market set an approximate price over which they could haggle.

As far as I could determine, the position of the Bhāgbāns in the jajmāni system in 1957 differed little from what it had been in 1927 or even earlier. District records reported the Tuesday and Friday bazaar in Lālbārī existing back in the 1800s. Although nothing as such was said about Rājpur's Bhāgbāns, they presumably were participating in the bazaar then too.

DHĪMAR (WATER CARRIER)

In 1927 the Dhīmars had occupied a relatively secure place—primarily as kām karnewālās—within Rajpur's jajmāni system. Their task had been to draw water daily for their Jāt jajmāns and, in certain circumstances, to help with food preparation and other chores. In return they had received fixed allotments of grain after each harvest from their jajmāns.

But with the advent of relatively cheap, convenient hand pumps, an increasing number of Jāts and other wealthy farmers had installed pumps in their own courtyards. Now they could have an ample supply of water whenever they needed it. What to the Jāts was a convenience, to the Dhīmars was a disaster. As one Dhīmar told me: "Our traditional job was drawing water for people to drink. . . . Nowadays we have been forced out of our livelihood." When their services as kām karnewālās were suspended, so were their fixed allotments of grain.

As a result, the Dhīmars were in as precarious an economic position as any of the castes in Rājpur. For the 5 per cent of the village population they constituted, they owned only 1 per cent of the cultivated land; so few of them could fall back on farming as a means of subsistence. Three Dhīmar man had left Rājpur in search of employment elsewhere. Of the sixteen remaining men, eight had found regular employment (three subsisted by farming, four held jobs in the nearby sugar mill, and one worked as waterman at the railroad station), while the remaining eight did a variety of odd jobs (net fishing in small ponds, gathering and selling water nuts, cooking curried stews and selling them for a few annas, or peddling bananas and guavas bought from wholesalers). They managed to live, but with little margin, and the future holds small promise for them.

KUMHĀR (POTTER)

In 1927 the Kumhārs had been the village potters, serving as the kām karnewālās of the wealthier Jāt families. They had periodically provided their jajmāns with a fixed number of clay water vessels and cooking pots and had received in return bags of grain at harvesttime. On the side the Kumhārs had made a variety of other clay vessels—grain containers, jars, cups, saucers for lamps or liquid foods, tobacco pipe bowls, and cattle troughs. These they had sold for cash to anyone who wanted them.

Several years before I came to Rājpur, the last of the Kumhārs had given up pottery as a livelihood, sold his donkeys, and allowed his pottery equipment to fall into disrepair. The Kumhārs gave a variety of reasons for abandoning their traditional occupation: farming was more profitable than pottery; the demand for clay pots was declining in the face of cheap, mass-produced vessels of brass, aluminum, stainless steel, or bell metal; inexpensive kerosene lanterns had virtually eliminated the demand for clay lamps; glass jars were now available for storing condiments; and the new galvanized steel buckets were better for drawing water from wells than the clay jars could ever be.

The Kumhārs of Rājpur were not the only potters in the area to abandon their trade; most Kumhārs had done the same. Only in the village of Tehrī could one find a family of Kumhārs still employed as potters. They had gone into large-scale production of clay vessels of all kinds—including the "disposable" clay teacups so popular in railroad stations. If people in Rājpur or other neighboring villages wanted clay pots, they could go to Tehrī to buy them from the Kumhār family, or they could stop by the Kumhārs' stall in the Lālbārī bazaar on Tuesday and Friday afternoons.

DHUNĀ (COTTON CARDER)

In 1927 the Dhunās had been considered the cotton carders of the village, although I was unable to discover how many of them ever actually engaged in cotton carding. In 1957 they were still considered the village cotton carders, although only two of the eight Dhunā men ever did any carding. As far as I could discover, the relationship between the Dhunās and the rest of the village had typically been on a piecework basis; for an agreed-upon quantity of cash or grain they would card anyone's cotton.

The busiest time of year for carding was in October and November, when the monsoons had ended and villagers wanted their soggy bedding dried and fluffed or when they purchased fresh cotton that needed to be cleaned before being stuffed into new quilts or mattresses. For much of the remainder of the year the Dhunā's carding instrument lay unused in one corner of the hut, while the two carders farmed their small plots.

This part-time nature of the Dhunās' carding activity was a feature of their trade in 1927 as well, and in both 1927 and 1957 they had to support themselves through supplementary means. Of the Dhunās who were not carding in Rājpur when I was there, two had taken up tailoring and worked together in a small shop in the center of the village, three found regular or occasional employment in the sugar mill, and one peddled curried sauces and fresh fruits. On the whole, life was hard for the Dhunās. Within the preceding decade two brothers had moved with their families to Delhi, where they had finally found employment as movie projector operators for the government.

CHAMĀR (LEATHERWORKER)

The Chamārs formed the largest single caste group in Rājpur, constituting 35 per cent of the village population. In 1927 they had typically worked as farmers (if their lands were large enough) or as field servants for the Jāts, plowing their lands, harvesting their grain or sugar cane, repairing their homes, and running their errands. In return they had received reimbursement in cash or kind. In addition, they had been at the beck and call of any government official arriving in Rājpur. If his horses needed grass, the Chamārs cut it; if he needed an extra cart, they provided it; if he required a larger retinue for the next lap of his trip, they went along.

The job from which the Chamārs had acquired the greatest amount of stigma was their leatherwork. In 1927 they had skinned the animals that died in the village, dried and tanned the hides in a crude way, sold them to dealers, repaired their jajmāns' sandals, and patched other leather items in the village—such as the large leather bags used in those times for irrigating the fields or sprinkling down the dust in the village lanes. In view of the aversion orthodox Hindus have for the handling of carcasses, the leatherwork activities of the Chamārs "justified" their exclusion from higher-caste Hindu society. They were not allowed to draw water from any wells but their own, and Brāhmans would not perform sacrifices for them.

By 1957 the lot of the Chamārs had improved. Land reform had given them hereditary tenancy and sometimes full ownership of land they had been farming; of the ninety-three Chamār men, forty-eight supported themselves and their families by farming either their own or others' lands. The Indian constitution had abolished untouchability;

government officials no longer exacted involuntary service from the Chamārs or other Scheduled Castes. Furthermore, Chamār leatherwork was now a thing of the past—at least in Rājpur. Galvanized buckets had replaced the leather bags used formerly for irrigation; so Chamārs were not needed for leather patch work. Muslim entrepreneurs had taken over the task of skinning dead animals and shipping the hides by train or truck to tanneries in Agra and Kanpur. Inexpensive machine-manufactured shoes were available in the Lālbārī shops, and hand-stitched sandals could be bought in the Tuesday and Friday bazaars. Three or four full-time sandal and shoe repairmen—all of them Chamārs, but none from Rājpur—had set up shop close to the gate of the nearby sugar mill; for a few annas they would replace a broken strap or resole a sandal. Along with the fact that for ideological reasons the Chamārs were eager to abandon leatherwork, the economy had shifted so that there was little leatherwork for them to do. What needed doing could be attended to by specialists.

Of the forty-five Chamār men who did not live from farming, thirty-four worked as regular employees in the nearby sugar mill, and the remaining eleven were scattered through a range of occupations: two were tailors in Rājpur, one worked for the railroad, one was a goat trader, another sold fodder and dung cakes, one ground grain, and the remaining five were unemployed, blind, or too old to work.

BARHAĪ (CARPENTER, MUSLIM)

In 1927 each Barhaī family had been firmly established in a jajmāni relationship with one or more of the wealthy farmers in Rājpur. In return for keeping their jajmāns' plows in constant repair, the carpenters had received a fixed quantity of grain or flour at each harvest. But maintaining the plows was only the minimum service. In addition, the carpenters were expected to prepare handles for the jajmāns' iron implements, repair their doors, door frames, and well beams, maintain their carts, replace damaged wheel rims or spokes, and generally see to the upkeep of any wooden articles belonging to their jajmāns. In what free time they could find, the carpenters had made wooden toys, lids for vessels, bread boards, and rolling pins which they sold for cash at occasional fairs or in the Lālbārī bazaar.

In 1957 the picture was undergoing a dramatic change. To be sure, eight of the fourteen Barhaī men were still carpenters—a high ratio for a traditional craft. But 1957 saw the first Barhaī family in Rājpur permanently turning over its jajmāns to other Barhaīs and setting up its carpenter shop close to the sugar mill about a quarter of a mile from the village. The family's reasoning was straightforward enough: there was no longer sufficient work in Rājpur to support all its carpenters. It was better that one family leave the jajmāni system and take its chances on the open market than for all the Barhaīs to starve slowly. Besides, it might be possible to survive on the open market. Wagons coming to the mill from neighboring villages with loads of sugar cane frequently broke down and needed repairs. With a strategic location and a certain amount of luck, the family might be able to make ends meet.

At the end of the first year, the little carpenter shop had set no business records. It had, however, paid for itself well enough so that a second Rājpur carpenter family distributed its jajmāns among the remaining carpenters and set up its small carpenter shop beside the road adjoining the sugar mill. In the meantime, the first carpenter shop began to diversify its products, making benches and desks that it hoped to sell to the local school.

It was too soon to tell if the rearranged jajmāni system in Rājpur could work to everyone's satisfaction. But at least for the time being a crisis had been averted.

LOHĀR (BLACKSMITH, MUSLIM)

In 1927 the Lohārs had participated in Rājpur's jajmāni system by maintaining their jajmāns' iron plow bars, fodder choppers, pick-shovels (phaurās), sickles, and grass cutters. In their courtyard was a small, improvised furnace where, by means of bellows or a blower, they had heated iron hot enough to shape it on their anvil. In return for their efforts, they had received harvest payments in grain from their jajmāns.

By 1957 this had changed. The surviving Lohār's father had practiced his trade while he was alive, but the iron-repair work had gradually fallen off. Better steel equipment was becoming available, requiring fewer repairs. Machine shops were appearing in Lālbārī, with grinding and welding equipment that could maintain the more complex metal implements like the crank-handle fodder choppers and Persian-wheel bucket chains. Then the Lohār father died, followed by the younger son, who left a wife and three small children to support. The last remaining Lohār decided he could not keep up the blacksmith work and still take proper care of his ten acres of farmland. So he informed his jajmāns with due apologies that he could no longer continue doing ironwork. His decision brought no loud complaints. Villagers wanting their blunted iron plow bars or sickles sharpened took them to the Barhaīs, who had the requisite skills and equipment for rudimentary metalwork. Those requiring more complicated repair work took their problems to the machine repair shops in Lālbārī. The only time the Lohār fired his furnace while I was in Rājpur was when he had to repair his own iron implements.

NAĪ (BARBER, MUSLIM)

The Naīs' activities in 1927 differed little from their activities in 1957. As village barbers they were expected to provide the shaves and haircuts for all Rājpur residents except the lowest castes. The quoted rule was that every jajmān should receive a shave twice a week and a haircut every two weeks, although as a matter of fact this varied considerably depending on the status of the jajmān and the commitments of the barber. During both periods the Naīs received at least a portion of their income in prescribed grain allotments from their jajmāns. During both periods they served as messengers of auspicious news, carrying feast and wedding invitations to their jajmāns' relatives in other villages and assisting in the marriage ceremonies themselves, for example, by making leaf plates. For these extra services they received additional compensation in clothes, cooked food, or cash.

Although the basic framework of the Naīs' jajmāni associations was similar during the two periods, there were differences in detail. One difference was that in 1957 most of the Naīs had supplementary means of income. Of the thirteen Naī men, six farmed land, four worked regularly in the sugar mill (and a fifth did so occasionally), one was a servant in a Jāt home, and one cleaned trucks for a Husainpur trucking outfit. Only one of the older Naīs lived exclusively by barbering. All thirteen still gave shaves and haircuts, but the ones with full-time jobs had to fit their barbering into free days or early mornings or evenings. This was no great handicap for them, but it did at times inconvenience their jajmāns.

Another difference in 1957 was that cash payments for shaves and haircuts were more popular. A haircut cost six or eight annas, a shave one and a half or two annas. This "contractual" arrangement freed both partners from the suspicion that they were being taken advantage of by the other.

In the meantime, barbershops had sprung up in the town of Lālbāri, where a man could get both a shave and a haircut for the fixed price of eight annas. These were frequented primarily by the lower castes in the villages who, under the traditional arrangements, had to wait till the higher-caste jajmāns had been taken care of, or who, like the Bhangi sweepers, could not receive haircuts from the village Naīs because of their ritual pollution. As yet the Lālbāri barbershops posed little threat to the Naīs of Rājpur. Most jajmāns preferred the convenience of being shaved as they sat in the comfort of their own courtyards—even if it meant a slightly higher price or a delay until the barber was free from his other commitments.

TĒLI (OIL PRESSER, MUSLIM)

In both 1927 and 1957, the Tēlis maintained a strictly "contract" relationship with the rest of the villagers. Farmers brought the Tēlis their rape, mustard, sesamum, or castor seeds to extract the oil, paying the Tēlis a share of the oil and possibly some of the crushed seeds for fodder. Or farmers sold their seeds to the Tēlis, who extracted the oil and sold it on the open market. This oil could be used for cooking, caring for the hair and body, or lubricating the moving parts of wagon wheels, fodder choppers, and other machines.

In 1927 the relative need for seed oil had been greater than it was in 1957. In addition to its current uses, it had been needed as fuel for lamps and as a softener for leather waterbags. But by 1957 kerosene lanterns had displaced clay lamps, and galvanized buckets had made leather waterbags obsolete. Even where seed oil was still used it faced competition, such as from the lubricating oils available at the filling station near the sugar mill, or from the cooking oils and shortenings available in many shops. In 1957 only two of the Tēlis had sets of seed-crushing machinery in working condition, and most of the year these lay idle.

Neither in 1927 nor in 1957 had the Tēlis been able to subsist on oil pressing alone. When I was in Rājpur about half the Tēlis (twenty-four out of forty-one men) farmed for a living, although their landholdings were characteristically small. Five worked for the railroad; two had jobs in the sugar mill; the remaining ten did odd jobs around the factory or hired themselves out as day laborers. Their lot was not a prosperous one; many of them blamed it on the fact that they were Muslims and were being unfairly discriminated against by the Hindus.

BHANGI (SWEEPER)

Sometime prior to 1927 the former Bhangi lineage in Rājpur had died out, leaving the village with no sweepers. Rājpur's Jāts had traveled to the village of Ināyat (where there were surplus Bhangis) and, by offering nearly two acres of farmland, talked one Bhangi family into coming to Rājpur. Since the Bhangis were of too low a caste to farm, they arranged that a Chamār would work their fields—for which he received half of every harvest.

Both in 1927 and in 1957, the Bhangis moved each morning with their pigs through Rājpur's streets, raising the dust with their brooms, gathering peelings and refuse from courtyard drains and night soil from the latrines, and dumping them beyond the village walls. When an animal died, they were called to drag the carcass outside the village where the vultures, dogs, and jackals disposed of it. For their efforts the Bhangis received fixed allotments of grain at harvesttime. In 1927 this grain had been given by the jajmāns whose drains they had cleaned and whose streets they had swept. By 1957 the system had been modified. Now the village panchāyat gave the Bhangis their grain—four bags every six months. In addition to receiving grain, there was a general understanding in the village that whenever the Bhangis needed funds—for a wedding, feast, or cremation—they were entitled to go from door to door collecting donations, the amount of the donation depending on the status of the giver.

In addition to their sweeping and scavenging, the Bhangis performed other services. In both 1927 and 1957 the senior Bhangi woman was village midwife. When the message came that a woman was in labor (and therefore in ritual pollution), the senior Bhangi woman donned old clothes and attended the delivery, cutting the umbilical cord with her penknife. For her obstetrical services she received cash: one rupee if she delivered a boy, three quarters of a rupee if she delivered a girl, nothing if the baby were stillborn, and five or ten rupees if the baby died in the womb and she managed to extricate it. In addition to the cash, she sometimes received clothes or food, depending on the family's generosity.

When news of a death had to be carried to relatives in other villages, it was the Bhangis' responsibility; for this they received cash or food. A number of Bhangis wove straw winnowing trays that they peddled in the bazaar. And occasionally they sold one of the pigs from their herd to a low caste that had no compunctions against eating a pork banquet.

One difference between the Bhangis' activities in 1927 and 1957 concerned handling the carcasses of water buffaloes or cows whose skins were large enough to warrant processing. After the withdrawal of the Chamārs from leatherwork, when a large animal died, a Muslim entrepreneur came from Nīlganj with a few Bhangis. These, along with Rājpur's Bhangis, carried the carcass outside the village and skinned it. The Muslim then paid all the Bhangis a rupee each, while he bundled this hide along with others to the tanneries in Kanpur or Agra.

The above descriptions present the interrelations of Rājpur's eleven castes. However, like the Wisers' Karimpur and Oscar Lewis's Rampur, Rājpur did not have a full contingent of necessary castes within its boundaries. For certain services it depended on two castes from other villages—the Brāhman (priest) and the Dhobī (washerman).

BRĀHMAN (PRIEST)

For generations more Brāhman families had lived in the village of Tehrī than could possibly be supported by its jajmāni system. Over the years some of these families had received the right (hak) to serve as priests in neighboring villages that lacked their own resident Brāhmans. This was the case with Panditjī Mohan Lāl's family. In 1927 one of their members had been serving as Rājpur's priest, attending feasts, officiating at weddings and cremations, and receiving the annual payments of grain.

The right to serve Rājpur was not strictly a hereditary one. Every time a family member died, this right was shuffled, along with the right to serve other villages, and reallocated. A decade or so before I arrived, there had been a death and a reallocation. Panditjī Mohan Lāl had emerged with the right to serve three villages: Nayām, Chitalgarh, and Rājpur. He still retained his fields in Tehrī, but both his Brāhman status and the demands for his priestly services forced him to hire a lower-caste farmer to work for him.

As Rājpur's priest, Panditjī performed certain duties for the entire village. The most dramatic of these was the annual lighting of the Holī fire. On the night before Holī, after the village men had gathered where the combustibles were piled, Panditjī arrived, examined the heavens, recited sacred verses (mantras), ignited a faggot, and walked around the pile with the faggot. At the appropriate moment he pushed the burning faggot into the pile, and in a few minutes the flames were reaching higher than the village rooftops. Then, on the basis of the direction the smoke was drifting, Panditjī predicted Rājpur's fortune for the coming year. As the men proceeded to embrace each other or join a shuffling dance, Panditjī hurried off, for the villagers in Nayām and Chitalgarh were waiting for him to light *their* fires.

For serving the entire village, Panditjī received compensation from the entire village. Every harvest he collected a double armful of grain from each farmer, and occasionally he received cash donations from those not owning land. Furthermore, when farmers set up their bullock-driven sugar-cane presses each winter, Panditjī was entitled to tumblers of cane juice.

Panditjī's services to, and compensation from, Rājpur as a whole would hardly have supported him. It was from his activities as the priest for any Hindu family in Rājpur (except the Bhangis and some of the poorer Chamārs) that he received greater compensation. He officiated at weddings, child-naming ceremonies, and cremations; he chose auspicious dates and hours for special events; he performed fire sacrifices for families concerned about the health of their children or cattle or the state of their crops; and he made special offerings at festival times for those who commissioned him. In return he received gifts of all sorts, depending on the generosity of his jajmān—blankets, clothing, cash, sweets, pictures of deities, fruit, and nuts. And he was always prepared to let a higher-caste householder earn religious merit by feeding him at a feast.

DHOBĪ (WASHERMAN)

In both 1927 and 1957, since Rājpur had no resident Dhobīs, those who wanted their clothes washed had to approach the Dhobīs in neighboring villages—Dakkāri, Jagorā, or Āmabād. When they found a Dhobī who could include them with his other jajmāns, they worked out some mutually satisfactory arrangement—periodic payments for the bulk washing of clothes, payments by the piece upon return, or some combination. Typically the Dhobīs preferred periodic payments while their jajmāns preferred to pay by the piece.

Both in 1927 and in 1957 the relationships between Rājpur's families and their Dhobīs were tenuous. There were frequent complaints about incompetence and delays in the return of the wash, and no one was surprised when a family dropped its Dhobī and hired another. During both periods the Dhobīs refused to wash the clothes of the lowest castes such as the Bhangis, and in both periods the majority of Rājpur's castes washed their own clothes.

The residents of Rājpur used the services of other nonresident castes as well–weavers, bangle makers, grain parchers, goldsmiths, and candy-makers, to mention a few. However, their relationships with these outside castes were generally on a "cash-contract" basis, and require no further elaboration.

These, then, were the outlines of Rājpur's jajmāni system—the "interrelation of services [in a North Indian Hindu village community] which carries with it certain responsibilities and rights," to use Wiser's definition. This definition is broad enough to include all of Rājpur's castes within the jajmāni system, from the Barhaī carpenters who serve specific Rājpur families for periodic payments of grain to the Bhāgbān vegetable growers and Telī oil pressers who deal with anyone on a "cash-contract" basis. In fact, if "North Indian Hindu village community" were not a part of Wiser's definition, it would be broad enough to include economic activities in many rural areas of the world.

Within Wiser's "interrelation of services," however, a number of associations are more unique to India and possibly even North India. These are the hereditary relationships between two or more families in which periodically gross quantities of grain are exchanged for recurrent services or products. The grain and the products of services are not exchanged on a one-to-one basis. Rather, the grain is given by the jajmān to his kām karnewālā as a type of "retainer fee"; in return the kām karnewālā provides his services rarely or frequently, depending on the needs of his jajmān The unique features are the *hereditary* relationships between *two or more families* in which *periodically* gross *quantities of grain* are exchanged for *recurrent services or products.* I shall label relationships that fit within this definition "core" jajmāni relationships, and in the following section these are the relationships that will be analyzed. From now on "non-core" kām karnewālās will be treated only peripherally or not at all; these include the Bhāgbān vegetable growers, Dhunā cotton carders, Chamār leatherworkers, and Telī oil pressers.

The fact that a kām karnewālā family maintains a core jajmāni relationship does not mean it cannot carry on cash-contract activities as well. Thus, the Barhaī carpenters were kām karnewālās for certain Jāts and received bags of grain. But they also made bullock carts and wooden household implements that they sold for cash. And the Bhangis were core kām karnewālās for the entire village, while in addition the senior Bhangi woman received payment for her midwife services from families of babies she delivered.

A striking feature about core jajmāni relationships during the years from 1927 to 1957 was the decrease in kām karnewālā castes maintaining such relationships. For details, see Table 2.

Table 2: Kām Karnewālā Castes with Core Jajmāni Relationships

1927	1957
Brāhman (priest)	Brāhman (priest)
Dhīmar (water carrier)	Barhaī (carpenter, Muslim)[a]
Kumhār (potter)	Naī (barber, Muslim)
Barhaī (carpenter, Muslim)	Bhangi (sweeper)
Lohār (blacksmith, Muslim)	
Naī (barber, Muslim)	
Bhangi (sweeper)	

[a] Although between 1927 and 1957 the portion of Barhaīs performing core kām karnewālā services declined, the fact that some of them still rendered such services seems to justify their inclusion in this column.

PATTERNS OF CHANGE IN CORE JAJMĀNI RELATIONSHIPS

In both 1927 and 1957 the Jāts and a few wealthy members of other castes were the jajmāns in the core jajmāni relationships. Although between those years the number of kām karnewālā castes serving them had diminished, in 1957 the Jāts retained their core jajmān position toward some castes; so for the moment we shall bypass the Jāts in our search for factors generating the diminution of core jajmāni relationships.

The key question that needs to be asked is: Why did the Dhīmars, Kumhārs, Lohārs, and certain Barhaīs abandon their core jajmāni relationships while the Brāhmans, Naīs, Bhangis, and certain other Barhaīs did not?

Three factors seem to be relevant in explaining the differences between the two groups of kām karnewālās:

1. THE APPEARANCE OF COMPETITIVE TECHNOLOGY RENDERING CERTAIN KĀM KARNEWĀLĀS' SERVICES OBSOLETE

Perhaps the most dramatic illustration of termination of a core jajmāni relationship for technological obsolescence was the displacement of the Dhīmar water carriers by hand pumps installed in courtyards. Once the price of a hand pump came within the range of the Jāt families, its convenience spelled the end of the harvest grain payments to the Dhīmars, and with it the end of their core jajmāni relationship.

Similarly the Kumhār potters were bypassed by technology. Once inexpensive, unbreakable metal pots were available, the Kumhārs were no longer required to produce annual supplies of clay water vessels and cooking pots.

To a certain extent, technology also spelled the end for the Lohār blacksmiths. The Lālbārī machine shops could sharpen or weld better than the Lohārs could, and the maintenance of the new mechanical devices required technical skills beyond the capacity of the Lohār to handle. What little ironwork the villagers wanted done in Rājpur could be tended to by the Barhaīs.

Competitive technology also played a part in the decline in traditional activities of certain non-core kām karnewālā castes. Shoe factories in Agra and Kanpur had so modified the leatherware economy in the area that few Chamārs now did any leatherwork. The Tēli oil pressers competed at a disadvantage against canned oils, shortening, and lubricants. Their days as oil pressers may well be numbered. In time the Dhobī washermen may find themselves threatened by washboards and tubs that enable families to do their own wash and remove the need for carrying dirty clothes to a stream or pond. Domestic irons and someday even washing machines may further diminish the need for Dhobīs. But as yet these are things of the future.

One may ask how much of a threat competitive technology poses for the four castes still performing core kām karnewālā services. The Brāhmans appear safe—at least from *this* threat. So long as people view rituals and ceremonies as an important part of their lives, and so long as Brāhmans are the only ones trained to perform these rituals and ceremonies, their services will be needed.

For the Barhaī carpenters, the technological changes in carpentering have so far been largely noncompetitive. When a wealthy farmer wants to build a brick house, he calls on an outside carpenter to shape and fit the beams and, since the introduction of electricity, to install the wooden backboards for the house wiring. But this supplements rather than competes with the services of the village Barhaī. The power saw installed in the wholesale lumberyard near the sugar mill may reduce the demand on Barhaīs to saw tree trunks into planks, but Barhaīs still have to cut down the trees in the first place, and they can use the finished planks for their own work; so the effects more or less cancel each other out. In time the specialized carpentering in which the non-core Barhaīs are beginning to engage (for example, cart building and repair) may deprive the core Barhaīs of some of their extra income. Also the introduction of steel plows, metal wagons with rubber-tire wheels, or any mechanization of farming that reduces the need for draft cattle (with their wooden equipment) will deprive the Barhaīs of some of their work and probably, in time, their grain payments.

The Naīs have survived their first technological threat—the introduction of safety razor blades. Fortunately for the Naīs, the foreign-manufactured blades were unavailable or expensive, and the India-manufactured blades did not have a good reputation. A few of the younger Jāt men had begun to shave themselves (the Naīs shaved them at best only twice a week, and the younger Jāts' own sense of style required more frequent shaves). But even they needed barbers for haircuts. Barbershops had appeared in Lālbārī, complete with perfumed hair oil and shampoos. But someone contemplating a visit to the Lālbārī barber had to weigh the (possibly) superior quality of the service against the convenience of receiving a shave and haircut during a leisure moment back in the comfort of one's own courtyard.

Until village streets are paved, proper soakage pits are dug, and homes have flush latrines, villagers are going to need the services of the Bhangis. Technology may ease the Bhangis' work somewhat (for example, cleaning a cement drain is simpler than cleaning an earth drain). And the establishment of maternity clinics may someday displace the senior Bhangi woman from her position as village midwife. But for the forseeable future the Bhangis appear safe in their core jajmāni relationship.

Table 3 presents in summary form the effects of competitive technology on core kām karnewālās. It may be worth noting that, as a rule,

Table 3: Effects of Technology on Core Kām Karnewālās

Castes Not Experiencing Reduced Demands from Competitive Technology	Castes Experiencing Reduced Demands from Competitive Technology
Brāhman (priest)	Dhīmar (water carrier)
Barhaī (carpenter, Muslim)	Kumhār (potter)
Naī (barber, Muslim)	Lohār (blacksmith)
Bhangi (sweeper)	

where core jajmāni relationships have ended in the face of competitive technology, the terminating initiative has come from the jajmān clients rather than the kām karnewālā workers. It was the Jāt jajmāns who dismissed their Dhīmar water carriers—not the Dhīmars who voluntarily resigned. Likewise it was the Jāts and other jajmāns who decided they preferred metal vessels to the Kumhārs' clay pots, manufactured shoes to hand-stitched leather sandals made and repaired by Chamārs, and commercial shortening to the Tēlis' oil. In this regard, the termination of core jajmāni relationships reflects Beidelman's observation that "the locus of power in [the jajmāni] system lies with the jajmān."[10] Only with the Lohār blacksmith did the initiative come from the kām karnewālā rather than from the jajmāns. In this case the Lohār had a strong bargaining position, for he had enough farmland with which to support himself and his family.

2. THE INCREASE IN POPULATION WITH NO PARALLEL INCREASE IN LAND

The appearance of competitive technology explains only part of the reduction of core jajmāni relations in Rājpur. A second factor concerns population growth. In the 1931 census the population of Rājpur was 603. In 1941 it had risen to 791. By 1957, when I took my census, it was 938. Rājpur's population increase between 1931 and 1951 was 46 per cent, compared with a 30 per cent increase for the surrounding Lālbārī *tahsil.* Part of this rapid population increase could be attributed to improved irrigation facilities from the government tube well. Part could be attributed to the building of the sugar mill, started in 1939. This mill pro-

[10] Thomas O. Beidelman, *A Comparative Analysis of the Jajmani System* (Locust Valley, N.Y.: J. J. Augustin, 1959), p. 75.

vided employment for villagers who might otherwise have had to migrate to one of the larger cities in search of work.

For certain types of kām karnewālās, an increase in population merely expanded the quantity of work to be done by a larger number of people, with little net change in the kām karnewālā-to-jajmān ratio. For example, there were more barbers in 1957 than there had been in 1927, but so were there more people needing haircuts and shaves.

A key difference between barbers and, for example, carpenters (for whom population growth had meant a loss of business) was the fact that barbers served persons independent of land, whereas carpenters served persons on the basis of their land. Typically, a carpenter received his payment of grain on the basis of the number of plows he was responsible for maintaining. As population increased, and as fields were divided and subdivided between relatives, a few more plows might have been added to the total number in the village. But there is an eventual ceiling on this, and after the ceiling has been reached, no additional plows are added to the village total. At this point a population increase means that a fixed amount of work (and grain) must be divided and subdivided among the kām karnewālās. It becomes only a matter of time before some kām karnewālā must leave the jajmāni system. The two new carpenter shops on the mill road dramatized this fact for Rājpur's Barhaīs.

Table 4: Effects of Population Increase on Core Kām Karnewālās

Castes Not Experiencing Reduced Demands from Population Increase	*Castes Experiencing Reduced Demands from Population Increase*
Brāhman (priest)	Barhaī (carpenter, Muslim)
Dhīmar (water carrier)	Lohār (blacksmith, Muslim)[a]
Kumhār (potter)	
Naī (barber, Muslim)	
Bhangi (sweeper)	

[a] This had been the case when the Lohār father and two sons had all been alive. After the death of the father and younger brother, only one Lohār was left; so the kām karnewālā-to-land ratio became what it had been a generation earlier.

Table 4 presents in summary form the effects of population increase on core kām karnewālās. This table illustrates the principle that population increase as such does not threaten all kām karnewālās in the same manner. If their services are linked to persons (e.g., officiating at worship services, cutting hair, cleaning refuse), their position remains unaffected by population growth; if their services are linked to land (e.g., maintaining plows and farm implements), they are apt to experience difficulties. Applying this to non-core kām karnewālas, one could predict that population increase would *not* affect Dhobī washermen adversely; whereas it *would* be detrimental to the Tēli oil pressers.

If one superimposes Table 3 on Table 4 one sees that the three castes appearing in both left-hand columns ("Not Experiencing Reduced Demands") are the Brāhman priests, the Naī barbers, and the Bhangi sweepers. These three castes still exist in Rājpur as core kām karnewālas (see Table 2). The other castes, the Dhīmar water carriers, Kumhār potters, Barhaī carpenters, and Lohār blacksmiths, appear in either Table 3 or Table 4 in the right-hand column ("Experiencing Reduced Demands"). All of them but the Barhaīs have abandoned their core kām karnewāla activities, and even the Barhaīs have survived only by extracting some of their members from Rājpur's jajmāni system.

Although these two variables—technological competition and population increase—seem able to explain why certain kām karnewāla castes retained their core jajmāni relationships between 1927 and 1957 while other kām karnewāla castes abandoned them, a third variable may be useful in making predictions regarding Rājpur's jajmāni system in the future.

3. AN IDEOLOGY AMONG THE KĀM KARNEWĀLAS OF NONPERFORMANCE OF "POLLUTING" SERVICES FOR OTHERS

The Chamārs of Rājpur had never occupied a core jajmāni position. However, by tradition they had possessed the right to skin animals that died in the village and to dry and sell the skins for a modest profit. They also had occasionally repaired leather articles. Had they wanted to, they could probably have continued supplementing their income with leatherwork. However, the Chamārs had recognized that if they wanted to rise in the social hierarchy, they would have to abandon their "polluting" leatherwork. When they abandoned their traditional occupation, they did so not only because of the technological competition of factory shoes (the shoes still needed to be repaired) but also because of ideological reasons.

The only core kām karnewālā caste in Rājpur that might be affected by this ideological variable would be the Bhangi sweepers. Sweeping as such was not "polluting"; the women of most households swept their own courtyards. Pollution attached to one who swept somebody else's refuse, or removed somebody else's feces, or handled animal carcasses. The Bhangis were aware of this. Yet any desire the Bhangis might have had to raise their status by abandoning these tasks was offset by their knowledge of the sanctions that could be imposed on them by the higher-caste villagers—termination of their grain payments and possibly banishment from the village. Should this ideology become stronger in the future, and should alternative means of employment be available, the Bhangis might be willing to pay the price of abandoning their "polluting" kām karnewālā activities; if so, it would spell the end of another core jajmāni relationship. Rājpur would then have to hire someone on a cash-contract basis to clean the village streets and remove the carcasses.

So far we have been discussing three variables associated with the decrease of core jajmāni relationships: (1) the appearance of competitive technology rendering certain kām karnewālās' services obsolete; (2) an increase in population with no parallel increase in land; (3) an ideology among the kām karnewālās of nonperformance of "polluting" services for others. We have implied that each of these variables is a sufficient (but not necessary) condition, that is, that other things being equal (which they rarely are), the appearance of any of these variables will be associated with the decrease of core jajmāni relationships, although the decrease may occur in the absence of any (or all) of these variables.

A word needs to be said about the rate of this decrease. Once one of these sufficient conditions is present, I would suggest that the rate of decrease is contingent on the kām karnewālās' alternative means of economic survival. In the context of Rājpur, this would mean the quantity of land they possessed or their job possibilities in the wider economy. The fact that the Lohār owned ten acres of land helps account for his fairly rapid withdrawal from his core jajmāni relationship. The fact that the Bhangis had less than two acres of land helps account for the slowness of their withdrawal from the system. In a similar manner, if the nearby sugar mill were suddenly to expand and require five hundred extra workers, one could predict the end of core jajmāni relationships not only in Rājpur but also in neighboring villages.

In his pioneering work in 1936 Wiser stated: "The Hindu Jajmāni

System cannot continue as it now exists."[11] In 1959 Beidelman stated that massive economic and political changes had occurred in India "in a combination and on a scale and intensity sufficient to cause grave conflict within such a system, a conflict which will ultimately make the jajmāni system obsolete."[12]

This paper has tried to take one step beyond predicting that the jajmāni system will end. It has suggested specific patterns one can look for in the decrease of core jajmāni relationships. Whether or not these patterns hold in other villages and other regions in India is a matter for empirical investigation.

[11] Wiser, The Hindu Jajmani System, p. 115.
[12] Beidelman, A Comparative Analysis of the Jajmani System, p. 79.

KATHLEEN GOUGH

Pālakkara:
Social and Religious Change
in Central Kērala

THIS PAPER IS ABOUT social and religious change in Pālakkara, a village of
former Cochin State in Central Kērala. It focuses mainly on Harijans
and their relationships with the dominant caste of Nāyars. I shall concentrate on continuity and change between 1949, when I spent eight
months in Pālakkara, and April to June, 1964, when I restudied the village.[1] The period before 1949 is introduced to provide a historical context.

THE SETTING

My chief interest is in the village goddess temple. I shall try to
show how the changing relationships of the various castes to this temple
have been connected with their economic, legal, and political relations
with one another and with the wider society.

Most of the religious changes I shall discuss could be regarded as
examples of Sanskritization.[2] Thus, during the past forty years, the non-

Kathleen Gough is Professor of Anthropology at Simon Fraser University, British
Columbia, Canada.

[1] My fieldwork in 1947-49 was made possible by the grant of a William Wyse Studentship from Trinity College, Cambridge, and of an Anthony Wilkin Studentship
from the Museum of Archaeology and Anthropology, University of Cambridge.
Fieldwork in 1964 was financed by an Auxiliary Research Award from the American
Social Science Research Council. I wish to express my gratitude to all these bodies.
In all I have spent 28 months in Kērala, 10 of them in Pālakkara. I have given
pseudonyms to villages and individuals in an effort to protect the identities of my
informants. I am indebted to my husband, David F. Aberle, for many helpful sug-
gestions in writing this paper.

[2] A fruitful concept introduced by M. N. Srinivas, *Religion and Society among the
Coorgs of South India* (Oxford, Oxford University Press, 1952), pp. 30-31 *et passim.*
In a recent work Srinivas defines Sanskritization as "the process by which a 'low'
Hindu caste, or tribal or other group, changes its customs, ritual, ideology and
way of life in the direction of a 'high,' and frequently 'twice-born' caste." *Social
Change in Modern India* (Berkeley, University of California Press, 1966), p. 6.

Brāhman castes of Pālakkara have all ceased to offer animal sacrifices and alcoholic liquor to their gods and spirits. They now offer vegetarian food, flowers, incense, water, fire, and libations of a type prescribed in Sanskrit religious works.

In a recent treatment of Sanskritization,[3] Srinivas recognizes that there are several kinds, depending on the social context of the caste, and that it is necessary to locate the reference group among the upper castes whose ceremonies are adopted by the lower caste. He notes that the model is often the region's dominant caste, which may be, but need not be, Brāhman. Srinivas emphasizes that Sanskritization has been occurring since Vēdic times. Sanskritization is not, moreover, a unique process but may be compared with any form of adoption by lower status groups of the mores and beliefs of higher status groups. It is clear from the work of Srinivas and others that Sanskritization is a regular, although not an invariant, feature of upward mobility in Hindu society. I would argue, further, that it is always connected with change in the legal, political, or economic content of the relationship between the Sanskritizing caste and one or more higher castes which serve as reference groups.

Srinivas writes that "the mobility associated with Sanskritization results only in *positional changes* and does not lead to any *structural change*."[4] This may be true of some of the examples that Srinivas gives in chapter 1, for he is here concerned mainly with Sanskritization in pre-British India. Even in these cases, however, the distinction is hard to draw. Whether we speak of positional or of structural change depends partly on the variable with which we are concerned. I suggest, for example that (as in the case that Srinivas quotes from my work[5]) considerable change in economic and political structure was occurring with the growth of overseas trade in the period of European mercantilism prior to British rule,[6] although in most areas the basic principles of caste ranking were not challenged. These changes in economic and political structure must have been relevant to many instances of Sanskritization. When

---

[3] *Social Change in Modern India*, pp. 1-45, 89-94, *et passim*.

[4] *Ibid.*, p. 7.

[5] *Ibid.*, p. 39, referring to the rise of Nāyar chiefs and petty Rajas in North Kērala in the seventeenth and eighteenth centuries under the impact of trade with European companies (Gough, in *Matrilineal Kinship*, ed. D. M. Schneider and Kathleen Gough [Berkeley, University of California Press, 1961], pp. 386-87).

[6] See, e.g., Ramakrishna Mukherjee, *The Rise and Fall of the East India Company* (Berlin, VEB Deutscher Verlag der Wissenschaften, 1958), pp. 174-257.

we come to British rule, moreover, Srinivas acknowledges that the rise of large-scale and competitive caste associations—which certainly involved structural changes—was associated with reforms that "were generally aimed at Sanskritizing the style of life and ritual."[7]

The modern Backward Class movement as a whole, however, Srinivas regards as "inevitably a secular movement."[8] While it is true that the Self-Respect Movement in Madras was antireligious, I would suggest that the majority of non-Brāhmans in Madras retained their religion, even while seeking social advancement through opposition to the Brāhman. I am unable to say under what conditions modern non-Brāhman movements for upward mobility have been religious or secular, but it does seem that many such movements have been both religious and Sanskritizing, at least in their early phases. This is notwithstanding the fact that in South India many have also been anti-Brāhmanical. In Kērala, the movement founded by Sri Nārāyana Guru is a prime example, involving the complete Sanskritization of Īzhava ritual. At the same time, Sanskritization was linked with the founding of Īzhava monasteries and temples. In creating their own priesthood, the Īzhavas dispensed with the need for a Brāhmanical priesthood altogether.

I would also emphasize that some of these modern forms of Sanskritization are more complex than mere adoption of the customs of a higher caste. They may involve new or syncretic beliefs and ceremonies, as well as the usual adoption of Sanskritized rituals, vegetarianism, teetotalism, and widow celibacy. The Īzhava S.N.D.P.[9] is again an example. It was influenced by Christianity and by such all-India figures as Swāmi Vivēkānanda, as well as by the religion of the local Nambūtiri Brāhmans and Nāyars. Some writers would perhaps not regard such a new religion, with its egalitarian "One God, One Caste, One Religion," as a good example of Sanskritization. It partakes so heavily of Sanskrit influences, however, as to require consideration.

Thus, while I agree that most lower-caste movements have become

---

[7] Srinivas, *Social Change in Modern India*, p. 92.
[8] *Ibid.*, p. 114.
[9] The Srī Nārāyana Dharma Paripālana Yōgam, or Association for the Protection of Virtue, founded by Srī Nārāyana Guru of Quilon district, Travancore, in 1903. See A. Aiyappan, *Iravas and Culture Change* (Madras Government Museum Bulletin, 1945), pp. 170-72, 188-94; Kathleen Gough, "Kērala Politics and the 1965 Elections," *International Journal of Comparative Sociology* (Leiden), September, 1967.

increasingly secular and political in the past thirty years (and the Īzhava movement is again an example), my point is that caste movements have been prominent in this century which combined religious fervor and Sanskritization with rejection of the Brāhman, belief in social and religious equality, and profound social structural change. The religious changes among Pālakkara Īzhavas and Harijans that I shall discuss are local examples of such structural change.

In Pālakkara, there have in fact been three main types of Sanskritization in the last forty years, among the Nāyars, Īzhavas, and Harijans respectively. Nāyar culture has been partly Sanskritized for centuries, but since about 1930 the Nāyars have come into a closer ritual association with the Nambūtiri Brāhmans and have also given up some non-Sanskritic rites. The Īzhavas entered their all-Kērala, autonomous, Sanskritizing caste association, the S.N.D.P., during the 1940s. The Harijans tried a kind of small local version of an autonomous caste association in the early 1950s, but abandoned that for a more radical approach in the 1960s.

Changes in the relationships and content of ritual in the village studied reflect changes already accomplished in the legal, political, and economic spheres. At the same time the religious changes often anticipate further political and economic change. The ceremonies announce a new morality appropriate to these further developments, clarify the issues, and point a direction. Ritual events, finite in time-span, rich in symbol, and compact in meaning, dramatize "real life" changes already wrought, and galvanize the participants for changes to come.

The village temple and its festival provide a focal set of ceremonies. Bhagavati, the goddess, has been worshiped by all the village from time immemorial. She is the fount of human, animal, and crop fertility, of war, smallpox, and other pestilence—in short, of good and evil happenings which may strike all men, regardless of their caste. Her courtyard has been the site for the meting out of village justice for many centuries. Sins against the goddess—especially those infringing the traditional laws governing the relations between castes—have been punished not only by human justice but (it is believed) by epidemics, the deaths of parturient women and cattle, failure of rain, or fouling of the village's pools and wells. For the Harijans to try to revolutionize the village temple ceremonies therefore meant a stab to the heart of traditional village order.

THE SOCIAL SYSTEM

THE CASTES

Pālakkara is a village (*dēśam*) in Central Kērala, three miles from a town of 80,000. The population increased from 1,289 to 1,932 between 1949 and 1964.

There are four main blocks of castes. (1) "Good," or "clean," upper castes in 1964 comprised one household of Nambūtiri Brāhmans, two of temple servants, and 99 of Nāyars, mainly of the high-ranking Sūdra Nāyar subcaste. These upper castes formed 32 per cent of the villagers in 1964. (2) Fifty-one households of Roman Catholics formed 17 per cent of the total. (3) Sixty-eight households of the "backward" but nowadays powerful caste of Īzhavas, together with 53 culturally cognate households of village servant castes such as washermen, barbers, stonemasons, and astrologers, formed 39 per cent of the villagers. (4) Three Harijan castes of Mulayans or Veṭṭuvans (34 households), Pulayans (1 household), and Paraiyans (3 households) fall at the bottom of the social scale. Harijans accounted for 12 per cent of the village population in 1964.

TRADITIONAL SOCIAL ECONOMY

Before British rule, most of the land in Pālakkara was owned by the Nambūtiri Brāhman household, Pālamana. The Nāyars were hereditary noncultivating tenants (*kāṇamdar*). They gave personal services to the Nambūtiris and policed the village. Through an assembly (*kūṭṭam*) of heads of matrilineal households, the Nāyars dispensed justice among themselves and the lower castes. Young Nāyar men trained in arms in a village gymnasium and, in wars, fought for the Maharaja of Cochin.

The Īzhavas and their congeners were subtenants (*verumpāṭṭamdar*) under the Brāhmans and Nāyars. The village servants served castes of higher or of similar rank to themselves. Each servant caste held a village right (*dēśam avakāśam*) in a hereditary system comparable to that of the *jajmāni* system of North India.

Among the Harijans, the Veṭṭuvans and Pulayans were slaves of the Brāhmans and Nāyars. Slaves did most of the wet-rice cultivation and performed other menial tasks.

The Paraiyans were village servants on terms similar to those of the higher village servant castes. They were, however, at the bottom of the religious and social scale. Paraiyans made baskets, removed and skinned dead cattle, and had special roles as magicians.

CHANGES DURING BRITISH RULE

In 1809 the Nāyar armies were disbanded. In Pālakkara, a few Nāyar families became prosperous cultivators of subsistence and export crops. Today, almost all Pālakkara Nāyars work in the nearby town, chiefly in white-collar or service occupations.

With the development of the market economy after the mid-nineteenth century, Pālakkara's Īzhavas, too, moved into wage work and urban occupations. Today they include tenant farmers, factory workers, shop keepers, and casual laborers.

The Christians entered Pālakkara from a nearby village about eighty years ago. They are descended from Harijan and Īzhava converts who, in the early nineteenth century, raised their rank and widened their economic horizons by attaching themselves to the urban Syrian Christian commercial community. Today the Pālakkara Christians rank socially between the Nāyars and the Īzhavas. Their occupations are similar to those of the Īzhavas.

The Harijans were freed from slavery in 1864 and became agricultural wage laborers. The religious pollution ascribed to them by the higher castes prevented them from entering other forms of work. In 1949, 31 out of 33 Harijan men were landless laborers or basketmakers. Most Harijans occupied shacks in gardens owned by the higher castes and could be evicted at will. In spite of the impoverishment of the Brāhmans and Nāyars and the mediocre success of the Īzhavas, the Harijans in 1949 were still much poorer and socially less privileged than almost all other households. None were literate, and none of their children attended school.

THE NEIGHBORHOOD AND ITS TEMPLE

Until about 1890, Pālakkara formed part of a larger unit comprising four neighboring villages, called a kara. Throughout Kērala, the kara or tara, which I translate as "neighborhood," was the main unit of intermarriage and intracaste administration of the Nāyars. The village (dēśam), by contrast, was normally an area owned by a single landlord (janmi) in which most of the servant castes had their field of service.

South of Pālakkara lay Nāyakkara; to the west, Puḷḷapura; and to the east, Āyyakkode. Each village had its Brāhman landlord house. Nāyars of the neighborhood intermarried closely and had a unitary caste assembly. Some of the village servant castes, such as astrologers, served the neighborhood; others, a single village.

The neighborhood jointly owned a temple dedicated to Bhagavati in the form of the fierce Bhadrakāli, managed by the Nāyars. The temple occupied a prominent position on a large green between Pālakkara and Nāyakkara. Such Bhagavati temples (kshētrams) are found throughout Kērala, Bhagavati being both the patron of Nāyar soldiers and the guardian of village prosperity and laws.

Village or neighborhood Bhagavati temples differ from the private temples (ambalams) of Nambūtiri Brāhmans or royalty. The latter are usually dedicated to the Sanskrit gods, Shiva, Vishnu, or Subramania, or to the benign forms of their consorts. Most of these private temples of Brāhmans and royalty were traditionally closed to Nāyars as well as to the lower castes, only Brāhmans, temple servants, and Kshatriyas being allowed within them. Pālamana's Subramania temple, situated on another green in the north of Pālakkara near the Nambūtiri household, is an example of such a private temple; comparable temples are owned by each Brāhman landlord house in the other three villages of this neighborhood.

In village Bhagavati temples, Nāyars could proceed as far as the door of the innermost shrine. Some village temples had, indeed, a special non-Brāhman priest (Pidāran) similar in rank to the Nāyars, who sacrificed chickens and offered toddy to the goddess within the shrine itself. Such shrines were avoided by Brāhmans and were virtually innocent of Sanskritic rites.

In the great majority of Bhagavati temples in Central Kērala, however, there has been for many decades an intermingling of Sanskrit and other elements. The Pālakkara shrine is an example. On the one hand, the goddess is represented not by a carved stone figure, as in most Brāhmanical temples, but by a womb-shaped stone similar to those found in many Nāyar lineage-goddesses' shrines. Near it is a phallic stone lingam representing Kshētrapālan, the "protector" of Bhagavati. The idols stand in an open courtyard similar to that in a Nāyar house, whereas the inner shrines of Brāhman temples are enclosed. On the other hand, only the neighborhood's Embrāntiri Brāhman priest may make offerings to the goddess, and only he and the temple servant castes may approach her. The larger building surrounding the inner shrine was traditionally open to the Sūdra Nāyars. The outer yard of the temple, surrounded by a wall, was open both to the Sūdra Nāyars and to their lower-ranking personal servants, the Nāyar oil-mongers, the Nāyar barbers, and the Nāyar washermen.

The mixture of Brāhman and non-Brāhman elements is seen again in the portable "image" of Bhagavati. In Brāhman temples a small brass statuette of the deity (vigraham) stands on a shelf near the inner shrine. It is taken out in procession on the back of an elephant during the temple festival. In the Pālakkara shrine, Bhagavati's "statue" is simply a hand-mirror similar to those used by Nāyar women in their toilet and in household ceremonies. It is, however, encased in a skirt and headdress.

The daily offerings to Bhagavati are entirely Brāhmanical. The Brāhman priest garlands the image of Bhagavati and, while chanting Sanskrit verses, offers cooked rice and vegetables, incense, water, fire, blossoms, and sandalwood paste. He presents the residue of these offerings to the Nāyar worshipers.

At the annual festival (vēla) in Dhanu (December-January), the Nāyars hire an array of temple servant musicians from the city to play panchavādyam, music with five instruments traditionally reserved for high caste functions. They bring five beautifully caparisoned elephants, with teams of Brāhmans to ride them, bearing aloft colored plumes, fans, and silk umbrellas. On the neck of the central elephant a fourth Brāhman mounts the "statuette" of Bhagavati supported by a golden shield. In ceremonial procession the goddess is borne slowly through the high-caste lanes of the village on the eve and the afternoon of the festival day. This procession is a shortened replica of those carried out at the traditional festival (uḷsavom) of a Brāhman or royal temple. Quite probably the Nāyars introduced it into the neighborhood temple ceremonies in the early nineteenth century in the course of their own "Sanskritization," for it is known that in pre-British times, when the Nāyars were soldiers, they had fewer Sanskrit elements in their ritual, and Bhagavati, the bloodthirsty war-goddess, required animal sacrifice as the central feature of her rites. It is interesting to notice that even today, only lower-ranking Embrāntiri Brāhmans from South Canara, and not native

Nambūtiris, serve as priests and ride the elephants at Nāyar-managed Bhagavati shrines.

Until recent times, moreover, Bhagavati remained the focus of various non-Brāhmanical institutions and ritual events. Before the festival, a Sūdra Nāyar oracle (veḷichappād) visited each Nāyar house with a company of musicians to collect para—measures of rice, coconuts, fruits, and money—to finance the festival. Para was obligatory for the Nāyar household. Failure to pay it meant excommunication from caste for the duration of the year.

At the festival, the oracle became possessed by the goddess and danced frenziedly, chopping his forehead with a sickle until the blood flowed. In a hoarse voice he declared the goddess's will to the people and blessed them by throwing rice on their heads.

While the Brāhman priest was restoring the goddess to her shrine a second priest-oracle (karami) of the Nāyar oil-monger subcaste sacrificed chickens and offered toddy outside in the temple yard. This priest was especially concerned with Bhagavati as the bringer of smallpox; he visited and performed sacrifices at the houses of smallpox victims of high caste in the course of the year.

In front of the temple gate at the festival, the Īzhavas and village servants performed a stick-dance on the village green. These castes made their own offerings of chickens and toddy to the goddess through the medium of another priest-oracle (kōmaram), a low-caste washerman. Even the Christians had some association with Bhagavati. Their own festival to ward off smallpox is addressed to St. Sebastian and occurs within a few weeks of the goddess's festival. In Pālakkara, some old Christians believe Bhagavati and St. Sebastian to be sister and brother. Hindus, especially Īzhavas, traditionally contributed to the Christian festival, and washermen, Pulayans, and Paraiyans played music for it. Christians gave money for the Bhagavati festival and many attended it along with the Īzhavas.

The Harijans had special roles in relation to Bhagavati. The Mulayans and Paraiyans worshiped two male godlings, Pōttōttan and Kandan. Pōttōttan is represented by a square stone slab set in the village green about 150 yards east of the Bhagavati temple. On it a male figure is painted in white. Kandan, the Paraiyan god, represented by a phallic stone, was housed in a small shrine farther to the east. The Paraiyan

headman of Pālakkara was Kandan's priest-oracle. A Pulayan priest sacrificed to Pōttōṭṭan and three Mulayan oracles became possessed by him
at the festival.

Appropriately, Pōttōṭṭan and Kandan were believed to be slaves of
Bhagavati. The Harijans made special offerings of chickens and toddy
to their gods after the harvest in Magaram (January-February), after
the New Year festival (Vishu) in Mēdam (April-May), and at the
sowing of the first crop in Kanni (September-October). For the
last festival the Mulayans drove the villagers' buffaloes wildly round
Pōttōṭṭan's stone on the green after refreshing themselves, the deity,
and the beasts with toddy.

In December, at the annual festival of the goddess, the Harijans
assembled near their own shrines, being forbidden to approach the village deity because of their religious pollution. While the ceremonies for
Bhagavati were in progress, the Harijan priests sacrificed chickens and
offered toddy to their godlings. Teams of Paraiyan youths arrived dressed
in palm fronds and red cloth costumes, with grotesquely painted faces,
and danced near the Harijan shrines. They represented *bhūtams*, demon-
servants of Bhagavati who at her bidding sowed the "seeds" of smallpox
among the people. Other teams brought stuffed cloth figures of oxen and
horses which they placed on the green as offerings, facing toward the
goddess's temple.

Toward the end of the festival, when sacrifices and offerings were
finished and the goddess was restored to her shrine, all of the village
oracles danced out into the spaces between the caste groups and com-
municated with each other. Higher-caste oracles shouted to those of
lower caste, expressing satisfaction with their rites. They shouted injunc-
tions about offerings to be made in the future, and about how, through
correct observance of the customs, villagers of every rank might ward
off disaster and pestilence. At last the oracles fell, exhausted, to the
ground. In a burst of general rejoicing, the festival ended with fireworks,
gambling, and drinking.

The myths of the village godlings refer to old-time misfortunes and
village conflicts. Bhagavati is the ghost of a girl of the Nāyar oilmongers'
subcaste who died of smallpox. Kshētrapālan was a Brāhman *sanyāsi*
(ascetic), or, some say, a clandestine Brāhman lover, who died at the
oilmongers' house. Kandan and Pōttōṭṭan were Harijan slaves, murdered
by their Nāyar masters. The ghosts of all these unfortunates were ele-

vated as village deities after various disasters and miraculous happenings had persuaded the villagers that this was essential.

Kandan and Pōttōttan were traditionally Nāyar as well as Harijan godlings, for the Nāyars built Kandan's shrine, financed the Harijan ceremonies, and granted permission each year for them to be performed. If the Nāyars had refused permission the godlings would have brought sickness upon them and perhaps on the village at large. Therefore, the Nāyars feared these low-caste godlings and in a sense were at the mercy of their Harijan priests and oracles, as they were also of the Paraiyans who impersonated Bhagavati's demons. On the other hand, if they neglected their godlings the Harijans had cause to fear the wrath of Bhagavati through them. Elsewhere,[10] I have suggested that various institutions associated with such minor godlings and demons served as a check on Nāyar abuse of their low-caste servants, as well as providing a safe means of handling aggressive motives between high and low castes —motives aroused by the political and economic systems which institutionalized the oppression of the low castes by the high. I have also suggested that the cults of these minor spirits provided a kind of ritual compensation for the lower castes, as well as reflecting both their servitude and their indispensability in village life.

CHANGE AND CONTINUITY BEFORE 1949

In 1885 the neighborhood split into two. Ayyakkōde, a growing village on a new main road to the town, formed one half and Pālakkara-Nāyakkara-Pullapura the other. In 1905, with further population increase, the western kara split again. Pālakkara, near another new paved road, formed one half, and Nāyakkara-Pullapura the other. There were now three Nāyar assemblies. Ayyakkōde staged the festival of the goddess in alternate years. Pālakkara and Nāyakkara-Pullapura took the off-years in turn, with each of them financing the festival one year in four.

The splits in the Nāyar assembly accompanied a decline in its judicial powers. With population increase, the Nāyar elders' geographical spheres were divided, but with the expansion of the market economy, the range of economic and political relations was widening. In the early nineteenth century the government had already introduced a system of

[10] Kathleen Gough, "Cults of the Dead among the Nāyars," in Milton Singer, ed., *Traditional India: Structure and Change* (Philadelphia, American Folklore Society, 1959), pp. 463-74.

"revenue villages" to collect the land tax. Pālakkara fell within a revenue village which did not coincide with the kara. In the 1930s, Pālakkara was incorporated into yet another kind of unit—the modern statutory panchāyat—for public works and village development projects. This covered a different area still—most of the old kara plus three other villages nearer to the town. Both of these modern units had government-appointed personnel, not all of whom were Nāyars or Brāhmans.

Meanwhile, more villagers went to work in the town or found themselves working for absentee landlords. Such people took their disputes to the urban courts and could no longer be fully controlled by the Nāyar assembly with respect to their crimes. The last case of ex-communication from the Nāyar caste took place in 1925, but the boycott of the erring household was not fully effective. With the spread of vaccination in the early 1900s, the fear of smallpox as a divine punishment gradually decreased. In 1949 ad hoc groups of Nāyar elders still occasionally settled disputes among the lower castes and levied fines, payable to the temple funds. But their powers to do so were reduced. By 1964 they had lapsed altogether.

The Nāyar assemblies continued, however, as temple managements. Annually, each village assembly met near the temple to elect a dēvaswom committee of nine. These committees levied para from their villages, paid the temple officiants, and organized the festivals.

Meanwhile changes in intercaste relations were occurring. These involved (1) reduction of the social and ritual distance between Nāyars and Brāhmans; (2) growing emancipation and autarchy of the Īzhavas; and (3) incipient moves toward emancipation by the Harijans.

NĀYARS AND BRĀHMANS

Each of the Nambūtiri Brāhman households of the old neighborhood owned a private temple dedicated to a god of the Sanskrit pantheon. Entry was forbidden to Nāyars. By the 1930s, however, all the Brāhmans had become more or less impoverished through lack of modern education and sales of land. One after another, they ceased to conduct their temple festivals. The several Nāyar assemblies then made a bargain with the Brāhmans: the Nāyars would finance the festivals, and in return the Brāhmans would open their temples to the Nāyars. In addition, at the Bhagavati festival, the goddess began to be carried on her elephant to the Brāhman temple of whichever village was performing the festival, ceremonially borne round that temple three times, and brought home again.

These ritual changes reflected a growing economic parity between the Nāyars and the Brāhmans. They were accompanied by other changes, for example, a decline in the rate of hypergamous marriages between Nambūtiri Brāhman men and Nāyar women,[11] and laws[12] that obliged Nambūtiri men to maintain their Nāyar wives and children and gave such children rights in their Brāhman fathers' estates.

IZHAVA EMANCIPATION AND AUTARCHY

Pālakkara Izhavas ceased to play formal roles in the Bhagavati festivals about the end of the 1930s. The Congress Party's agitation for temple entry was at its height in Cochin, but most "public" temples were not opened to the lower castes until 1947. The Izhavas, few of whom were any longer economically dependent on local Nāyars, argued that their traditional cock-sacrifices and stick-play outside the temple were degrading. If they could not enter the village temple equally with the Nāyars, they preferred to support their own.

In the late 1930s such a temple was built in a village six miles away, and some local Izhavas began to frequent it. Dedicated to Subramania, it was fashioned after the Nambūtiri Brāhman temples and employed a Sanskrit-trained Izhava priest. By 1944, the Izhava all-Kērala caste association, the S.N.D.P., had established an office in a village next to Nāyakkara together with a shrine dedicated to Srī Nārāyana Guru, who died in 1920. Pālakkara and Pullapura were formed by outside organizers into a local branch of the S.N.D.P., and every Izhava household joined it.

Joining the Izhava association involved employing only Sanskrit-trained Izhava priests for life-crisis rites, attending only Izhava temples, and abandoning "primitive" ritual customs such as animal sacrifice or offerings of alcohol. Izhavas were in theory required to cease trading in palm wine and to become teetotal. They were required to adhere to

---

[11] Traditionally, only the eldest son of a Nambūtiri Brāhman patrilineal family married within his caste and begot children for his family and caste. Younger sons had liaisons with women of the matrilineal royal, temple servant, or Nāyar castes. Children of these unions were affiliated to the mother's family and caste (Gough, *Matrilineal Kinship*, pp. 357-58; Joan P. Mencher, "The Nāyars of South Malabar," in *Comparative Family Systems*, ed. M. F. Nimkoff [Boston, Houghton Mifflin Company, 1965], pp. 170-82).

[12] In Cochin the most relevant act was the Cochin Nambūtiri Act of 1939 (Act XVII of 1114, Malayālam Era).

monogamy; fraternal polyandry and polygyny, already fast dying out with the coming of independent wage-work, were now forbidden. Izhavas under their new priests were asked to study the teachings of Nārāyana Guru and to believe in "One God, One Caste, One Religion." Finally, they were expected to live frugally for the future benefit of their families and caste. This meant giving up costly life-crisis ceremonies, paying regular dues to the S.N.D.P. for its educational and welfare programs, and attempting to save and to invest money in land or profitable commercial enterprises.

By 1949, therefore, Pālakkara's Izhavas were living in a kind of parallel, back-to-back relationship with the Nāyars and Brāhmans. No longer subservient to the latter except when their individual jobs demanded it, the Izhavas ran their own ceremonial life, credit associations, drama clubs, teashops, temples, and reading rooms. They did not attack Nāyar dominance head-on, but evaded it by self-organization.

The village servants were divided between the desire for a similar autonomy and their continuing dependence on the Nāyars. Among the astrologers, low-caste washermen, Nāyar oilmongers, and Nāyar washermen there were men who served the Nāyars as heretofore and, correspondingly, played their roles in the Bhagavati festival. Each of the servant castes had, however, its own statewide caste association clamoring, like the S.N.D.P., for government jobs and representation in the legislature. Younger village servants left their traditional work or transformed such work into a contractual, market-oriented occupation. Such men sought social equality with the Nāyars and avoided the ritual hallmarks of servitude.

In 1947, the granting of temple entry by the Cochin government affected ceremonial relations between the castes. Within a year, the larger temples in towns were fully opened to all castes. Izhavas, village servants and Harijans flocked into them during the annual festivals. Things moved more slowly in villages. During 1948, a half-dozen young Izhavas, astrologers, and washermen began to bathe in pools attached to the Bhagavati temple and to certain government-managed temples of the neighborhood, and presented themselves for worship. They were served grudgingly by the Brāhman priests, who knew that by law the game was up. Nāyar elders grumbled in private. Old women prophesied that the rains would fail and that mothers and cattle would miscarry. When a slimy weed appeared in one of the bathing pools, Nāyar women stayed at home, believing it to be a sign of the deity's wrath. At the festival of Bhagavati in 1948, however, large numbers of Īzhavas and village servants passed into the temple. Correspondingly, except for the Nāyar oilmonger priest-oracle who sacrificed the chickens, no persons of rank below Sūdra Nāyars arrived to make their traditional forms of obeisance outside the temple.

THE HARIJANS ATTEMPT EMANCIPATION

Until the late 1940s the Harijans, employed inside Palakkara, confined to landless labor, untraveled, illiterate, and still much dependent on local Nāyars, kept up their traditional ritual roles. In 1948, however, the Temple Entry Act affected them. During that year Pālakkara's Harijans refused to hold their special ceremonies to Pōttōṭṭan and Kandan in February, May, and September, and did not take part in the Bhagavati festival in December. Like the Īzhavas a decade earlier, they argued that it was degrading for them to assemble at a great distance from the Bhagavati temple to perform their old-fashioned rites.

At the Bhagavati festival of 1948, however, no Harijans were seen to enter the temple yard, although it was feared that some might do so. The Harijans evidently felt that to tempt the Nāyars' wrath in this way would not be to their advantage. In 1948, therefore, the Harijans temporarily suspended all their public ceremonies, uncertain which way to turn. Among the more "modern" villagers in general, there was a sense that the old order was passing. As one Nāyar of thirty-five put it, "Prohibition is near, and this cock forbidden;[13] what will be the position of our Kandan, then?" The Harijans had not decided.

In 1949, however, a strange event brought Kandan to the forefront of public consciousness again. Twelve years before, the youngest son of the Puḷḷapura Brāhman house had run away from his work as a temple priest to join the Congress Party at age thirteen. He later became the neighborhood's first Communist. After a period in the British army and in union work, Viśvanāthan married and claimed a share of his ancestral property. It happened that Kandan's shrine lay on a grassy plot on this land, which its Communist scion wished to fence and turn into a garden. A militant atheist, "Communist Nambūtiripād" demanded that the villagers move Kandan out of his sight. The Nāyar assembly met in

---

[13] The Congress government was considering the prohibition of alcohol in Cochin and had already prohibited animal sacrifice, although it was still widely practiced.

consternation and decided, with oracular help from Bhagavati, to move Kandan's shrine out to the common land near Pōttōṭṭan's stone. This event was elaborately accomplished in March, 1949, a few weeks after the "mad Communist" was arrested for political agitation and put in prison. It required the selection of an auspicious time by the astrologer, special *pūjas* to Bhagavati and Kandan, pronouncements by the oracles of both gods, and the presence of both the Nāyar committee and elders of the Paraiyan community.

CONTINUITY, 1949-1964

When I returned to Pālakkara in 1964, the village had not changed markedly to the eye of the casual observer. Some dozen new families had entered, many households had divided, and a few of the old ones had left, but the residential arrangement of castes was only slightly more mixed than it had been in 1949. On average, the Nāyars and Brāhmans were still slightly wealthier than the Christians and Īzhavas. While the proportion of wage workers had increased in Nāyar, Christian and Īzhava castes, the Nāyars remained predominant in white-collar work and the Īzhavas and Christians in manual and service work. The Brāhman land-lords and a half-dozen Nāyar cultivators retained substantial acreages. Among the Harijans, 44 out of 51 men were still landless laborers or traditional village servants, working mainly in Pālakkara.

The Bhagavati temple was still managed by a Nāyar committee and the festival held in December. Some Īzhavas continued to worship at the Īzhava temples in other villages; some regularly attended the Bhagavati festivals and worshiped inside the temple with Nāyars.

CHANGE, 1949-1964

ECONOMICS

Continuity was most marked in the economic relations of villagers. There were changes, but there was no cataclysmic upheaval. After 1949, more land was sold out of the village, and more Nāyar families became paupers. The indigenous Īzhavas and village servants had become poorer than before, except for a few factory workers and carpenters. A new, wealthier urban upper class of five families of various castes had bought gardens and built houses in the village, accentuating the deepening poverty of most of its indigenes.

On the whole, unlike the other castes, the Harijans had improved their living standards, approaching and even surpassing those of some Īzhavas. In 1964 only three Harijan families lived in their old-fashioned shacks. The rest had thatched cottages with verandas and windows. Harijans used soap and hair oil, drank coffee, and ate modern "snacks." The women wore blouses and *sāris*; the men, shirts and long *muntus*. These improvements came mainly as a result of the fixity of tenures and minimum agricultural wages instituted by the Communist government in 1957-59. They were accompanied by greater social equality for Harijans, who in 1964 walked freely in the streets, ate in the teashops, and no longer observed distance-pollution in relation to the higher castes. At the same time, it would be hazardous to say that the Harijans had made an all-round or permanent economic improvement, for during the early 1960s unemployment became more common than before and food prices were rapidly rising. Despite a bold front of modernity, many Harijans (and some families in the other castes) starved for days together during the rainy season of 1964.

POLITICS

It was in the political sphere that change had swept through Pālakkara, revolutionizing the villagers' conceptions. In 1949 there was only limited franchise in Cochin, and political parties had made little headway in the village. A few educated Nāyars supported the Congress Party, but most were cool to the party because it had opened the temples to the lower castes. About six youths, Nāyars and Īzhavas, supported the Communists. They worked in a textile mill, belonged to a Communist union, and in town demonstrations marched proudly behind the party flag. They sat in low-caste teashops and played cards in the roadway, greatly infuriating the elders. It was some of these youths, together with four young Socialists, who "tested" the Temple Entry Act by bathing in the high-caste pools.

At that date most of the Īzhavas' political energies went to their caste association, and, although few could vote, they supported Īzhava candidates recommended by the S.N.D.P. The Christians were absorbed in their parish church and supported only church-approved candidates.

In 1949 the Harijans had no interest in political parties. Engaged in local relations with small landlords or owner-cultivators, they had never been reached by the Communist peasant unions, which, on the larger estates, were in 1948 attacking the privileges and the granaries of wealthy landlords. Viśvanāthan had burst upon the village scene, but he was already in prison and no one suspected what his future role might be. Most villagers thought him mad, and he thought them hopelessly backward.

Major political change came to Pālakkara in 1951 with universal franchise. Villagers refer to this period as "when the isms came." The Congress and Communist parties set up permanent units in Pālakkara and neighboring villages. By 1964, the Congress Party had 76 members in its Pālakkara branch. The Communist Party, which restricts its membership to proven loyalists, had only three members but a much larger number of active supporters.

The party units became firmly entrenched with the first panchāyat elections in 1953. By 1964 Pālakkara formed a ward within a panchāyat of 20,000 people covering seven traditional villages. Eight of the panchāyat board's members, including the Pālakkara representative, were Communists or Communist supporters; two were Congressmen. Viśvanāthan, who had soared to meteoric fame among the urban manual workers, landless laborers, and poorer tenants, was the panchāyat president and the ward member for Nāyakkara. Pālakkara's Communist ward member was a Nāyar owner-cultivator from the village's largest and oldest matrilineage. His Congress rival was also a Nāyar from another well-established lineage.

In the 1963 panchāyat elections, 38 per cent of Pālakkara voters supported the Congress Party, and 62 per cent the Communists. There is a moderately strong and highly significant relation between caste and party affiliation, with higher castes favoring the Congress Party, and lower castes, especially Harijans, the Communists. There is a similar relationship between economic class and party affiliation.[14]

Communist rule in Kērala from 1957 to 1959 greatly strengthened low-caste and lower-class support for the Communists and stiffened high-caste and upper-class resistance against them. The Communist government introduced a number of laws and programs that benefited the propertyless. These included debt relief and higher minimum wages

[14] For statistical details see Kathleen Gough, "Village Politics in Kerala," *Economic Weekly* (Bombay), February 27, 1965, pp. 415-16.

for agricultural laborers, fixity of tenure for all classes of tenants, free housesites for propertyless families, and an act that placed ceilings on land-ownership and permitted some tenants to buy fields from their landlords. At the local level, Communist panchāyat board members brought new wells, bathing pools, roads, irrigation works, and a number of other small but tangible benefits to the poorer and lower-caste sections of the village.

In Pālakkara, most Nāyars, Christians, and Izhavas support political parties individually, making their choice on the basis of personal advantage or conviction. The men of these castes have a lively interest in state and national politics. They read newspapers, attend political rallies, and follow state elections with fascination. It appears to me that, among the Communist supporters in these castes, belief in communism and the "ceremonial" participations (such as demonstrations and rallies) attendant on party support have largely replaced religion in the individuals' lives. This is especially true of younger men, few of whom now worship in the temples, although some still perform their household rites. Significantly, the local S.N.D.P. building, which used to be primarily a religious center, has been taken over by an elected Communist committee and now functions mainly as a library, a shrine where inter-caste marriages take place, and a center for party propaganda.

The younger Congress supporters, too, tend toward secularization, but they are less iconoclastic than the Communists. Nāyar Congressmen still give para to Bhagavati and help to elect the temple committee, whereas most Communist Nāyars have ceased to pay para and attend the festival only as spectators. In 1953 Viśvanāthan made a microphone speech on the village green in the middle of the festival, exhorting the villagers to abandon their foolishness. Congress supporters were disgusted with this performance.

The Bhagavati temple committee is nowadays made up of older Nāyars and temple servants. All are Congressmen, and as such, profess support for temple entry and Harijan uplift, but all of them are also landowners with "old-fashioned" interests in traditional institutions. The committee is headed by a newcomer from the nearby town, a wealthy, retired government servant of the temple drummer caste who inherited land in Pālakkara and built a large house near the temple in 1950. He and his wife devote themselves to charity in connection with a clinic in Nāyakkara, recently built by absentee landlords, and exhort the villagers toward unity, thrift, and industry in the framework of traditional institutions. In 1956, when Kērala became an integrated state, this gentleman persuaded the temple committees of the old kara to reunite and conduct the festival jointly henceforth in a "proper" manner. Collecting funds to refurbish the Bhagavati temple and to improve the festival has, for the more conservative and propertied Nāyars, become a kind of counterweight to the Communist-dominated panchāyat board's collection of taxes to finance "upstart" ventures among the poor.

The Harijans play a different role from the other castes in the village's political life. They vote mainly, although not entirely, in caste blocs and by local communities. Whereas the Īzhavas, Christians, and Nāyars have long since lost their caste assemblies for the settlement of disputes, the Harijans retain a loose association of male household heads who consult on important matters. Each local cluster is led by one or two "big men" of forceful personality. Of late, the leadership has passed to young, literate men who favor the Communist Party[15] and are impatient for change.

These men are not, however, wedded to the party in the way that Īzhava, Christian, or Nāyar supporters are. They are "brokers" who muster votes in return for services to their community. The Harijans have learned that franchise gives them power, as a village minority, to manipulate the parties and thereby gain certain small but tangible benefits. Most of them have in fact supported the Communist ward member since 1957, but their support depends on the fulfillment of promises. Before the panchāyat elections of 1963, both the South and the West Pālakkara Harijan settlements were temporarily influenced by a Harijan Congress Party member of the Legislative Assembly who came to campaign for the local Congress candidates. In the end, however, most people in the two communities renewed their support for Viśvanāthan and the Pālakkara Communist leader, after receiving promises of a new road and a public well. These were being built by the panchāyat board, with hired Harijan labor, in 1964.

The Harijans' awareness of their voting power has led to greater

---

15 The Communist Party of India split between right and left wings at about the time of my arrival in Pālakkara in April, 1964. In Pālakkara and the surrounding neighborhood almost all the Communists went with the left group. For discussions of these two parties see J. B. Wood, "Observations on the Indian Communist Party Split," *Pacific Affairs* (Spring, 1965), pp. 47-63; Gough, "Kērala Politics and the 1965 Elections."

self-respect and to an urgent demand for social equality. This might have happened had any two parties competed for their support, but there is no doubt that Communist policies particularly enhanced their self-confidence. Although both major parties preach social equality and uplift, it is the Communists who eat in the homes and teashops of Harijans, organize drama clubs among them, file suits on their behalf, and agitate for fixed tenures, higher wages, and a share in the land. The Harijans' demand that they be treated "like men" has been re-inforced by these efforts and by the Communist belief in a classless society. The Harijans have phrased this belief in terms applicable to their village life.

RELIGION

After I left Pālakkara in 1949, the Harijans continued to stay away from the Bhagavati festival, but resumed their own festivals in February, May, and September. During the early 1950s they turned Kandan's shrine into a small "Sanskritic" temple. The Paraiyan priest-oracle began to make daily offerings and to recite *mantras* in imitation of Brāhman priests. In 1952, animal sacrifice was strictly prohibited by the government. This ended such sacrifices in Pālakkara as a whole; today, for example, Bhagavati's Nāyar oilmonger priest severs pumpkins at the annual festival instead of beheading roosters. In 1956, when the neighborhood was reunited and the Bhagavati temple repaired, a wealthy temple servant benefactor from Ayyakkōde rewarded the Harijans' piety by rebuilding Kandan's shrine. When I visited it in 1964 the old Paraiyan priest-oracle proudly offered me *prasādham* and told me that Kandan is an aspect of Shiva, just as Bhagavati is an aspect of Pārvati, Shiva's consort.

It might be wondered why the Harijans maintained their own shrine and did not simply avail themselves of temple entry and join the higher castes in worship of Bhagavati. The reasons are, I think, first, that many Nāyars cold-shouldered the Harijans and made them feel unwelcome in the village temple. The attitude of religious Nāyars is one of contempt for Harijan ignorance of Sanskrit ritual and of derision when Harijans enter temples and (as one Nāyar woman put it) "bow at everything they see." The Harijans are sensitive to this treatment and have preferred to practice their Sanskrit rites on their own.

Second, the Harijans already had their own oracles, shrines, and festivals, which the Nāyars continued to finance. The old Harijan officials resented any move to abandon the minor godlings. Although he has given up eating beef and skinning dead cattle, the Paraiyan priest-oracle is still a village servant and might have met difficulties in selling his baskets if he had gone against the Nāyars' wishes in the matter of festivals. Today, it is the Paraiyan priest of Kandan and the old Pulayan priest of Pōttōṭṭan who most favor keeping these godlings alive. The priests' sense of their own importance in village eyes is also involved.

Eventually, however, the larger caste of Mulayans became impatient of these minor shrines. They were no doubt emboldened by the fact that, after 1958, they could no longer be evicted from their house-sites. During 1963 they conceived the idea that, as Bhagavati is the village goddess, they have equal rights in her temple and an equal claim to stage festivals in her honor. A movement had already begun locally for young Harijans to learn panchavādyam, the special type of music formerly reserved for high-caste festivals. On the festival day, Pālakkara's Harijan leaders hired a caparisoned elephant from the government Dēvaswom Department. All the Harijans assembled outside the Brāhmanical Subramania temple and proceeded thence southward through the village to Bhagavati's shrine. They marched the elephant through the entrance to the temple yard, flocked into the temple to worship, then "rounded" the temple three times with the elephant, marched out again, and formed up close beside the temple wall. The festival ended with a session of panchavādyam playing and oracle dancing, followed by a display of fireworks.

After the festival the Nāyar Temple Committee met and discreetly discussed this exhibition. Their first act was to clean up the temple yard from the day's depredations and to whitewash and purify the temple. Next they built a steel gate across the entrance, with a padlock. Some weeks later they quietly made it known that, while they did not propose to take action in the case just cited, they would not sanction a repetition of "last year's irregularities." Hearing of this, the Ayyakkōde Harijans in February, 1964, staged only their usual festival to Kandan and Pōttōṭṭan with offerings, traditional drumming, oracular demonstrations, the presentation of stuffed oxen and horses, and "demon" dancing.[16] Pālakkara Harijans derided these stale efforts and held themselves in readiness.

---

[16] Although the Nāyars reintegrated their neighborhood in 1956, the Harijans retained a division of labor in organizing their festivals. Ayyakkōde Harijans take major responsibility for the February festival; Pālakkara Harijans for the May festival; and Puḷḷapura Nāyakkara Harijans for that in September.

In March, a delegation of Pālakkara Harijans presented a petition to the Temple Committee president. It was signed by sixteen literate young Harijans and by a large number of other villagers, mostly Communist supporters. Viśvanāthan did not sign it, perhaps because having thrown off his temple priesthood he refuses to look back toward religion. Pālakkara's Communist ward representative's name topped the signatures, however, followed by those of ten other Nāyar Communist supporters. (A Nāyar Congressman pointed out to me slyly that none of them paid para to the temple, showed up to elect the committee, or ever offered a grain of rice to the deity.) The petition prayed that the Temple Committee would grant full rights to the Harijans to enter the temple, take out the goddess's emblem, proceed through the village with it, and "round" the temple with it on an elephant three times at the Harijan May festival.

The Temple Committee president seated the Harijans on one side of his living room ("he has no caste prejudice," as a Nāyar remarked), placed the Temple Committee on the other side, and received opinions. The Harijans argued that the temple was public property, that they were "as good as anyone," and that therefore they had the right to conduct their festival in the same way as any higher caste.

The Nāyars did not argue (although some of them said afterwards) that the Harijans were inferior and should not enter the temple. They argued that, with temple entry, Harijans could already enter the temple at any time, "just like Nāyars," and should properly worship there on the village festival day. Beyond that the Harijans had separate rights only to conduct ceremonies to their minor godlings. The Nāyars pointed out that from time immemorial the elephant procession has occurred only in December. It takes place on an auspicious day determined by oracle and astrologer. The idol must be bathed in gingelly oil by a special tantric priest, and priest and oracle must purify themselves for forty-one days in advance of the festival. Bhagavati cannot simply be lifted out and aired at any time when any private group thinks proper. More important, only Brāhmans may enter the innermost shrine and touch the idols, and only they may mount the elephants and man the sacred shield, plumes, fans, and umbrellas. No Nāyar would dream of doing so! Why then should Harijans?

One Nāyar suggested that the Harijans become "regular" members of the temple community by paying para on the same terms as Nāyars and running for office on the temple committee. (Other Nāyars thought this too revolutionary, but said nothing, perhaps because they knew that Nāyar voters outnumber Harijans.) The Harijans refused this offer, saying obstinately that they could not afford to pay para and that they wished only to exercise their rights of ownership and management one day a year, at their festival. They could not see why, now that "all of us are men," they should not handle the deity and mount the elephant with the same freedom as any Brāhman.

A Nāyar government servant then made a witty speech burlesquing the Harijans' demands. "Our friends the Pālakkara Harijans have asked that they should process the goddess with one elephant. Suppose that the Izhavas now arrive and ask to parade her with five elephants? Is it allowable? Shall the temple be opened to the Ayyakōde Harijans on yet another day? Shall anybody in the village be allowed to conduct a marriage at any time with an elephant arriving from the temple? Moreover, it is possible that next year our Christian friends may arrive and request to conduct mass in the temple. Is it allowable? And the year after, no doubt we shall be asked to transform it into a Marxist reading room!" He ended by speaking bitterly against the Harijans' practice of entering temples with "no plunge-bath and no neatness" and said that if they cared for religion they would study to preserve its sacred laws and forms.

A deadlock was reached, and the Harijans left without satisfaction. Some days later the Temple Committee president called a general meeting of about 100 Nāyars, who voted against the petition. The committee sent a letter to the Harijans informing them that "under present circumstances" they were free to conduct their festival in any way they pleased outside the temple walls. They would not, however, be permitted to enter the temple with an elephant.

Shortly afterwards I returned to Pālakkara and saw the Harijan festival in May of 1964. As in the previous year, the magnificently caparisoned elephant wended its way solemnly along the village lanes from the Subramania temple to Bhagavati's green. On it were mounted four young Mulayans, proudly bearing the golden shield (but not the goddess), the soft plume, stately fans, and beautiful pink umbrella. In front marched a dignified company of Harijans playing panchavādyam. The whole neighborhood appeared to be watching. Thick crowds of men and children lined the streets or sat on rooftops, and women gazed over walls and through bedroom windows. At intervals, the procession stopped, the horns sounded mightily, and the four elephant riders, flushed and trembling, rose majestically to their feet and held aloft the sacred symbols.

None of the Communist leaders attended the festival. As they explained to me, they did not feel that they had a role in religious ceremonies, although they did feel they had been bound to support the Harijans' "democratic rights." Viśvanāthan was nowhere visible, but Pālakkara's Communist ward member watched eagerly from a teashop, and many Communist supporters joined the procession. A small group of Īzhava Communist supporters, well known for their fisticuffs, walked near the elephant; one of them told me they were there to "protect" the Harijans in case a fight broke out.

At the Bhagavati temple, the gate was locked, and seated quietly on the wall was a line of white-robed Nāyars, including several Congressmen and members of the Temple Committee. In front of them stood a row of uniformed police with lathis, summoned from the town. The Temple Committee president was absent. A ceremonial confrontation took place. The elephant halted directly facing the temple gate, and the musicians formed up on either side. For two hours, a vigorous panchavādyam performance assaulted the ears of the high-caste spectators, while the Harijan elephant riders periodically raised and lowered their sacred emblems. Behind the elephant, Kandan's Paraiyan priest-oracle made offerings and danced in a state of possession. Paraiyan and Pulayan "demons" arrived in their costumes, and a team of gaily-dressed Pulayan youths, bearing the traditional stuffed oxen, created a pleasant diversion with their spirited dance. At dusk, fireworks closed the performance and the village went quietly home.

As we returned, a Communist Īzhava factory worker told me that, had they wished to, the Harijans could have stormed the temple and entered it by force. But then of course they would have been arrested and put in prison. The Nāyars, he said, were "bad" not to open the temple because it belongs to the whole neighborhood, and Harijans have a right to enter if they wish and to parade their elephant. "But under this capitalist government the people cannot exercise their rights." A Nāyar schoolboy waited judiciously till he had gone and then remarked that the Harijans did not, in fact, have the right to enter the temple *with an elephant* under the Temple Entry Act. Entry is one thing, he said laughingly, but an elephant (with a shield and no goddess!)is nonsense. "But these Harijans are always doing strange things these days, and no one can predict their mischiefs."

It must be noted that the Harijans' rebellious act was not simply a piece of Communist subversion. The Nāyars themselves are in a similar legal confrontation with the Puḷḷapura Brāhmans. Since the 1930s, Embrāntiri Brāhman priests hired by the Bhagavati Temple Committee have been taking the Bhagavati idol out on an elephant in the December festival and, in the appropriate years, entering the yard of Puḷḷamana temple and marching round it, just as the Harijans wish to march around the Bhagavati shrine.

During the 1950s, however, the landlord of Puḷḷamana (Viśvanāthan's oldest brother and a Congress leader) angered the Nāyar community by impregnating a Nāyar woman and refusing to maintain her or her child. (By modern law he should do so; by traditional law he need not.) The Nāyar family, with community support, filed a suit against the Brāhman. The following year, he locked his temple gate against the Nāyar procession. Shortly afterwards, the Communist government made an inquiry into the ownership and property of temples in villages and ordered that those traditionally in public ownership should be brought under the supervision of the government Dēvaswom Department. The Puḷḷamana temple was of special interest because (unlike the Pālakkara temples) it owns substantial land. The Nāyar Temple Committee and the Dēvaswom Department filed suits against the Brāhman landlord to compel him to reopen the temple and hand over its property to the government. The suits are still pending. The Nāyars' grounds are that for over thirty years they have entered the temple, helped to finance its festival, worshiped there, and entered its yard with their elephant, and that therefore it is a public temple. The Brāhmans' grounds are that the temple was built and endowed by a single household and that Nāyar use of it was a privilege which could at any time be withdrawn.

The Harijan and Nāyar cases are similar in appearance, both stemming from modern pressures toward upward mobility. There are, however, differences. The Nāyars active in the Temple Committee wished to raise their caste rank closer to that of Brāhmans but did not challenge Brāhman ritual supremacy. They did not claim that men are equal, either before God or in society. Their own claim to rank rested, indeed, on their ability to hire Brāhman priests to do their ceremonies, bear aloft their goddess, and ride their elephants. They thought it impious that non-Brāhmans, let alone Harijans, should claim these rights. Moreover, although to gain their private ends they were willing to place the Brāhman temple in the care of a government department, they did not claim that all castes had equal rights in it.

The Harijans took literally the Communist teaching that members of a community should have equal rights in its property and public assets. For them this meant dividing out the property so that each man, or in this case each caste, had a separate but equal share. Just as, in their eyes, the Communist slogan "land to the tiller" meant that all cultivators should own private plots of equal value, so also the idea of temple entry came to mean that each caste should own temporally specific rights in the goddess, to worship her as its members pleased. In reaching this interpretation the Harijans, like the Īzhavas before them, were no doubt influenced by the knowledge that in fact they were not welcome as equal participants in temple worship, and that, no matter how they conducted themselves, they would never persuade Brāhman priests to officiate at their caste festivals. Whereas the Īzhavas thirty years ago went off to build their own temples and install their own priests and idols, the Pālakkara Harijans laid claim to equal rights in the village temple.

ANALYSIS

The analysis of social change in a local community requires investigation of (a) the community's changing relations with its subsistence base, especially through change in its technology or demography, and (b) the community's changing relations with the wider society, especially its economic relations and its relations with the national and local governments or other prominent centers of power.

The changes that take place in these two sets of "external relations" (with the subsistence base and with the wider society) give rise to changes in the community's internal social structure, that is, in the structure and functions of its groups and in the relations between them. Some of these changes are brought about by force through the operation of laws or other pressures from external centers of power; others, by the exigencies of changing technology, demography, or external economic relationships. Still other internal changes take place because, as the conditions of their lives change, individuals and groups actively and sometimes creatively strive to attain new kinds of self-realization through increasing their power, wealth, talents, or knowledge or through struggling toward new kinds of freedom. Such struggles take place partly in terms of values already held by existing groups, but of course new values, as well as new groups, also develop as the character and activities of the community's members undergo change.

In agreement with Marx,[17] I regard changes in the organization of production as the most significant in society as a whole, forming the basis of legal and political changes and the prime mover behind changes in the ideological and ritual spheres. When, however, we confine our perspective to a part-society (and anything less than world society is a part-society today), legal, political, or religious changes may in a given instance precede or occur relatively independently of changes in technology or economic organization, as a result of pressures from some center in the wider society or as a result of competition with other social units of like order. The introduction of universal franchise, of the modern panchāyat system, and of temple entry into Pālakkara by the Cochin government exemplifies such relatively independent legal or religious changes imposed from outside. Whatever their source, all of these kinds of social change involve conflict, creation, and struggle. When, moreover, the underlying technological, economic, or demographic changes are profound, as in the case of Kērala's vast development of export crops, its great population increase, and the proletarianization of large masses of its people in the past century, I would expect new power groups to arise and old elites to be overthrown or submerged.

The value of studies of change in local communities is that they illustrate some of the local details involved in the broad sweeps of change occurring in the total society. Community studies are not very illuminating unless made within the framework of knowledge and theory about what is happening to the larger society—in this case, to Kērala, beyond that to India, and beyond that still to the relations between former colonies and both new and old power-centers in the Western and Communist worlds. Understanding of the wider society in turn requires a grasp of its main structural features in successive periods.

The events that I have described for Pālakkara fall, it seems, into three historical periods each characterized by a distinctive kind of social

[17] Karl Marx, A Contribution to the Critique of the Political Economy, ed. N. I. Stone (Chicago, Kerr, 1904), pp. 10-12.

structure. We may for convenience call these (a) feudal,[18] (b) colonial capitalist, and (c) democratic state-sponsored capitalist. Obviously, periods do not begin and end on well-defined dates. There is ragged overlapping, and there are continuities throughout. Periods can, moreover, be differently dated according to the subject and scope of analysis. Kērala's ports and their hinterlands came under the influence of a form of colonial capitalism with the Portuguese arrival in 1492. The region as a whole passed irreversibly into "the colonial capitalist period" with the British conquest of 1792, although the effects of the new system did not seriously undermine many of the institutions of villages like Pālakkara until the late nineteenth and early twentieth centuries. Similarly, it can be argued that Kērala (and India) is in the grip of a kind of neo-imperialist capitalism, centered in the United States today, although political independence and democratic electoral processes arrived in 1947. In spite of these complications, we may distinguish the three types of system because they do help us to pinpoint fundamental qualitative changes in social structure and thus to bring order out of the details of change that have been outlined for Pālakkara.

The feudal system was characterized by the division of Kērala into petty warring principalities. The village or small village-cluster was almost self-sufficient for food and daily necessities. Ranked castes owned hereditary, differential rights in the produce of village lands and practiced hereditary, interdependent occupations. Under the Brāhman landlords and the Rājas, the dominant caste of Nāyars governed most villages in the economic and religious as well as in the legal spheres. Economic processes were those of reciprocity and redistribution,[19] channeled through the Nāyars and Brāhmans. Market relations were few or absent in inland villages and there was no free market in labor or land. The village festivals reflected and reinforced the interdependent and hierarchical relations between the castes.

[18] I use "feudal" not to refer indiscriminately to all the preindustrial agrarian states of India, but specifically for Kērala because of its similarities with feudal principalities of Western Europe in the late eleventh century. The similarities include government through relations of servitude between lords and vassals, fief-holding by vassals and by members of a religious hierarchy spread over many independent principalities, and frequent warfare between principalities and their component fiefs.

[19] See Walter C. Neale, "Reciprocity and Redistribution in the Indian Village," in Karl Polanyi, ed., Trade and Market in the Early Empires (Glencoe, Ill., The Free Press, 1957), pp. 218-36; Gough, Matrilineal Kinship, pp. 314-23.

The colonial capitalist system, whose impact on Pālakkara became strong after about 1860, brought private ownership and free marketability of land. It brought marketability of labor, both in the village and in new urban occupations, together with new forms of capitalist enterprise. In Kērala, the production of export crops such as tea, rubber, and coconuts formed the main basis of colonial capitalism, but gradually all crops, including food, were drawn into the market system. Among other technological changes, modern transport facilitated the movement of people, and the beginning of power-based industry created new urban classes. The foreign government imposed a new bureaucratic administrative structure, only indirectly based on caste, which reached into the villages through its system of appointive offices. The Nāyar-Brāhman and the Īzhava blocs of castes lost their interdependence and became competing and to some extent autarchic groups, each with its own bourgeoisie. Villages lost whatever self-sufficiency they had had, and local government by the dominant caste decayed. Land wealth, however, remained predominantly in the hands of the higher castes, while the erstwhile Harijan slaves turned into a rural proletariat. Many villages like Pālakkara became dependencies of the new urban bourgeoisie, their former aristocracies being partially pauperized at the same time that they were partially urbanized.

After independence, the new democratic national government modified the economy and social system less radically than the British had done in the nineteenth century. It retained a predominantly agrarian, raw materials-producing economy organized mainly through private enterprise and wage labor. With modifications, it retained the bureaucratic administration established in colonial times. For villagers, the principal change was the introduction of universal franchise and its application to a strengthened local government in the form of the elected panchāyat board. In Kērala, especially under the Communists in 1957-59, the state government also interfered with market relations to the benefit of the rural proletariat by introducing such measures as fixity of tenures, minimum wages, and free house-sites. In Kērala also, the fierce competition between the Congress and Communist parties brought awareness of their potential voting power to even the lowliest citizens, together with the hope of an eventual revolutionary reallocation of land, wealth, and political power. Between 1949 and 1964 it was these changes, stemming from universal franchise, political party competition, and the Communist concept of class struggle, that most affected the social system in Pālakkara and neighboring villages.

In Pālakkara, the responses of the Nāyars, Īzhavas, and Harijans to these wider systemic changes took different forms, appropriate to the ranks and power of these castes. In the colonial period, the Nāyars, having lost their roles as a feudal militia of landholders, gradually merged with the Brāhmans into a modern, internally less differentiated, high-caste, local "ruling class." The changes in the economic and legal spheres found expression, in the 1930s, in the Nāyars' achievement of virtual co-dominance with the Brāhmans in running the Brāhmans' temple festivals.

In taking over partial management of these Brāhman temples, and in gradually assuming sole responsibility for the village Bhagavati temple, the Pālakkara Nāyar community ceased to be a status grade in a feudal hierarchy and became a voluntary association, combining some of the features of a joint-stock company with those of a religious sect. The payment of para became voluntary among Nāyars, and those who paid it formed, as it were, the membership of a modern "church." They elected a committee with president, secretary, and treasurer to replace the old, multifunctional ascriptive assembly of heads of households.

At the same time, the Nāyars, being near the top of modern as of ancient society, retained certain feudal relics and sanctions. They approached closer to the Brāhmans and usurped their authority, but maintained the ritual supremacy of the Brāhman and the hierarchical form of worship.

During the 1950s, with the coming of democracy, the Nāyars's views about their own and the Brāhmans' temples changed toward a kind of welfare-state conception. The Nāyars became willing, at least in theory, to integrate lower-caste people as worshipers and to accept state supervision of and state aid for religious institutions by the Dēvaswom Department, provided that they retained the controlling voice. Faced, in the case of the Puḷḷapura Brāhman temple, with a choice between a reversion to old feudal rules of temple management by an autocratic landlord authority, and modern state supervision of religious properties, they opted for the latter, which offered them more prestige and power.

The Īzhavas, starting out from a lower rank in the feudal system, necessarily followed a different path. For them, whether locally or throughout the state, there was no integrating into the new Nāyar-Brāhman ruling class; the laws of both Travancore and Cochin states under the Maharajas precluded this. The Īzhavas, however, did develop an urban bourgeoisie, and even in villages new forms of wage work and petty private enterprise released most Īzhavas from their feudal dependency. The Īzhava response in religion was to set up, in its purest form, the independent "church" as voluntary association, joint-stock company, and religious sect, in the form of the S.N.D.P. They could do this because they had a literate, statewide bourgeoisie. Many Protestant, or rather Puritan, features appeared in this new religion, for example, an inner-directed morality, an ethic of saving and investment, a stress on personal initiative and on the potential equality of men, on private enterprise and upward mobility, and a rejection of the traditional priesthoods of feudal society. Throughout the 1930s and 1940s the S.N.D.P. flourished as a religious reform movement, helping poor Īzhavas like those of Pālakkara to lift themselves out of the feudal matrix. In that period a combination of intellectual liberalism and economic competitiveness characterized the movement's ideology.

In the 1950s, however Kērala's failure to effect a noticeable economic expansion, coupled with rapid population increase, brought a new impoverishment of many rural Īzhavas, a deepening of class struggle all over the region, and a widening gulf between propertied and propertyless classes within each caste. The state S.N.D.P. leadership, capitalist and associated with the Congress Party, eventually lost its control over most of the Īzhava poor. While keeping hold of the movement's capital and larger properties, it released a large number of rural branches and temples into local Communist hands. The S.N.D.P. ethic of equality and personal commitment could then be harnessed in the service of a revolutionary socialist ideology among wage-working Īzhavas and others of lower caste. With their urban economic ties and literacy, and their already established consciousness of state unity, such Īzhavas now transferred their energies to the political ends of class struggle as outlined by the Communists. For the individual, belief in and commitment to the socialist brotherhood began to replace the more mystical religious formulations. Concomitantly, in the Pālakkara neighborhood, the S.N.D.P. buildings became a combination of Communist clubhouse, registry office, and library.

The Pālakkara Harijans shook off feudal religious forms much later than the Īzhavas. This was probably because they were restricted to landless labor under high-caste masters, because of the universal social discrimination against them, and because of their confinement within a small-scale rural setting, their illiteracy, and their lack of an urban bourgeoisie. Until the end of the colonial period, those who did not become Christians acquiesced in their low status and preserved their traditional attachment to the village temple. With independence, however, first temple entry and then universal franchise encouraged the Harijans to hope for upward mobility. Communist teachings about equality nourished these hopes in the 1950s. Under the Communist government of 1957-59, new laws freed the Harijans from some of their dependence. Meanwhile, in the 1950s and early 1960s, the competition between the political parties accorded them a new bloc-voting power and awakened the idea of independent control of a portion of village resources.

In the 1950s the Harijans responded to the new conditions of democracy by severing themselves from the main village temple and Sanskritizing their own godlings and festivals. They thus tried to produce a kind of localized Harijan replica of the Īzhava S.N.D.P. This was not, however, satisfactory to them for long. The reason was, perhaps, that while Sanskritization is always an attempt to validate upward mobility, the validation can be made to "stick" only if there is an outside public that accepts the caste's new rites as proof of its claim to higher rank.[20] The Īzhavas achieved this kind of public recognition. The temples they built were bigger and more splendid than many Brāhmanical ones. Their literati were in touch with the national and international intelligentsia and with modern all-India Hindu mysticism. Their shrines were places where Īzhavas could marry, not only each other, but persons of other religions and castes. Their guru, Srī Nārāyana, acquired international fame. For the Pālakkara Harijans, by contrast, the Sanskritization of their local godlings, while reflecting their own self-esteem and improved legal status, went unrecognized by their fellow villagers and did not change the low esteem in which they were held by the public at large.

Meanwhile, it is probable that Communist teachings about the sharing of property prompted the Harijans to seek other ways of validating their new sense of equality. Confined as they were within the village, it was natural that they should turn around and demand a share in its central institution, the goddess's temple. Although they did not achieve

---

[20] Homer G. Barnett makes this point with reference to the potlatch of Northwest Coast American Indians. See "The Nature of the Potlatch," *American Anthropologist*, XL (July-September, 1938), 351.

their object, they did make a dramatic confrontation and succeeded in arousing the interest and partisanship of all in their neighborhood.

The Harijan festival, although a small and (from a pan-Indian viewpoint) trivial occurrence, compactly set forth a whole complex of Harijan claims. The four Harijans mounted atop the elephant said to the Nāyar and Brāhman elite, "We are as good as you; why will you not accept us as your equals?" With their hands grasping the sacred plumes and umbrellas, they also said, "We are as close to God as you," while the panchavādyam musicians gave out the message, "We are as clever, talented, and artistic as you." The very presence of an elephant, hired for Rs. 100, showed that the Harijans had acquired some ability to accumulate money. The whole pageant brought home to the villagers the fact that, for one day at least, Harijan organizational ability was equal to that of the highest castes. The presence of the elephant and the sacred symbols was, moreover, a proof to the village that the traditional religious symbols of high rank were no longer accepted and validated as such by the wider society, but had been "democratized." That the modern dēvaswom board should permit the Harijans to hire an elephant at all, not to mention the accompanying plumes and other symbols of Brāhman supremacy, meant that the Harijans were able to prove to the village that their "sacrilege" had at least partial government support. By stretching the modern law to the utmost they were thus able to overthrow some of the village's existing rank-restrictions, while also making new demands which went beyond presently accepted interpretations of the law.

These new demands of the Pālakkara Harijans somewhat resemble current demands for Black power on the part of American Negroes—who, incidentally, form roughly the same percentage of the total population as do India's Harijans, and who have a similar history of slavery and extreme social and economic discrimination. In its unsophisticated way, the Pālakkara Harijan usurpation of the village temple in 1963 was an instance of "Black power" appropriation of local resources, as contrasted with the kinds of "integration" provided for in the Temple Entry Act. Propertyless Harijans do not wish to be "integrated" into village society as the bottom layer of the cake, just as propertyless Negroes are disinterested in being legally integrated into American society unless this brings gains in wealth, opportunities, and power. Both propose a form of separatist power which they see, at present, as involving maximal self-government of their own neighborhood, bloc voting, and the exercising of a due, but separate, control of public institutions. The Pālakkara Harijans' search for power takes place, of course, within a very narrow framework, that of the village to which their work, poverty, and near-illiteracy have so far confined them. Like the local demands for Black power in America, the Harijans' demands do not yet mesh with a program for the national economy and polity, although the Harijans are willing to use both Congress and Communist policies for their own local ends.

The Harijan festival that I witnessed dramatized a state of class confrontation and temporary stalemate in Pālakkara. As I have explained elsewhere,[21] the situation in Kērala in 1964 struck me as one of comparable stalemate throughout the state as a whole. It was a condition resulting from the demands for change made by the Communists in 1957-59, and the owning classes' refusal to grant these demands. In Pālakkara the Harijan festival dramatized a demand for equal rank, power, and ownership on the part of the landless laborer castes. It was rejected by the local upper class of landlords, priests, and more prosperous owner-cultivators. In 1957-59, and again in the 1965 elections,[22] the Communist-led propertyless classes as a whole made similar but more sweeping bids for social, economic, and political equality throughout the state. They were rejected and contained by the landowners and the bourgeoisie of Kērala, supported by conservative caste and religious organizations.[23] The Īzhava factory worker was expressing a hidden wish of the Harijans when he said, "They could easily have stormed the temple." Like them he recognized, of course, that if they had done so they would have been arrested. He generalized further than the Harijans were wont to do when he said, "Under this capitalist government the people cannot exercise their rights." In Pālakkara, as in Kērala, most of the "rights" that the propertyless people demand were actually promised to them in theory by the leaders of the Congress nationalist movement two decades ago. They involve equal political power, economic opportunity, social status, and access to symbolic institutions. When propertyless groups try to claim these rights in ways that are meaningful to them, however, they are blocked by two forces that successive Congress governments have failed to modify: the economic power of a property-owning elite, and the armed

[21] See Gough, "Kērala Politics and the 1965 Elections."
[22] For an analysis of the significance of caste and class in these elections see *ibid*.
[23] Chiefly by the Catholic hierarchy, but also by leaders of the Nāyar Service Society, the S.N.D.P., and the Muslim League.

police power that property owners command through their roles in the political structure. Until they can organize with other propertyless groups to overcome these forces, it seems unlikely that the Harijans will gain the equality and the power they demand, even in the village temple. At the same time, I am doubtful whether the Communists, or any other revolutionary or reform movement that may arise, could unseat the present propertied classes without the full and organized support of Kērala's agricultural laborers, among whom, in many areas, Harijans are the most prominent element.[24]

CONCLUSION

Since 1964, the Pālakkara Harijans have ceased to perform any of their religious festivals. The reasons are unknown to me but are probably partly economic. Increased inflation, food scarcity, and unemployment in Kērala since 1964 have enhanced deprivation among the propertyless and reduced their ability to spend on luxuries and festivals. Under these conditions, there is evidence that class struggle is deepening and becoming unified throughout Kērala, overriding other group loyalties. If these condition persist, I would expect the Harijans' parochial and symbolic demands eventually to become submerged in a generalized struggle by the propertyless for land and political power.

[24] In Travancore and Cochin in 1951 landless agricultural workers and their families formed 20.16 per cent of the total population and 39 per cent of the population dependent on agriculture. The proportion of landless laborers is higher in Malabar (northern Kērala), reaching 48 per cent of the agricultural population in some districts, and it has probably increased throughout the state since 1951. Harijans were recently estimated at 9 per cent of the total population (Democratic Research Service, *Kērala under Communism: A Report* [Bombay, 1959], p. 9).

K . I S H W A R A N

Mallūr:

Internal Dynamics of Change

in a Mysore Village

I

MOST STUDIES OF INDIAN villages tend to account for the social and economic institutions, the group dynamics of the village, and the changes in village life mainly in terms of external factors. The role of internal sources of change does not seem to have been given adequate attention. By internal sources, I mean physical phenomena which may affect the lives of the villagers, phenomena which are, in a sense, part of the village setup and almost inseparable from it.

First, this paper proposes to direct attention to natural and ecological phenomena which still play an important part in peasant life and history.[1] Indeed, the keen struggle between nature and the peasant is a never-ending one. The peasants may have no written records of this battle, but they have proud folk-memories of their heroic encounters with nature. They have a sense of having made history with their own rugged hands.

Second, the paper examines the concept of dominant caste in relation to the problem of maintaining social equilibrium in the village and in bringing about change. This concept is found to be inadequate as an explanation of how in practice the village manages to maintain itself.

Third, the paper also draws attention to the deep-felt dilemma of the peasant, torn between his loyalty to the land and tradition, and his pragmatic urge to utilize the resources of modern technology and ideologies.

The study centers upon Mallūr, an ancient village in the south

[1] The fieldwork for this study was first begun by the author in 1964, and, with interruptions, it was carried on till the summer of 1966.

Indian state of Mysore, and takes as its central point of reference the splitting of the village into two villages—the old one and its offshoot, the new village. First I shall describe the social structure, religion, economy, and the political process as they might be observed prior to the village split in 1950. I shall then give an account of the split and its consequences as observed up to the summer of 1966. On the basis of the empirical analysis of these changes, I shall attempt to arrive at certain conclusions regarding (1) the internal dynamism and change-potential of the village social system and (2) the conceptual framework within which the changes might be explained.

Mallūr is a medium-sized village, with a population of 1,258, according to a census carried out by the author. This figure is based on the entire village, old and new. The demographic and other details that follow refer to the village taken as a unit, since it is not necessary, unless specific focus demands it, to give figures separately for the two villages. Indeed there is a certain ambiguity about the situation—the two villages can be regarded as both separate units and a single unit.

The population was divided into as many as eight caste groups. Of a total of 207 families, 66 per cent could be described as elementary and 34 per cent as extended families. The total land area cultivated by the villagers was 1,795 acres, an average of 8.67 acres per family and 1.43 acres per person. Of the cultivated land, 1,350 acres were cultivated by owners and the rest by tenants. There were 115 landowning families, which means an average of 11.74 acres owned by a family. The remaining 92 families were landless labor families.

The land is fertile, and it varies from black to red soil. Black soil is predominant, accounting for 80 per cent of the land cultivated. The main crops are jowar, wheat, cotton, and pulses, though a little paddy is grown in the adjoining Malenād area (the wet belt). The village receives regular rainfall of about 850 to 900 millimeters. The livestock in the village numbered 640.

The village was spread over an area of twenty acres, of which the actual living area was only about five acres. About three quarters of this area was covered with temples, wells, roads, and public buildings. If one takes into account the fact that the families were large and that the livestock shared living space with the villagers, it is clear that the villagers lived in cramped conditions.

In the southeastern part of the village flows a rivulet, known as the Mādi; it flows from north to south. In the rainy season it bounds the village on three sides. When the monsoons come, the waters of the Mādi inundate the village and virtually cut it off from the rest of the world. But the Mādi is also the life-stream of the village, even though it becomes a source of trouble during the months of July, August, and September. During those months its deep waters wash all the garbage into the village, heighten the pollution of the water in the village well, and flow into the homes of the farmers. The mud huts of the Muslims and the Talwār, the official village servants, are worst hit because they are closest to the rivulet. The untouchables are also regular victims of the seasonal fury of the Mādi because their huts dot the southern fringe of the village, and every rainy season they have to repair their huts.

The *tālūka*, the administrative headquarters of the unit above the village, is situated four miles away and is not connected with the village by any regular road. The only communication line is a rough, circuitous bullock-cart road which takes at least two hours to negotiate at the best of times but becomes impassable during the rainy season. The district headquarters, the unit above the tālūka, is thirty miles away. A whole day is needed to reach it, and even as recently as 1945 such a journey involved the carrying of packed food.

The two nearest market centers for the purpose of commercial transactions and for long-term shopping are twenty miles to the north and eight miles to the south respectively of the village. The annual supplies of jaggery, clothes, and kerosene are purchased at the nearer of the two centers. These provisions are supplemented by material bought from itinerant traders. On special occasions like weddings the villagers make trips to the distant market at Hubli to buy their special requirements.

The first primary school was established in the village as early as 1889. The original school building, located near the rivulet, was washed away by the floods in 1940. After that the school was shifted to a local temple. Originally the school had two teachers, but their number was increased to three in 1950. The staff was further increased, and at the time of this study it was four strong. According to the latest figures available, those for 1966, there were 217 students on the roll. Of these, 91 were girls. The attendance register showed that only about 162 students actually attended the school. Of these, 101 were boys and 61 were girls.

When the author personally counted the students, he found that the figure dropped to 89, made up of 59 boys and 30 girls.[2]

The village has a cooperative society which was started as long ago as 1916. The function of the society is to borrow money from the district cooperative bank, and then lend it to the villagers. Therefore, the society depends on an outside agency and actually comes under its control to a considerable extent. The villagers resented such outside control. In its long history, the society has taken different names. In 1928 it was called the Cooperative Credit Society, and since 1961 it has been called the Village Seva Sahakara Sangh (literally, the Village Service and Cooperative Society). In 1950 its membership comprised 109 heads of households, rising to 142 in 1961, and then dropping to 138 in 1966. From conversation with the villagers one gets the impression that they regard the society with pride and hope.

II

The following account of the caste and occupational structure of the village as it existed prior to the village split is based on information collected directly from interviews with caste leaders and the representative sections of the population, on participant observation, and on official and private records. The ranking of the groups (see Table 1) is based on both subjective and objective criteria. It takes into account both how each group regarded itself in relation to other groups and how other groups regarded it. Broadly speaking, the hierarchical model of the classical varṇa system in its structural principles, though not in details, operated in the village.

The social structure of the village was both hierarchical and pluralistic. There was a clear sense of the higher and the lower, but this was to some extent offset by a degree of autonomy enjoyed by the groups. Each group was left to itself considerably, and when there was intergroup action the hierarchical principle tended to manifest itself. However, the pattern of group interaction was a fairly complex and intricate one in

---

2 Such discrepancies and inaccuracies are quite frequent in many records of the Indian countryside. Officials keep records to please higher officials, and they are likely to lose their jobs if entries are not made. This is a major handicap for both planners and administrators. Anyone studying Indian villages will soon realize the difficulties of interpreting records and of using the questionnaire method, the latter because people are not accustomed to express their experience in objective, measured terms.

which both vertical and horizontal principles, that is, of hierarchy and of autonomy, operated. Prima facie, a situation like this rules out any simple pattern of power concentration or dominance. Instead one sees a tendency toward diffusion of power between groups with regard to matters affecting the village community as a whole.

The caste and occupational structures of the village coincided, though this does not mean that there was a one-to-one relationship. While a single subcaste tended to engage in one particular occupation, there might be more than one subcaste engaging in a common occupation. But this happened (see Table 1) only in the case of agriculture, and within the Lingāyat caste. We may therefore observe that there was a strong caste-occupation congruence.

It may also be noted that the classical varṇa system as such did not obtain, though its principles of hierarchy and endogamy existed. In the classical model there is a hierarchy of four castes in a descending order— Brāhman, Kshatriya, Vaishya, and Shudra. In Mallūr there were no Brāhmans, no Kshatriyas, and no Vaishyas. This is a situation generally true of the villages in the northern areas of Mysore State.

There were eight caste groups hierarchically arranged, from the Lingāyat down to the untouchable. Some remembered or knew of only one intercaste marriage in the village in the last hundred years or so. In Shivapur,[3] another village in this district, I have had occasion to record five intercaste and interreligious marriages. This fact may be attributed to the greater geographical proximity of Shivapur to an urban center.

The occupational structure of the village reinforced the hierarchy based on endogamy. Each person could be placed on the basis of his traditional calling. Table 1 illustrates the hierarchical and occupational structure of the village.

The Lingāyat subcastes were hierarchically related, and they practiced hypergamy. The first two subcastes never took brides from any of the castes below them. Also no group took brides from the last two subcastes since they were associated with menial and impure occupations.

Before the pollution-purity norms which governed the relations of the caste groups and subcaste groups are described, a brief comment needs to be made about the occupational structure. In Mallūr there was no prohibition against anyone engaging in agriculture. The untouchables

---

[3] For details see K. Ishwaran, *Tradition and Economy in Village India* (London, Routledge and Kegan Paul, 1966).

Table 1: Caste and Occupational Structure

Castes	Subcastes	Traditional Occupation
I. Lingāyat		Agriculture
	Hiremath	Priest
	Pujār	Lesser priest
	Panchamsāli	Agriculture
	Sādar	Agriculture
	Kudavakkaliga	Agriculture
	Agasa	Washerman
	Hadapada	Barber
II. Panchāl		Artisan
	Badiga	Carpenter
	Kambhār	Blacksmith
III. Rajput		None
IV. Muslim		
	Sayyad	None
	Sheikh	None
	Pinjār	Mattress-maker
V. Kuruba		Shepherd
VI. Talwār		Village servant
VII. Waddar		Masonry
VIII. Holeya (untouchable)		Sweeping and leatherwork

were not prohibited from agriculture and there were, at the time of this study, thirteen untouchable families cultivating twelve acres of land which had been granted to them by the government. There was one family which cultivated land as a tenant. Besides the occupations mentioned in Table 1, the untouchables were also employed to perform such village duties as carrying the news about village ceremonies and rituals.

From my study, it appears that the occupational structure of Mallūr did not register any sharp changes over the years. Callings other than agriculture, for example, were pursued by the same families for four generations.

Turning to the pollution-purity norms, one finds that they characterized the social life at all levels. Some of these norms divided the people, while others drew them together.

Life-cycle rites, village and family festivals, and the relationship with the gods outside the village involved ritual observance for all groups. When ritual pollution occurred, cleansing could be performed only by a priest. The belief was strongly held that ritual pollution brought bad luck and bad health. Smallpox, for instance, was believed to result from a visitation of the goddess Devi. Skin disease, barrenness, lean harvests, droughts, famines, and floods were all regarded as the consequence of the violation of the pollution-purity norms.

The priest was the custodian of ritual purity for all groups. Only the Lingāyats and the Muslims had regular priests of their own. The other groups obtained their priestly services either from outside their group but within the village or from outside the village itself. The groups below the Muslims were served by the Lingāyat priests, though the Talwārs and the Kurubas went to Lingāyat as well as Muslim priests. The Rajputs and the Panchāls claimed with pride that they had their own priests, but their priests lived too far away to be of any use to them.

The pollution-purity norms involved prohibitions against interdining and interdrinking. Among the Lingāyats interdining and interdrinking were permitted only up to the Kudavakkaliga subcaste. Those below this group might take drink or food from those above, but those above did not reciprocate. Muslims were regarded as unclean because they ate meat and meat was associated with ritual pollution. A washerman informant said that he did not wash for the Muslims because they took meat.

Among the Muslims there was no prohibition on interdining and interdrinking between the groups. It is an indication of the prevailing village norm that the rest of the village did not approve of such a situation. In fact, they referred to the Muslims sarcastically as a sea caste (Samudra Jāti).

With regard to the untouchables, there has been an interesting development which points to the ability of the social system to change itself, even if it be only on a small scale. Under the impact of the Gandhian movement, the untouchables were allowed to draw water from the village well, but characteristically this was a conditional concession. In return for the privileges, the untouchables had to take an oath in a temple, declaring that they would give up meat. An untouchable informant claimed that they had not touched meat since then. It was believed that if they violated the oath taken in a temple they would be inviting the wrath of the gods, which might eventually engulf the entire village in some dreadful calamity.

Though there have been minor modifications in detail, there were no sharp changes in the pollution-purity rules over the years.

The spatial distribution of the groups, both with regard to the residential settlement and with regard to seating arrangements at community gatherings, tended to strengthen the general social pattern of hierarchy and group isolation. It is significant that the various groups were found concentrated in particular localities.

The Lingāyats were split into the village headman lineage and the non-headman lineage. The headman lineage was broken into several households, and they resided on one side of the main street. The non-headman lineage households resided on the other side of the street.

The Talwārs were concentrated in the southeast part of the village, while the Pinjārs and other Muslims inhabited the northwest part. The untouchables lived in isolation in the southern part.

It is no less significant that the temples of Hanumant (the monkey-god) and Basava (the bull-god) are located in the very center of the village, close to the Lingāyat houses.

This hierarchical location pattern was often reflected in the seating arrangement at village community meetings. The Muslims and the other lower castes took seats farthest back. From observation and subsequent investigation, I detected no noticeable resentment on the part of these groups against such a situation. However, there can be suitable degrees of acceptance, and I found that the maximum of acceptance and resignation was found among the untouchables. Therefore, it may reasonably be said that the arrangement of "social space" corresponds to, and underlines, the social structure of the village.

How is one to go about describing the religion of the village? The problem is complicated because the social structure and the religious system are interconnected in a complex way. In a sense the whole village belongs to a common value-system, but in another sense this is not true.

Primarily the complication arises because of the Muslims. If the rest of the community is regarded as Hindu, then logically the Muslims are not part of it. But this is only a partial truth. The Muslims did function as a caste, and they also functioned as an articulated part of the total social structure. To that extent, they were part of the social system, though the system was based on non-Muslim religious sanctions. Also one has to bear in mind that there were areas, such as religious festivals, where the Muslims and the Hindus did meet at some level of interaction. A further complicating factor is that each caste had its own specific set of gods, dogmas, and rites. However, there were also broad religio-ethical norms like *dharma* (duty) *and karma* (fate) that bound the whole village, perhaps loosely, but nonetheless perceptibly.

Each group had its own gods, festivals, and rituals. There were also common gods and common festivals. There were festivals which might belong to one group, but which also drew in other groups.

Basava, Hanumant, and the Prophet (the Muslim religious founder) are community gods. The importance of Basava arose from the fact that the bullock is an important element in the village agricultural economy, and the bull-god, who symbolizes this fact, commands universal reverence.

The mosque, though it is a specifically Muslim institution, had become a center of attention for the Hindus as well. Indeed, the Hindus had come to look upon it as a kind of temple. During Moharrum, an important Muslim festival, the Hindus offered worship and fulfillment of vows made earlier, while the Muslims joined the Hindus at devotional singing parties in the Hindu temple. There was greater social interaction between the Muslims and the castes below them. This could be attributed to the close physical proximity and the common social and economic background of the Muslims and these casts. As one descends below the Muslim level, the allegiance to the Prophet and the Moharrum festival increases progressively. For instance, the lower orders performed the religious tiger-dance during the Moharrum festival. This dance is performed as part of a religious vow by persons naked except for a loincloth, with red, yellow and green stripes painted over the body, a tiger marking, and a tail. However, the untouchables normally did not perform the dance.

Socially, the Lingāyats were at a considerable distance from all these groups. This distance was emphasized by the fact that the Lingāyats are vegetarians, whereas the other groups are nonvegetarian like the Muslims. However, the Lingāyats also associate themselves with the Moharrum festival by contributing toward the expenses of the ritual carriage of the god. One Lingāyat bore as much as a quarter of the expenses involved. The Muslims, however, took part in the *bhajan* (devotional singing) groups of the Lingāyats.

The untouchables had their own deities, who were exclusively meant for them, but when exceptional crises such as epidemics or droughts occurred, the members of higher-caste groups offered worship to the goddess Karevva, a deity of the untouchables.

Each caste group had its own festivals, just as it had its own pantheon. But then festivals also attracted participation from others. The Lingāyats celebrated the Kārahunnime (bullock procession) festival on the day of the full moon. Their season festivals for the year opened with the worship of the snake-god. We have seen that the Muslims had their Moharrum. The Rajputs celebrated the Shivajayanti (birthday of Shivaji). Then there were festivals common to all the Hindus—the Deepāvali (the festival of lights), the Mahānavami (the festival of nine nights), the birthday of Basava, the festival of the goddess Devi, the festival of the lap-filling of the goddess Devi (the ritual filling of her lap with gifts), and the Holi festival. But non-Hindus also took part in these festivals. The Holi festival is the merriest of all Hindu festivals; it is meant ostensibly to mourn the death of Kāma (the God of Love), who is burnt to ashes by Shiva (the God of Cosmic Destruction). During this festival everybody had a good time, beating drums or chanting bawdy songs or sprinkling colored water on others. Usually there are wrestling programs during these festivals.

The foregoing account shows that there is considerable intergroup action at the level of religious festivals. This may be regarded as one of the factors loosening the rigid-seeming, hierarchical social structure. But going a little further, we may ask whether additional ties exist between the religious groups. This is a problem that needs greater investigation, but on the basis of my own observation I would hazard the view that there may not be any such interaction. There may be parallels between the two religious practices, but these occur only at a surface level. For instance, the Lingāyats have the custom of washing hands during the betrothal ceremony, and the Muslims have the custom of washing feet. Among the Lingāyats the betrothal ceremony is held at the bridegroom's place, whereas among the Muslims it is held at the bride's place, as it is among the Brāhmans in this part of the country. But these are stray parallels, which may not amount to much. As for the untouchables, they live outside the main Hindu system but share features of it. On the Holi day, they have their own Kāma, who is known as the Holeyara Kāma (the Kāma of the untouchables). Part of the fuel collected jointly for burning the village Kāma is used for the burning of the Holeyara Kāma. There is a legend that a Hindu had illicit relations with an untouchable woman, and this is said to be the reason why the Hindus carry the fire to their Kāma from the Holeyara Kāma, who is burnt first. This practice also implies that the two Kāmas function separately.

On the question of theology we encounter an interesting situation. In their theological literature the Lingāyats have rejected the belief in rebirth (*punarjanma*). The philosophy of Lingāyat religion emphasizes the here and now more than the life beyond, unlike the traditional Hindu philosophy. The Muslims certainly do not subscribe to Hindu theological or metaphysical doctrines. Yet in Mallūr, all groups believed in rebirth in practice, or, at any rate, their verbal behavior points to such an interpretation.

The economy of Mallūr is similar to that of other villages in this area.[4] It is essentially an agricultural economy. Land is its central focus, and the traditional occupations are all related to land. In economic terms, landownership is a key to power and status. But the economic system and the social system broadly coincide. The hierarchy of the social structure both contributes to, and derives its strength from, the economic system. However, this coincidence should not be overstressed because the economic relations of Mallūr cannot be understood purely in terms of the motive of economic interest. The social structure regulated the economic relations to a considerable extent, though economic and occupational mobility did take place on a limited scale.

The economy can be described as one which involves the āya system. Economic relations are governed by the principle of gift-exchange. Āya means a gift that is unmeasured and not conditional. The system involves

4 *Ibid.*

a series of transactions between the *āyada kula* (the giver) and the *āyagāra* (the recipient of *āya*). There are different levels of *āya*, broadly paralleling the hierarchy of the caste system in the village. Though the quantum of *āya* is customarily determined, this fact is never explicitly referred to. The principle is that a gift is not measurable in economic terms but is associated with the notion of dharma. Though "normal" economic processes like production, buying, and selling may be noticed, they invariably involve noneconomic norms of religion and morality. The basic ideal is that one must share things with others.

Besides the *āya* system, there is also a market economy and a limited monetary economy. There were commercial transactions which did not fall within the *āya* system. In these cases a monetary economic system was clearly at work. Though the village produces primarily for consumption within the village, it does manage, on a limited scale, to produce for export and for monetary, commercial purposes. The situation may be best expressed as a dual economy, in which a predominantly agricultural, gift-oriented, and closed economy, coexists with a monetary, cash-oriented, and open economy.

Can one speak of the political system of the village? The view taken here is that the concept of a "political system" may be misleading in the context of Indian village society for two reasons. First, the various activities which make up the totality of what may be described as "political activities" do not structure neatly into a single political system. Second, it may also be the case that a structural pattern with a minimum of system vitality may be in the process of emerging, in which case to talk of "a political system" would be to prejudge an issue that is yet fluid. Therefore, it is more helpful and certainly less misleading to refer to the political activities of the village. Under this rubric may be subsumed all group and intergroup processes of decision-making for various levels of group action which fall outside the traditional area of ritualistic or religious activities. It would be possible to refer to the political activities within a caste group or to political activities between different caste groups, which may eventually lead to village politics as a whole. The activities of the *panchāyat* or the involvement of the village in increasingly wider areas of political activity, eventually leading to the national political process, could be subsumed under this category. The "administrative" system of the village, which also links the village to the wider state and national administrative systems, should be included here, because the neat distinction between the administrative and the political, useful for certain purposes, may not be relevant. The village administrative system is political in the sense that it may not be subordinate to any other authority in the village or in the sense that its decisions are influenced by the group activities within the village.

Only two panchāyat elections were held in the period under study (in 1956 and 1961); thus the electoral process was not yet fully institutionalized in the village, and political activities centered rather upon (1) the administrative system, (2) the informal caste panchāyat, and (3) informal decision-making by joint intergroup action.

The administrative system comprised the offices of the *mulki pātil* (the revenue officer) and the police *pātil* (the police officer). The mulki pātil was the village headman. Both offices were hereditary during the period which is being discussed here; they were inherited by certain families which were originally invested with the titles by the government. Both offices were important in terms of village life, and it is not surprising that the villagers should surround them with a certain amount of small-scale, local political activity. Generally this took the form of influencing the officers for specific personal benefits. Of course, the two officials had rules and regulations to go by, but there was also considerable room for maneuverability within such formal rules.

The informal caste panchāyat was an important focus of political activities involving the particular caste group. Each caste had an informal caste council composed of caste elders and leaders. In terms of the average villager these constituted important decision-making bodies, affecting him either as an individual or as a member of the group. Their activities were not differentiated, and they combined administrative, rule-making, and quasi-judicial functions.

Lastly, when decisions affecting the village as a whole or more than one caste group had to be made, the different groups got together informally in an intercaste council. In these councils satisfactory compromises were worked out by bargaining as well as by appeals to religio-ethical norms. When common problems like epidemics or floods arose, or when common action was needed for religious festivals, the informal intercaste council provided a setting for focused deliberation. A broad consensus could emerge out of these deliberations.

III

As already noted, the monsoon floods affect the village during the months of July, August, and September. But the actual onset of the monsoons may start earlier. We have also noted that the impact of the flood was marginal for the Lingāyats, while it was very grave for the other caste groups. However, the flood affects all equally in the sense that it prevents the preservation of fodder and the storing of grains.

Mallūr experienced one of its worst floods in June, 1948. The whole village was very nearly washed away, and even the homes of the higher castes were threatened with damage. The furious waters rushed into every house, with the result that there was no place to cook, eat, or sleep. Cooking was done on temporary raised platforms of stone. The unsanitary conditions resulting from the flood led to epidemics.

Indeed, the situation became so grave that in July, 1948, Mallūr was forced to consider seriously the need to migrate to a more secure place. Action followed soon after. A meeting of the people was called, and votes were taken in favor of moving to a safer site toward the northeast of the village. The local language (Kannaḍa) press was used to attract governmental attention to the desperate situation. Letters were addressed to the administrative head of the district, appealing for help. The public and the press in the area became so alive to the situation that a local daily (dated November 18, 1948) published the following report under the caption "Flood Disaster": "Fifteen houses at Mallūr have been totally destroyed. Fertilizers stored in the backyards have been washed away, and crops have been heavily damaged. The total loss has been estimated at about Rs. 20,000."

A petition, the result of a formal meeting of the village, was presented by the villagers to the district administrative head (the Deputy Commissioner), requesting a grant of 64 acres of land, on which they could start life afresh. The petition explained that the village had been isolated by the flood and that heavy losses were sustained by the people, and it complained that the government was delaying in coming to the village's assistance. It ended by requesting quick action from the government. It also contained a graphic account of the hardships actually suffered, and this might have moved the authorities to act in the end.

The organizing genius behind the developments noted above was a single individual. He was a person belonging to the Lingāyat non-headman (peasant) group. Sometime prior to the flood, the senior lineage headman had died, and his death led to a diffusion of authority in the Lingāyat headman lineage group. The organizer took advantage of this situation to some extent. In his efforts to get the village to agree to shift its location and in his efforts to organize the process, he was helped by the Muslims and the Talwārs. The Lingāyats belonging to the headman lineage extended no support to him. He was a forty-year-old local Congressman with an education as far as the primary grade level, and his participation in the nationalist movement gave him prestige in the eyes of the village and must certainly have given him training in organization. He represented the new nontraditional leadership. His household was forty-five strong and occupied three dwellings. He had been the chairman of the Village Cooperative Society from 1948 to 1960. He gave the village the leadership it needed, and he received from the village a good measure of response.

At last things began to move, and on May 25, 1949, government officers arrived on the scene. They chose a site different from the one the villagers had asked for. However, this proved to be a better site for the new settlement, and the villagers got their 64 acres. Though the government did not give the land as a gift, the price stipulated was below normal. The government told the villagers that they should deposit a sum of Rs. 21,000 as payment for the land. It is a measure both of the competence of the leadership and of the potentiality for village collective action that, within a week, as much as Rs. 15,000 was collected. Of this, Rs. 6,000 was raised by the personal efforts of the organizer, who had successfully appealed for help to his relations and friends in the surrounding areas.

He took charge of the moving operations. A committee of five was set up to supervise and organize the shift. On this committee there was one Muslim and four Lingāyats, with the Congressman as its secretary.

Out of the total of 207 families in Mallūr, all except 30 were against leaving the village. The untouchables were the group in which there was the highest willingness to move. In fact, 90 per cent of the untouchables bought sites in the new area; the rest did not only because they could not afford to do so, although they applied to the government for loans so that they could buy sites.

The actual shift took place early in 1950. As the families from the old village moved to the new, a pattern of settlement emerged that reflected the strength of tradition as well as a new dynamism.

In the old village nobody had a site exceeding 500 square feet, whereas in the new village one of the households belonging to the numerically important peasant Lingāyat group bought a site as large as two acres. The organizer himself bought a site of one acre. The minimum area each household had was ⅜ of an acre (13,900 square feet). As provided for in the plan of the new village, the houses were to be more isolated and independent. At the time of this study there were 87 families settled in the new village, which left 120 households in the old village. The process of moving was not a smooth one, and those who did move felt intense anguish at the thought of wrenching themselves away from ancestral roots. The figures for divided and undivided families in the two villages are shown in Table 2.

Table 2: Distribution of Family Types

Village	Divided	Undivided	Total
Old	88 (73%)	32 (27%)	120
New	49 (56%)	38 (44%)	87

The pattern of settlement in the new village was not haphazard. It was planned and supervised by a committee in which no caste was dominant. The Lingāyats took care not to impose their view on the rest for the obvious pragmatic reason that the new village could not be built without the active cooperation of every group. The decision to locate the untouchables in the southern part of the village was taken at a meeting of all the groups. The settlement committee decided unanimously that the allotment of the sites should proceed from the west to the east. It was also agreed that those who had lived in the western part in the old village should be allotted sites first, that is, in the west. Ritually, the right way of allotting the sites was from the north to the south. As a matter of fact, such a procedure was suggested by a retired primary-school teacher. However, he was overruled by the others on the committee. The dominant reason to allot from the west to the east seems to have been the desire to reproduce the same pattern of settlement as in the old village.

Three households belonging to the Lingāyat peasant lineage were the first to move to the new village. In accordance with the rules of settlement, they were allotted sites in the western part of the village. Along with them went other peasants. The decision of the peasants to move may be explained partly in terms of the push from one among them for change, and partly in terms of the desire for better accommodation. The Muslims moved because their houses had been damaged most by the flood.

The well-to-do headman lineage did not move because, for them, the old village was a symbol of security and prosperity. With them remained people dependent upon them—the priest, the craftsmen, and the village servants. The majority of the members of the headman lineage stayed behind for the obvious reason that they were sentimentally attached to their ancestral land and, more important, because they were a prestigious group in the old village. Moreover, the lands they cultivated were closer to the old village and moving to the new village would mean a shift farther away from these lands. Those dependent on them, the priest and the artisans, stayed behind in the old village for reasons of emotional and economic security.

The untouchables present a rather special case. Originally, as was noted, practically all of them seemed willing to shift to the new village. However, as things turned out, only one of the sixteen untouchable families actually moved. The head of this family was a village servant. It so happened that, within a week of his moving to the new village, his wife died. He saw this as a bad omen and made a hasty retreat to the old village. In an interview he explained that he had moved against his wife's will, adding, "I have paid the penalty for not listening to her!"

If we examine the spatial configuration of the new village, we find a similarity in basic features between the old and the new, but with modifications in detail. As in the old village, here also the houses were arranged from west to east, with the difference that the houses were not closely strung together as before. The new village spread three furlongs from west to east and had wider streets.

One can observe in the whole process of migration a compromise between the villager's attachment to his land and his pragmatic use of a chance to promote his self-interest. The attachment to the land was well symbolized in the fact that those who moved to the new site carried with them mud from the old village. We can also note here the pragmatism of those who stayed behind. They seized the opportunity to better themselves by buying up some of the property of their immediate neighbors who had moved.

Compared with the new village, the old one is more compact, nucleated, and congested, while the houses are closer together. In contrast, the houses in the new village are more isolated from each other, and they have hedges. A well-to-do peasant family even built an extensive compound for its house. The spatial configuration of the old village brought about a more vivid intimacy based on a closer network of relationships between the residents. But one should not exaggerate the role of physical factors, because those who moved to the new village carried over with them the relationships that had been forged in the old village. These were continued in some respects. In the new village, as in the old, the village elders and the priests were important and were held in respect.

However, there are significant differences. The inhabitants of the new village have developed to a considerable extent the urban attitudes of independence and aloofness. Sufficient evidence was found both of the existence of such attitudes and of dissatisfaction with them. One of the informants in the new village said that the people there did not care for each other as they used to in the old village. Many of our informants related incidents which people in the new village interpreted as showing an undesirable lack of neighborly and community feelings, feelings which were believed to exist in the old village. A few of these incidents may be mentioned. In one case, an elderly lady in the new village had died at a time when both her husband and her son were away from home, and the ritual ceremony necessary for the occasion did not start for hours after the death because no neighbors turned up to help in the matter. But the news of her death spread to the old village, and it was from there that extended kinsmen came to help the bereaved family. This gave rise to a feeling, in both villages, that the residents of the new village were self-centered.

In another case a house was robbed in the new village. Saris and jewelry had been stolen but were abandoned near the rivulet. The victims were an old woman and her children. When the burglar entered the house she had cried for help in vain. As against this there was the case of a Talwār who was caught while stealing chilies in the old village.

The people spotted this and reported the matter to the village headman, who handed the culprit over to the authorities. The culprit's relatives in the new village appealed for mercy. Leaders of the two villages deliberated and the Talwār was let off with a fine of Rs. 15 to be utilized for the temple in the old village. A more dramatic example contrasting the attitudes of people in both villages was reported. A cattle shed in the new village had caught fire, and one could see from a distance children fleeing from the scene. The flames were also visible from the old village. The people from the old village rushed to the spot, but none from the new village had bothered to come out. Before the people from the old village could reach the spot, the cattle had been burned to death. These incidents were understood as showing the self-centeredness of the new village against the higher sense of community involvement in the old village.

In the old village it was regarded as an unfriendly act if one was not invited to a marriage or to any ritual ceremony, for these are considered as community affairs. In the new village there was no genuine spontaneity about such invitations, which were taken to be formal, social gestures. One informant from the new village felt that they had no good human relations there, they could not easily borrow and lend money, they could not settle disputes through compromise any more. He concluded with a sigh: "We are fed up! We are isolated from each other!"

People in the old village had their own image of the new village. In referring to the housing pattern, they called the new villagers "city-folk, living on the hill, enjoying better air, eager to live all by themselves, and averse to common walls!"

It might be interesting as an indication of the attitudes of the old village people to look at some of their statements about the new village and its people. The following remarks are typical:

"Better be huddled and congested, and feel cozy, than live in spaciousness up there!"

"After all, what is life? A continuous process of give and take. To live is to share. I would not go up there to live just for myself."

While such remarks and incidents emphasize the difference between the two villages, one must not overlook certain common points. In both villages, men and cattle live in close proximity. This cultural continuity is all the more surprising in the case of the new village where there is no pressure on space. Here is an illustrative response from residents of the new village:

"We need to watch our cattle closely and constantly. Unless we live close to them, we cannot feed them properly."

In contrast, note the response from residents in the old village:

"Here in the old village we have only one house with a separate cattlepen. Once it happened that one of the cows in this cattlepen suddenly fell ill and died. The owner could not discover in time that the cow was sick because he lived so far away from it!"

When an informant was questiond whether he did not regard it as unhygienic to live close to the cattle, he said, "That is what the town people say. For us, contact with cattle betokens health!"

Here we see the persistence of a behavioral pattern. The new village has not broken with the traditions of the old village in all respects. There is a clear continuity of some aspects of the old village tradition in the new village.

IV

The splitting of the village has created certain problems in the key areas of politics, economy, and religion, and the attempts to cope with these problems have resulted in some changes in these areas. However, not all of these changes can be attributed to the split, and even in those cases where it is one of the causes, it can be seen to have exerted different degrees of influence in different cases. With regard to the political activities of the village, it is necessary to examine the panchāyat politics of elections as well as the process of community decision-making on issues which face the people as a whole. However, both panchāyat politics and the community decision-making process reflect a multicentered, variously caused pattern. In such a process, no single group can really dominate, though it may have a slight edge of advantage over the others. This has already been noted in connection with the operation of moving the village.

The two villages, new and old, do not have panchāyats of their own but are part of a group panchāyat which includes Mallūr (old and new) and two other neighboring villages. The first panchāyat elections were held in 1956, and Mallūr was represented by nine members. This was followed by another election in 1960, when Mallūr (old and new) was represented by eight members. The election results for 1956 and 1960 are shown below:

	1956	1960
Muslims	2	2
Lingāyats	5 + 1*	4
Untouchables	1	2

* One woman candidate was elected for a seat reserved for women. That she was a Lingāyat is incidental.

The composition of the two panchāyats reflects the proportionate numerical strength of the groups. All the groups lower than the Muslims in the social hierarchy could not contest because they lacked the necessary leadership and could not find people whose candidature they could support. The untouchables got elected because they had reserved seats on the panchāyat.

From the above figures, it is plausible to maintain that the Lingāyats dominate the political life and that they are a dominant caste. However, this would be a superficial inference because it leaves out the crucial pre-election deliberations as well as other factors which influence elections indirectly. In the first place, it should be noted that the Lingāyats did not function as a single unified block. On some issues personal conflicts came in the way of such consolidated action. But the issues that divided the Lingāyats could also be less personal in the sense of involving questions of what was in the best interest of the group or the village. In the 1960 election, 14 candidates contested, of whom six were defeated. Of the defeated candidates, five were Lingāyats and one was a Talwār. The defeated Lingāyats were opposed to the elected ones and this split them. There were further complications owing to shifting loyalties. Two of the four elected Lingāyats made an alliance with six defeated Lingāyats. One of the defeated Lingāyats was the Congressman who had taken the initiative earlier in the shifting of the village, and who was alive to the changes introduced by the new political and administrative decisions emanating from outside the village. Yet he suffered defeat, which rankled him. Being a resourceful person he set about to teach the people a lesson for defeating him. Using his skill in organization and negotiation, he succeeded in getting his own younger brother elected and saw to it that his brother became the chairman of the panchāyat. He supported his brother on condition that he agree to the location of the panchāyat office in a neighboring village. This was the way he showed the people of Mallūr that they had to pay for defeating him—the payment being the cost of the privilege of having the pānchayat office located in their village. The situation was even more intricate. Earlier the Congressman had negotiated with the elected members of another village and had brought about an agreement by which the chairmanship of the panchāyat should go to Mallūr but the neighboring village should have the panchāyat office. Also part of this bargain was the stipulation that the vice-chairman of the panchāyat should be from the neighboring village. While this served the purpose of the Congressman, it made both the panchāyat and its chairman, a man from their own village, highly unpopular with the people of Mallūr. The panchāyat and its chairman became indifferent to the people and, in following the elder brother's instructions, evaded meeting the visiting Community Development officials. At the time of this study the chairman had even turned against his elder brother.

The foregoing account shows two significant aspects of village politics. First, the political activities involved in elections cannot be explained in terms of the concept of dominant caste. Not only can no single caste dominate the political process, but mere caste identification is not sufficient for political support. There is no single group which can dominate because no single group can command a decisive majority. There are simply minorities of varying strength, and none can act without the support of other groups. Second, the new election politics of the village calls forth a new kind of leader who must effectively represent the old and the new order. At present, the chairman of the panchāyat is new because he comes from a group which is not the one that supplied leaders under the traditional order. He must therefore rely upon a different kind of organizational skill. At the same time we have to realize that the old village leaders also possess skills of negotiation and bargaining needed for coping with intergroup, village problems.

But panchāyat politics do not stop with elections, and it is necessary to go beyond them to see how the panchāyat functions. Though that would be a major undertaking by itself, some illustrative data may be given. From January to July, 1966, nine meetings of the panchāyat were called but they could not take place for want of a quorum. The records of the panchāyat proceedings show that a full quorum was an unusual event. The members attended only to promote specific interests such as a contract or construction of a road. The chairman, it was found, attended the meetings very irregularly. The result was that the vice-chairman, who belonged to a neighboring village, became powerful in the panchāyat, and used his position to the disadvantage of Mallūr. In fact, in the absence of the chairman he took action to impose a house tax, which affected adversely the people of old and new Mallūr who held property in both villages. The result was great apathy on the part of the members toward the panchāyat because they suspected that this act of legislation was not passed in good faith. They felt that it was a deliberate attempt to compel people of old Mallūr to sell their property and move to the new village. The inhabitants of new Mallūr in particular felt that it was all due to the sinister role of the chairman's brother. These distrustful attitudes make it difficult for the panchāyat to emerge as a common focus.

The second aspect of village politics relates to the way in which the villagers discussed problems affecting the village community and the way in which they arrived at compromises in solving these problems. The problems they endeavored to solve were raised by the division of the village. Here the bargaining process involved the adjustment of interests between the old and the new village. But one can also glimpse, even if dimly, the emergence of a common interest. In the wake of the split, the new village needed amenities such as a well, a school, a temple, a co-operative building, and a panchāyat building.

The final decisions regarding some of these matters were not made till 1965, after a lengthy discussion. To get a clear picture of the situation, it is necessary to keep in mind that the new village was the center from which the demands discussed here radiated, that it did not formulate them and articulate them until it became established in the new site, and that these demands involved the transfer of institutional assets from the old village as well as the establishment of new ones in the new village. The demand to raise a building to house the panchāyat may well be interpreted as a sign that the new village was outward-looking, and that it was anxious to develop links with the world beyond the village.

On New Year's Day in 1965, most of the heads of the two villages met informally at the temple in the old village to discuss these issues, and finally drew up a plan for a Community Hall, the Cooperative Society building, and residential houses for the village level workers. This was followed by the formation of a committee charged with the implementation of the decisions. It was also decided to ask for contributions for the purpose from the panchāyat and the government. By 1966, in fact, all these buildings were completed, and on August 15, 1966, they were officially inaugurated.

However, the new village still had its problems, while the old village had also its own needs. The new village had its own *bhajan* groups (devotional singing groups) and its own youth organization for conducting sports and games, but it lacked a temple and a school. The old village had a temple but no Community Hall. To discuss these issues, the heads of both villages met on New Year's Day in 1966. At this meeting, the representatives from the new village presented their demand for a temple and a school, while those from the old village presented their demand for a school and for a bridge over the Mādi.

Lengthy discussions took place over these matters at the meeting, which the author attended. On the question of a temple for the new village, the representatives from the old village argued that the new village should raise its own funds for the temple. The representatives from the new village countered this by saying:

"You have two temples, which you use, and a third which is not in use. At least give us the image of the God from the third temple. The problem for us is not merely one of building a temple, but it is also one of getting the deity for it."

At the end of the discussion, the heads of the old village agreed to part with the image in the third temple, and even agreed to contribute toward the building of the temple in the new village.

As regards the school, each village wanted a separate school building for itself. Neither of them had a school building, and they were naturally anxious to have one. However, a sense of realism soon prevailed, and the idea of two school buildings was abandoned. But the question of the site for the school remained. Two offers of a site were made, both from the old village. One of these sites was toward the west and away from the new village, which was to the east of the old village. The other site was midway between the two villages, and it was accepted as the most convenient location for the school. A decision was made to request grants from the government and to supplement them by contributions from the village. Connected with the school issue was the demand for a bridge over the Mādi. The bridge was necessary to enable those from the old village to attend the school. The meeting therefore voted for it. The villagers got busy with the collection of funds, and within a week they were able to collect their contribution to the estimated cost of the bridge. On August 29, 1966, the foundation stone for the bridge was actually laid at a ceremony, which the author personally witnessed.

The above account of the manner in which the villagers discussed common issues, arrived at mutually satisfactory solutions, and mobilized for action brings out two important features. First, it brings out the fact that the villagers can and do have a rational and realistic approach to problems concerning their lives. Second, it brings out the fact that they are action-oriented, and that they can mobilize for group action on the basis of commonly agreed-upon decisions.

In the economic domain, the new village presents a contrast to the old. Economic changes have, in their turn, brought about other changes such as those in the field of communication.

The new village has registered a remarkable rise in its cash crops and has become more cash-oriented. At the time of this study there were eight horticultural gardens which grew cash crops. Of these, six belonged to the new village and two to the old. Of the latter, one, the oldest in Mallūr, belonged to the family of the village headman. But it was not cultivated for commercial purposes; it served primarily as a symbol of prestige and only secondarily for self-consumption. The other garden was started after a certain economic momentum had gathered in the new village. But the gardens in the new village have become an important source of change in the economic life of the community, necessitating the importation of twenty gardeners. Cash crops like sugar cane, bananas, lemons, areca, and grapes were grown and marketed at the cities of Hubli and Dharwar. The gardens have thus initiated a money economy in the new village and have forged economic links between it and the world beyond.

The new village has grown economically more dynamic than the old village. The pace of living in the new village has increased, whereas in the old village it is slower and, by and large, traditional. At the same time, the old village is not entirely immune to changes. We have already noted that a horticultural garden was cultivated by the old village in a more commercial manner than previously only after the establishment of the new village and as a result of its impact.

In the transport system of the village there has been an increased use of the bicycle, especially in the new village. However, the bicycle did not lessen the over-all importance of the traditional bullock cart, which, for agricultural purposes, was dominant. In the new village even trucks are used to carry bananas and other crops to the marketing centers. The bicycle and the truck facilitate a widening use of the market by the village, both for buying and for selling. Formerly only two marketing centers were available but now an additional one is located closer to the new village. The villagers used to sell grains and vegetables in these markets and buy foodstuffs not grown in the village. But the new market to the northwest of the village was used less and less after it came under municipal taxation.

The market-consciousness of the village has also increased through the presence and use of three daily newspapers. The peasants, though mainly illiterate, now get the news from their children who can read and thus they become more alive to the fluctuating prices of food grains. This has sharpened the monetary attitudes of the peasants.

The traditional economic system of the āya, which involves the exchange of goods and services, has persisted in spite of the changes in both the old and the new village. Both were found to practice the giving of susāya (the overflowing gift), aḷegāḷu (measured grain), and āya (the unmeasured gift), which are all different kinds of gifts under the traditional āya economy.[5] The system of āya brings together under one economic order the peasant, the priest, the artisan, the landowners, and the landless. But in the new village the traditional order of āya does not function in the customary form for the simple reason that the population does not contain artisans, priests, and untouchables. While the old village gets its agricultural implements from the village artisans under the āya relationships, the new village buys some of them in a nearby market.

The traditional economy also involved the *jeeta* system, a form of contractual labor received from castemen. The jeeta laborer drew water and helped in domestic as well as farm work. The jeeta survives in both villages, though to a far lesser degree in the new village. The new village has resorted to the practice of hiring laborers on a daily basis to a larger extent than the old village.

[5] For fuller details of the system, see *ibid*.

The introduction of electricity made new facilities available to the peasants. The traditional system of lift irrigation was laborious, involving two bullocks and about four laborers on a small plot of five to ten acres. It was also more expensive compared to the electrical pump, which could lift well-water faster. Whereas the new village used electricity, the old village continued in the old way of using bullocks and bullock carts.

In the period following the split, the following changes in the economy can be noticed. First, there has been a difference between the old and the new villages with regard to the quantum of change accepted. The new village is far more dynamic and change-oriented. Second, while the new village is more monetized and commercialized, it has not totally abandoned the traditional āya system. Third, the old village has not been totally impervious to change. It has simply been more conservative in this field.

We may now proceed to compare the religious activities of the two villages. The main religious establishments of Mallūr remained in the old village. The temples, the mosque, and the sacred sami tree were all there. In consequence, the new village had to depend upon the old for these establishments. The importance of them is not merely religious, for they also involve social and economic relations within the traditional order.

On the day of Deepāvali (the festival of lights), millets are collected in the temple from the peasants for ritual treatment. Every peasant receives from the temple a small quantity of the ritual millet because it is believed that the sacred qualities of this millet will protect the grains from pests and ensure better harvests in the coming year. The peasants in the new village are drawn to the old village for this ceremony.

During the Mahānavami (the festival of nine nights), both the old and the new villagers come together to sing religious songs and to visit the sacred sami tree on the last day of the festival. It is expected on this day that all old enmities will be forgotten and good relations be established. This expectation is symbolized by the exchange of sami leaves between individuals.

The chariot which was used during the Basava Jayanti (the birthday of Basava, the founder of the Lingāyat religious movement) was also in the old village. Once again the new village comes to the old village to celebrate this important festival.

During the Hōli festival, both a sense of distinction and a sense of identity between the two villages was to be noticed. Each village had its own image of Kāma, though the new village set up a larger one. The custom, however, was that the first offerings should be made to the image in the old village. The interdependence between the two villages was further noticeable in the fact that youths from the new village went up to the old to steal cowdung and wood, while youths from the old village went up to the new in friendly retaliation for the same purpose. The material so collected was used in burning the images, which marked the end of the festival.

Religion seems to be the area in which there is least change, and also the area in which the old village dominates. Further, it is the old generation in the old village which is the chief agent in preserving the traditional religious practices. The old people in the new village, on the other hand, are lesser agents of conservation.

The role of the old people in the new village differs considerably from that of those in the old village. Though no dramatic changes could be observed, there was sufficient change in this area so that, taken together with other changes in the new village, it constituted a viable base for dynamism. In any case, it made the new village more receptive to new ideas and technological changes.

The old people are respected in the new village as much as in the old village, and they can influence the young people as much as in the old village. But, unlike the situation in the old village, the old people in the new village regard the younger people as sources of authority, and they willingly transfer part of their authority to them with regard to management of the family.

The chairman of the Village Cooperative Society, who lives in the new village, explained that he owed his position to the encouragement and help he received from his father. His father had not only voluntarily given up active management of the family in favor of his son, but he had also worked for the son's position in the community life.

In contrast to this, the old people in the old village show little willingness to transfer power to the young people. A retired primary-school teacher, who was controlling his son most effectively, was looked upon by the people as a model parent.

People in both the old and the new village regarded changes in terms of secular values, and both attributed to them certain specific gains—education, increasing transport facilities, and employment of the people in the village. Prior to the splitting of the village, there was only one matriculate for the whole village, but at the time of this study in 1966 there were ten students preparing for their matriculation, while there were already five who had matriculated. The number of primary-school teachers had risen from two before the split to four by 1966. In the same period the village had produced five undergraduates and two postgraduates.

Before the split there was no villager serving outside the village. But at the time of this study there were nine people working in rice mills, government offices, and the army.

The educated as well as the urban-employed have brought into the village secular values from the outside world. Such slight changes as could be noticed with regard to the relaxation of the ritual practices of pollution-purity rules were consequences of these new elements in Mallūr.

The preceding descriptive account, as well as its analysis, leads to certain tentative, theoretical conclusions that may be elaborated as follows:

1. The changes here studied are important not merely in themselves but also as causes of further change in social relationships. There is a danger here that one may miss change in social dynamics simply because one associates it too much with structured changes. In developing and "transitional" societies, there is the need to look for patterns of human interaction as manifested in social relations. It is from this point of view that we can make meaningful generalizations about empirical data collected in changing contexts.

2. It has been held that the dominant caste functions as a watchdog in maintaining a pluralistic culture and value system.[6] In this study I did not find any evidence for such an assumption. The process of escalation in the case of the peasant non-headman Lingāyat lineage group in the new village cannot be explained in terms of any single scale, ritual or otherwise. One has to use many scales—ritual, economic or political, or social-secular. The rise of the nontraditional leader of the Lingāyat peasant group can be accounted for partly in terms of his political ability and

[6] M. N. Srinivas, *Social Change in Modern India* (Berkeley, University of California Press, 1966), p. 15.

partly in terms of opportunity. It is clear that the change he brought about in the new village would not have been realized without the support of other groups.

I also failed to find any dominant caste model here. There could be neither a Brāhman nor a Kshatriya nor a Vaishya model here because these groups simply do not exist in the village. But I also failed to find any Lingāyat model. It could, of course, be argued that "dominance" means not absolute but "relative dominance." Even so there was no trace of any group being dominant, not even the Lingāyats. The concept of "relative dominance" presents difficulties, because "relative dominance" is not the same thing as "permanently (or at least reasonably stabilized) relative dominance." This is an important issue for a theoretical understanding of Indian traditional society. Suppose we have in the traditional pluralistic system groups A, B, and C, all of which are potentially capable of "relative dominance." There is "relative dominance" only in the sense that, at any given point in time, one of these three groups could use a situation, organize a coalition with other groups, and then transform "relative dominance" into effective dominance for a time, but always on the basis of coalition. Logically "relative dominance" should lead to a coalition model of dominance, which is not exactly a model of dominance. In other words, all that a theory of dominant group in the context of plurality would amount to is that at different times different combinations come to dominate the social system. In my view, this would be theoretically inadequate for an understanding of the social dynamics of Indian rural society. The very pluralistic nature of society goes against the possibility of either a permanent single group or a permanent coalition dominance.

There is another difficulty about interpreting Indian rural society in terms of the concept of dominance. In my view, there is a clear distinction between the way persons and groups in a system interpret their situation and the way an outsider may interpret it. This is a truism but one that is likely to be forgotten. The "dominance" notion seems to be an imposition on the system inasmuch as the people within the system do not see their situation in terms of dominance. A purely materialistic interpretation is inadequate in comprehending a society which has a tendency to look for nonsecular sanctions. It is possible that traditional Indian society is in the process of becoming one in which dominance subordination is a clear-cut notion. The efforts of minority groups to escalate themselves can be better explained in terms of what Eisenstadt has called "protest," leading to change.[7] The intention is not so much dominance as the acquisition of a minimally favorable position in relation to similar groups engaged in similar pursuits. It appears that social change can be more satisfactorily accommodated within such a framework.

3. Lastly, this study shows that the Indian rural society has considerable change-potential within itself. The manner in which the village responded to the challenge of the floods, organized the shifting of some of its members to a new site and faced up to the problems that arise out the splitting of the village shows that the villagers can think pragmatically about problems and can act to meet change situations. Though their reaction may not involve an over-all change, it certainly involves acceptance of some change. In this study, we find that the new village, which after all is part of the old village, was able to gain a sufficient momentum of change. The desire for change was certainly accelerated by external factors, but its initial stimulus came from within.

For the first time in the history of India, vast socioeconomic programs for change have been planned and initiated. To use the idea of center and periphery developed by Shils and Eisenstadt,[8] the periphery is being drawn closer to the center by these programs as well as by the legal-political developments at the national level. It seems imperative that those concerned with such instruments of change should have a grasp of what is taking place in rural India. From this study of Mallūr, it seems worth while to emphasize the following: (a) The village social system has sufficient inner dynamism and change-potential, which might be tapped by any program of change. (b) On an ideological level, social change cannot be explained in any simple terms of escalation along a single scale, ritual or otherwise, and also cannot be explained as being initiated by the dominant caste group. An awareness of these realities might go far in enabling those who direct the formulation and implementation of large-scale socioeconomic policies to cope better with the problem of social change.

---

[7] See S. N. Eisenstadt, *Modernization: Protest and Change* (Englewood Cliffs, N.J., Prentice-Hall, 1966).

[8] For details see E. A. Shils, "Centre and Periphery in the Logic of Personal Knowledge," in *The Logic of Personal Knowledge: Essays Presented to Michael Polanyi* (London, Routledge and Kegan Paul, 1961), pp. 117-31; idem, "Charisma, Order, and Status," *American Sociological Review*, XXX, No. 2 (1965), 119-213; and Eisenstadt, *Modernization*.

JOAN P. MENCHER

A Tamil Village:
Changing Socioeconomic Structure
in Madras State

THIS PAPER ATTEMPTS TO examine some aspects of social continuity, and factors leading to social changes, in the region around Kanchipuram (pronounced Conjeevaram) in Chingleput District, Madras State. It is based on data collected as part of a larger comparative study of Kērala and Madras.[1] The analysis focuses on two major variables: (1) the role of caste, and (2) the social structuring of economic roles. The data to be presented lead to the conclusion that, in this region, it is becoming less and less meaningful to speak of the caste system as a rigid, hierarchical, tightly linked socioeconomic system. However, this is not to say that the caste system itself is disappearing, or even weakening. While it is true that some of the traditional intercaste divisions are becoming attenuated, it is clear that these divisions continue to play a major role in people's lives, and in many instances have been strengthened.

An important methodological implication of all this is that any hypotheses which attempt to relate caste structure and change must be based on the realization that concepts such as *rigid caste system* and *Hindu orthodoxy*, or *cultural innovation* and *social change*, are all multifactored, and that an uncritical use of such concepts masks analysis. In India, particularly South India, it is meaningful to differentiate between the ritualistic and social aspects of caste behavior (such as attitudes about

Joan P. Mencher is an Associate Professor at Lehman College of CUNY and a Senior Research Associate at Columbia University.

[1] Work was done in 1963 under a postdoctoral National Science Foundation fellowship, and in 1966 on a National Institute of Mental Health grant through Columbia University. Professors Bernt Lambert and F. C. Southworth have provided useful comments on the materials. The author thanks Mrs. Chudamani Sundarajan for her help in collecting the materials.

pollution, insistence on caste endogamy, traditional food habits, and ritual prerogatives and restrictions) and the economic roles (the degrees of willingness to adopt modern technology or new types of employment, or other avenues to economic improvement). The well-documented tendency, among castes at all levels, to adopt new roles nowadays, in response to the changing socioeconomic and political scene, is not necessarily in conflict with the continued emphasis on orthodoxy in ritual and family matters. Apart from the methodological significance of these conclusions, it seems to me particularly important to focus on these questions at the present time because of the potential contributions of anthropologists in various fields related to development.

With regard to the relationship between orthodoxy and change in India, several different and often conflicting views are to be found in the current literature. The picture of orthodoxy as a factor inhibiting change is exemplified in the following quotation:

In countries like India and Pakistan a rigid caste organization slows cultural innovation. The prerogatives associated with each group are jealously guarded. . . . Role conflict, stemming from traditional caste patterns, may also hinder innovation.[2]

A contrary view emerges from Milton Singer's recent paper dealing with the modernization of cultural traditions in India:

The industrialization which is going on in India today is not only being seriously inhibited by characteristic Indian institutions, beliefs, and cultural values, but is, in some respects, beng facilitated by them. . . . Technical and social innovations are accepted not as displacements of the old but as additional alternatives, frequently set alongside of the old and labelled as "new" by as process of compartmentalization.[3]

In this connection my own observations indicate, perhaps rather surprisingly, that in South India (both Kērala and Madras) the individuals who are most eager to take advantage of certain aspects of modernization are often the most vociferous in insisting on the maintenance of "purity" of caste and family. This brings me back to my earlier point regarding the need to differentiate between those aspects of orthodoxy which are most resistant to change and those which appear to show some

[2] George Foster, *Traditional Cultures* (New York, Harper & Row, 1962), pp. 115-18.
[3] Milton Singer, paper presented at a conference on caste in South Asia, June 3-5, 1965, p. 127.

flexibility. In other words, if change is taking place, we must ask what aspects are changing, and how much they are changing. Certainly there have been changes in some of the traditional intercaste relations; however, as Dumont points out:

The fact of change is so taken for granted by most of us that any likelihood or any unverified statement, will pass for proof. . . . One thinks, among others, of Srinivas, who rebuked the current wishful thinking about caste weakening on its way to disappearance. He argued, on the contrary, that caste is actually seen as very resilient, that it adapts to new conditions, entrenching and reinforcing itself. This conclusion has been challenged . . . [but the question has been changed] to whether caste is becoming something else than what it was.[4]

It is clear that the caste system is becoming something other than what it was in the eighteenth and nineteenth centuries; indeed, in many respects it is being drastically remodeled. Today, the caste groupings do serve new functions in what is perhaps a more competitive sphere than before. In urban areas in the south, informal caste groupings help their fellows at least in providing a social forum, and on occasion, in more crucial matters. If a member of the caste has risen in importance either in government or in private business, he will make use of these informal relationships within his caste group in selecting recipients for favors (assuming that his close relatives are not in the bidding) or in deciding whom to hire. This is clearly recognized by the untouchable castes and is one reason why, in most cases, when an untouchable becomes a factory owner, he will try to help his own group exclusively.

It is true that in rural areas there has been only a partial lessening of the traditional *jajmāni* type of relationship. Indeed, at the village level, there is continued interdependence of castes in many parts of the country. Still, even in the rural context, there has been a tendency toward an increase in the solidarity of the caste group within larger regions. This sense of caste solidarity may be expressed in diverse ways: for example, it might be the rationale behind a march of Paraiyans to the village temple, led by the head of the subregional Paraiyan group, or a petition by Harijans in a particular village that they be provided with a government well; other instances are noted below. It is of interest in this respect

[4] L. Dumont, "Interaction and Comparison," *Contributions to Indian Sociology,* VII (1964), 13.

to note how caste organizations, especially among the lower castes, have worked to fight against the worst abuses of the caste system. The increased sense of caste unity may also play a role in the way in which members of each caste group look towards modernization. In spite of all that has been written about the lethargy of Indian villagers, it is clear that what often stands in their way is something socioeconomic and not attitudinal (e.g., the land tenure system in an area). Kusum Nair makes much of the fact that Harijans in Tanjore, when asked how much land they wanted, mostly requested less than five acres, sometimes even five on lease.[5] But what she failed to emphasize is that each man asked for more than he had, and that no one was being totally unrealistic and asking for something he knew he could never hope to have. If a farmer in the area of the lower Bhavani project area plants paddy and not cash crops in newly irrigated land, he is not necessarily being irrational. I suspect that he would not do so if there was enough paddy available so that a farmer could make a profit on the commercial crop and buy all the rice he needs. With present (1966-69) rice shortages, he is being quite realistic.

In the course of fieldwork it was clear that most villagers were concerned with improving their standard of living. People would phrase their goal in terms of not worrying about having something to fall back on when the rains fail, etc. But the goal of improving one's standard of living is conceptualized differently by members of different caste groups, or of different socioeconomic strata within a given caste. In part this difference is based on their different positions within the traditional hierarchy, in part upon a realistic appraisal of what is open to them. Put another way, while each of the caste groups evidences concern about change, the types of change envisaged vary from caste to caste.

In most parts of the south in which I have worked, the lower castes are not primarily concerned with intermarrying or interdining with higher castes, though one does hear occasional references to interdining among males. There was some concern about temple entry in the past, and today one still observes some tendency among the lower castes to favor the Brāhmanical "Sanskritic" deities. Since, however, there are now laws making it possible for untouchables to enter most of the major, more sacred temples, there does not seem to be too much time spent worrying about entering local village temples, which are not considered to be as

[5] Kusum Nair, *Blossoms in the Dust* (New York, Praeger, 1962), p. 31.

sacred anyhow. The prime concern can be phrased as "simple economic improvement," to have a chance to live better.

It is clear that in India the networks of social interaction have always been different for each caste group in a village. Although there has been relatively little change in attitudes toward orthodoxy and in intercaste relations and attitudes, the maintenance of these traditional features should not be regarded as simply *inhibiting* all changes. It is true, however, that the traditional structure does serve to *channel* change, that is, to determine where and under what circumstances different kinds of change can take place. The detailed study of this channeling is, in fact, a fundamental necessity for any understanding of what is going on in India, and probably has important implications for any attempt at economic development.

In the following sections I will examine briefly the historical background of the sample village, placing it in the larger regional matrix, and then compare the earlier situation with the present. On this basis, I will then discuss in detail the evidence for the conclusions I have just mentioned.

ILLUSTRATIVE MATERIAL

BACKGROUND

The illustrative material for this paper is drawn from both field and archival research dealing with Chingleput District of Madras State, and in particular in Kanchipuram and Sriperumbudur *tālūks*. The countryside around Kanchipuram lies in a gently undulating region with paddy-floored bottoms and low lateritic rises largely under poor grass and scrub.[6] Between the first half of the third and the end of the ninth century A.D. it was the seat of the Pallava empire; following the downfall of the Pallavas, it was one of the major cities of the second Chola empire. For a time it was ruled by Nāyaks of the Vijayanagar empire, then the area was invaded by the Marāṭhās, and finally at the turn of the seventeenth century it was annexed by the Muslims and ruled by the Nawāb of Arcot. Between 1750 and 1763 the Jaghire, as the district was then called, was obtained by the East India Company from the Nawāb in return for services rendered to him.

[6] See O. K. Spate, *India and Pakistan: A General and Regional Geography* (New York, E. P. Dutton & Co., 1954).

There was considerable dispute among the British as to how to manage the area, but in 1855 the government in Madras decided that an accurate survey of every village should be conducted. By 1886-87, according to Baden-Powell,[7] the survey of the majority of districts in the Madras Presidency was completed. It was then decided that a resurvey should be done every thirty years, and during the first decade of the twentieth century the resurvey of villages in Chingleput District was completed. Though rates of assessment have gone up during the past fifty odd years, and land has been further subdivided, the survey plots have not been altered in this area since that time.

According to one local tradition, originally only Veḷḷāḷās (the highest non-Brāhman caste in Madras) held the land, though they often had tenants, some with fixed tenures and others with short-term tenures, as well as agrestic (field) slaves and day laborers. But it is clear that even in the Pallava period there were some villages where the land was owned by Brāhmans, and there is some indication that at least part of the land was also in the hands of the Vaṇṇiyārs or Nāyakars as they are called in this district today), a caste group which ranks considerably lower than the Veḷḷāḷā. It is interesting that in a report of 1799, Place, a British administrator, notes that he found surviving Nattahs who were heads of groups of villages, evidently chiefs of a given region or nāḍu.[8] In at least one instance with which I am acquainted, there is good evidence that this traditional headship belonged to a family of Nāyakars called Nāṭṭu (after their traditional position) who were said to have been the "head of a circle of 32 villages before the Nawāb's time."

As opposed to the picture presented for Tanjore,[9] there were traditionally many sets of service relationships between the Brāhmans and Nāyakars and between the Nāyakars and Paraiyans, but none between the Paraiyans and Brāhmans except indirectly through the Nāyakars. It is significant that in the area where intensive work was conducted, Nāyakars either owned their own land or rented land from Brāhmans or Veḷḷāḷās

---

[7] B. H. Baden-Powell, *Land Systems of British India* (Oxford, Clarendon Press, 1892), III, 53.

[8] W. K. Firminger, ed., *Fifth Report from the Select Committee of the House of Commons on the Affairs of the East India Company, 28th July 1812* (Calcutta, R. Cambray & Co., 1917), p. 197.

[9] E. K. Gough, "The Social Structure of a Tanjore Village," in McKim Marriott, ed., *Village India: Studies in the Little Community* (Chicago, University of Chicago Press, 1955), p. 59.

to work as tenants, whereas Paraiyans, though occasionally owning small parcels of land, were never taken on as tenant farmers by Brāhmans.

DETAILED ACCOUNT:
BASE LINE OF COMPARISON

The village studied in detail is located approximately thirteen miles from the ancient temple city of Kanchipuram. The village itself dates to at least the end of the tenth century A.D. (on the basis of inscriptions on the wall of one small temple and on a stone built into the floor of the *mandappam* (pavilion) in front of the main Vaikunta Perumal temple). Brāhmans of the village claim that a cousin of the twelfth century Vaishnavite reformer, Rāmanujam, built the main village temple.

There has been considerable migration in and out of some of the villages in this region during the past 150-odd years, that is, during the period after it came under British rule, but there is at least some indication that intervillage movement also occurred earlier. In 1834, in Chingleput District, outsiders were allowed to take up land which was lying idle and this might have spurred on internal movement, but movement for this purpose only accounts for a part of the migration.

Many of the Nāyakars (the dominant agricultural caste in the district) can approximately date their arrival in the village as well as where they came from: some came from places in North Arcot District near Vellore, others from the region around Tiruporur on the coast between Madras City and Mahābalipuram. Gradually some of the newcomers acquired property in the village; some managed to retain their property, while others lost it again. Some individuals and families left the village in search of better economic opportunities. If a man had difficulties in one village, if he quarreled with his family, or if he lost his land, he might move to a place where he had affinal relatives (either a wife's mother, or a mother's brother, or a married daughter—marriages having in any case been arranged with kin, or at least with distantly related families). This spatial mobility was accompanied by the possibility of social mobility, since this region had adopted a cash economy much earlier than Tanjore; this made it easier for an individual to change his economic status, either up or down. Still, there is no reason to believe that some such movement, for similar reasons, did not go on in pre-British times.

This residential mobility has also been true for Brāhmans, at least up until twenty-five years ago. New Brāhmans originally came to the village either through adoption, or because one's wife's father was there and had no son, or, in the case of one currently wealthy family, because a distant relative without an heir had land there.

It is not clear what changes occurred in the caste composition of the village prior to the mid-nineteenth century, but the census of 1871 provides detailed information about caste composition on a village-by-village basis. Tables 1 and 2 indicate the caste composition of the sample village in 1871 and again in 1963. Two groups listed for 1871 have not been in the village since the early part of the twentieth century. These are the Sattāni, said to have been temple servants who performed menial tasks in Vaishnavite temples, and the Sembādavan, said to have traditionally been boatmen and fishermen. In addition, there are no Idaiyārs or cowherds, though there are many in adjacent villages. In the sample village

Table 1: Caste Composition in the Sample Village

Caste	1871[a]	1963[b]
Brāhman	125	128
Cheṭṭiār	14	38
Veḷḷāḷā	38	13
Naiḍu		27
Idaiyār (cowherds)	24	
Kammalan (artisans)	38	20
Vaṇṇiyār (Nāyakars)	418	916
Sattāni	7	
Sembādavan	23	
Āmbaṭṭan (barbers)	43	13
Waṇṇān (washermen)	6	10
Villi (Irulā) (semimigratory)		19
Kuravā (migratory)		4
Paraiyan	74	139
Others	5	2
Muslim	9	33

[a] Veḷḷāḷās in 1871 possibly included Piḷḷai, Naiḍu, Paṇḍāram, Devar, and Mudaliār. Idaiyārs do not live in this village any more, but there are numerous Idaiyārs in two adjacent villages, who own small amounts of land in the sample village. There are no Sattāni (a menial temple servant caste) or Sembādavan (fishermen) in the village at all.

[b] The 128 Brāhmans include a few outsiders (a school teacher and his family, a village level worker and her family) plus a preponderance of females, small children, and the aged. The 13 Veḷḷāḷās include 9 Mudaliārs and 4 Piḷḷais, all temporarily in the village. None of the descendants of the Veḷḷāḷās of 1871 live in the village today.

Table 2: Abstract of Census Data for the Sample Village, 1871-1963

Year	No. of Households[a]	Total Population	Brāhmans No.	%	Nāyakars .No.	%	Paraiyans No.	%	Others No.	%
1871	132	824	125	15.3	418	51	74	9	207	25.1
1891	158	1026	No data on villagewise caste breakdown							
1901	182	999	No data on villagewise caste breakdown							
1911	187	1089	No data on villagewise caste breakdown							
1921	190	1066	No data on villagewise caste breakdown							
1931	220	1070	106	9.9	No data		103	9.6	No data	
1941	238	1202	135	11.2	No data		121	10.2	No data	
1951	284	1053[b]	No data on villagewise caste breakdown							
1961	347	1280	No data on villagewise caste breakdown							
1963	306	1363	128[c]	9.4	916	67.2	139	10.2	179	13.1

[a] The criterion for the numbering of households has varied over the years. The criterion used by the anthropologist in 1963 differs from that of the census commission. In 1963, where two rooms were used by two independent families whether related or not, the families were counted as two separate households, whereas, when one man owned two or more buildings inhabited by his family, all of whom cooked and ate as one unit, this was counted as one household.

[b] The decrease in population between 1941 and 1951 is partly attributable to World War II, plus the severe cholera epidemic of 1942-43. Thus the death rate in Madras, which had declined to 21.7 in 1938, increased to 25.25 in 1943 and 25.4 in 1944. (See T. Krishnaswami, *Rural Problems in Madras* [Madras, Madras Government Press, 1947], pp. 18-19.)

[c] This figure includes 22 Brahmans now living in the village as temporary residents (schoolteachers and their families). Other figures also include temporary residents in the village.

the Nāyakars take care of cattle. There were several Veḷḷāḷā families in the village in 1871 but none of these families are there today; indeed, the only Veḷḷāḷās in the village are temporary residents employed by the government as teachers and in other positions. Of the 128 Brāhmans in the village today, 22 are temporary residents, and thus really outsiders.

It is clear that villages in this area were not self-sufficient in the past. The sample village has only a limited number of service castes, and this was also the case for each of the neighboring villages. Thus cloth was brought from nearby Kanchipuram, and the finer grades of rice were mostly sold there. Indeed, there has been for a long time a custom of growing the best rice on very good land and selling it in Kanchipuram, even if the farmer then had to buy a cheaper grade to eat. The nearest shepherds were in one of the adjacent villages, and sheep for sacrifices had to be brought to the village from outside. The nearest potters were about four miles away, and vegetables mostly came from three villages even farther away. Brass pots came only from Kanchipuram or farther south. The nearest leatherworkers were almost ten miles away, though indication of a Chakkli site on the survey map of 1911 arouses the suspicion that there may have been leatherworkers in this village before 1871. Usually, outsiders were brought in to recite the Mahābhārata at the non-Brāhman Draupadi Ammāl temple in the village. The census of 1871 for the whole of Kanchipuram tālūk makes it clear that this village was not unique in having only a limited number of service castes, even though the majority of large villages (including our sample one) did have their own barbers and washermen, and often their own blacksmith and carpenter, the four most essential workmen.

The records of the land survey and resettlement, printed in 1911 for the sample village, also furnish a basis for comparison with data collected in 1963. In this village, in 1912, between 27 per cent and 30 per cent of the land was owned directly by Brāhmans of the village, though individual holdings were larger than they are today. An additional 4.86 per cent of the land belonged to the main Brāhman temple in the village and two other Brāhman temples. Thus, the Brāhmans only had a maximum of 35 per cent of the land under their control even at that time. The majority of the land was owned by non-Brāhmans, mostly Nāyakars, though a few nonresident Veḷḷaḷās also owned land there. Fourteen landholders of paṭṭādārs each held over 20 acres at that time, and approximately 200 paṭṭādārs held about 2 acres each. Paraiyans owned about 2.3 per cent of the land, which is rather unusual for the area and possibly reflected pre-British māniyam rights (land given over to village servants, such as the men who watched the fields at night or were in charge of the irrigation waters—all jobs usually done by the lowest group of untouchables). Though not a large percentage of the village land, it was enough so that at least in this village the Paraiyans did have some economic independence.

This situation stood out in marked contrast to villages which had large Brāhman populations at that time, and perhaps relates to the fact that this village was part of a former nāḍu which had once had a Nāyakar head. The other types of Brāhman villages (there were, of course, many non-Brāhman villages) were ones which had a large wealthy Brāhman population (20-30 per cent of the total population) who owned almost all the land (with perhaps one or two Veḷḷāḷā landowners), with very little owned by Nāyakars or Paraiyans. In one of the two types, the Brāhmans let out most of the land on a sharecropping basis to Nāyakars; in the other they only let out part of it in this way, and had the remainder of the land cultivated by Paraiyans under Nāyakar supervision.

Even in the sample village, where the Brāhmans had less absolute economic power, they did occupy a dominant role in the social structure. Belonging to orthodox Vaishnavite sects, they were most strict about matters relating to ritual pollution, and even today the older Brāhman men adhere carefully to all of the rules regarding proper intercaste behavior. In fact, ritual behavior has not changed appreciably. But even traditionally the socioeconomic role of the Brāhmans in the village was influenced by the fact that in this region a considerable number of the cultivators owned all or part of the land they worked. Further, those with only small parcels of land, or no land at all, could work as tenants or day laborers for members of their own or other non-Brāhman or "clean" castes, as well as for Brāhmans. The man who owned even half an acre of his own land commanded a different position in his local society than the man who was totally landless.

THE PRESENT SITUATION: PROCESSES OF CHANGE

In Chingleput District in 1871, Brāhmans constituted 3.5 per cent of the population, but by 1931 they constituted only 2.3 per cent, and according to Dupuis[10] an even greater percentage left the rural areas after 1931. The city of Madras swelled from eleven thousand in 1871 to 1,729,141 in 1961.[11] In one village discussed by Dupuis,[12] where there were 66 families of Brāhmans in 1917, there were 23 in 1957. If one travels about in the three northern districts of Madras State—Chingleput, North Arcot, and South Arcot—one will find many former Brāhman streets or agrahārams which are partially or totally deserted. Many of these Brāhmans did retain their small holdings in the rural areas, usually

---

[10] Jacques Dupuis, Madras et le nord du Coromandel (Paris, Librairie d'Amerique d'Orient, Adrien-Maisonneuve, 1960), p. 49.

[11] Census of India, Madras State, Chingleput District Handbooks (Madras, Madras Government Press, 1961), p. 132.

[12] Dupuis, Madras, p. 353.

two to five acres, which are given out to tenants, but also in many of the villages more of the land is owned by owner-cultivators.

In the sample village there has been an exodus of Brāhmans, though they still constitute 8 per cent of the population (excluding temporary residents). However, this figure is misleading, since it consists largely of elderly couples, widows, younger widowed women, women whose husbands are employed outside, and children. Though Brāhmans still retain control of about 20 per cent of the land in the village (this figure includes land held by Brāhmans resident outside), they tend to see their future most clearly in terms of outside employment; if educated, in white-collar jobs; if uneducated, as cooks for urban Brāhmans. The majority simply hold on to what they have because they have no other source of livelihood, or else they are looking for a supplement to other income, or they stay out of sentiment for the ancestral property. Though they might invest in fertilizers, the majority are certainly not concerned with making indirect or long-term investments in the land. Striking here is the fact that most of the Brāhman absentee landlords live in Madras. If a Brāhman wants to set up a business, he is most likely to choose Madras, or some other larger town such as Kanchipuram or Sriperumbudur.

There are a few villages in this part of Madras State where close to 80 per cent of the irrigated wet land is owned by resident Brāhmans and little change may be observed. Such villages, however, are few and far between, and may be expected to change within the next five to ten years, as the older Brāhmans die and the younger ones refuse to remain in the village. The discussion here ignores these villages for the most part.

ANALYSIS AND CONCLUSIONS

EXTENT OF SOCIOECONOMIC CHANGE OBSERVABLE

Looking at economic roles in the village, one finds that there has been considerable change as many traditional roles have acquired a more temporary contractual nature. For example, there are still three families of blacksmiths in the village. They are paid in cash nowadays, except when they perform subsidiary roles such as trumpeter for processions of the deity. One of these blacksmiths moved from another village because his wife's sister, a resident of the village, convinced him that there was a good opportunity for business. The children of another blacksmith are in Madras, and it is likely that he will move there when he gets older. There is one carpenter, but carpenters from Kanchipuram are also called in for any major construction work. All of the former service *ināms* (endowed plots of land for members of service castes) have been given up and have reverted to the government; in some cases they have been transferred to members of other castes.

Wooden plows are no longer solely constructed in the village, but are also bought in market towns and transported by bus or bullock cart. Even in earlier times, all brass and earthen cooking utensils were bought from wandering vendors or in nearby towns.

There are two households of washermen in the village who are primarily paid in cash. One has only been in the village for a year and is planning to leave and stay with relatives near one of the larger towns.

Traditional economic roles for service castes are changing as modern technology, here including modern transportation, makes it feasible for both poor and middle-class people to resort to more impersonal services. On the other hand, the service castes remain endogamous, and at least within the village context only serve those castes which they served formerly. But I have been told that when there is no carpenter in a village, Nāyakars often do their own repairs, and sometimes even make repairs for others. There is a marked tendency for the service castes to congregate more and more in larger towns and cities as service becomes less personal and communication easier. But their traditional ranking does not change. Though the process is unformulated by the people themselves, it is almost as if the model of a guild or union, adapted to the Indian situation, which also requires endogamy, can serve as a basis for explaining their behavior.

While the percentage of Brāhmans has gone down and that of Paraiyans has remained relatively constant, the percentage of Nāyakars has increased markedly. This tendency for the proportion of people belonging to the dominant agricultural caste to increase has been noted for other villages in the region. It is indicative of the exodus of Brāhmans, as well as of members of other small caste groups, and leads to a relatively new village type resembling more that found earlier in Europe and China, where differentiation is based primarily on class criteria. One large village in this tāluk is of this type.

Paraiyans still continue to perform certain of their traditional jobs, such as regulating the supply of water to the fields, collecting the government assessment on the lands, watching the fields to see that grain or water is not stolen, beating the drum for Nāyakar funerals, helping with cremations, and removing dead animals and tanning their hides. Because such jobs are a source of income for them, and because they have a certain amount of economic security in their role in the village, they will obviously continue in these occupations for a long time. It is interesting that about twenty-five years ago, in an attempt to break up a feud between two Nāyakar brothers who are most influential in the village and have been the leaders of the two opposition political parties in the area, Congress and the Dravida Munnetra Kazhagam (D.M.K.), one of the Paraiyans led a successful boycott for six months. The Paraiyans refused to perform any of their traditional role activities. The Nāyakars somehow or other managed to get things done by themselves without the aid of the Paraiyans though they did finally beg the Paraiyans to return to their work and offered them various inducements. What is of interest here is that the Paraiyans were able to act as an organized corporate group against the Nāyakars, and only when the latter were able to present some semblance of agreement were they able to deal with the Paraiyans, who refused until that time to take sides with either of the two brothers. Today, the two brothers still do not get along, but in relations with other castes the Nāyakars present a more unified front and do not try to force the others to take sides except perhaps at election time.

On the whole, in this type of village relations between caste and social or economic status have undergone no marked change in recent times. While it is clear that in villages like the one described by André Béteille,[13] where in the past Brāhmans controlled all of the land, there has been considerable modification of the traditional congruent relationship between caste and social class, no such change can be observed in the sample village. To some extent one must take into account the fact that there was no perfect correlation between caste and land ownership in this sample village even at the turn of the century.

It is clear that here the relations among the three major castes, Brāhmans, Nāyakars, and Paraiyans, have not undergone significant eco-

---

[13] André Béteille, *Caste, Class and Power: Changing Patterns of Stratification in a Tanjore Village* (Berkeley, University of California Press, 1965).

nomic change. Perhaps one reason for the difference between this and Béteille's study relates to the fact that in Chingleput District 48 per cent of the workers are owner-cultivators (the figure goes as high as 60 per cent in the adjacent North Arcot District), 16 per cent tenant cultivators, 33.7 per cent agricultural workers, and only 23 per cent noncultivating proprietors. This contrasts greatly with a Deltaic region like Tanjore (where Béteille's study was conducted), which has a large rural proletariat and a small group of well-to-do landlords. Perhaps the striking difference between the Chingleput District and Tanjore lies in the concentration of holdings. In Tanjore the top 4 per cent of landowners, who own more than 30 acres each, hold 45 per cent of all cultivated land.[14] In Chingleput the amount of land owned by such large landowners is considerably less.[15] Just as striking, though, is the fact that many of the Chingleput landowners who own around 30 acres of land (for example, in the sample village) belong to the agriculturalist caste. As such, many of them work as much of the land themselves as possible, cultivating the rest with hired daily laborers under their direct supervision.

To the extent that there has been any change in intercaste relations, it appears in the attitudes of the Paraiyans: they are on the whole no longer content with their situation,[16] and in so far as thy are able to, they seek opportunities to improve their economic lot. They are also aware that their chances to do this in the village are severely limited. The percentage of land owned by Paraiyans has decreased in the sample village from 2.3 per cent in 1912 to 1.5 per cent in 1963, most of the decrease being due to the forfeiture of land as a result of unpaid loans. Paraiyans in this area can sometimes become tenants of Nāyakars or of the temple lands which are managed by a well-to-do Nāyakar, but on the whole most Nāyakars prefer to rent their land to members of their own caste where possible, stating the traditional myth that "Paraiyans are lazy, they do not work hard, they don't get good crops." In any case, many of these tenants have no fixity of tenure.

[14] Luchinsky, "Tenurial Conditions," p. 6.
[15] For a general comparison between this region and Tanjore, see Dupuis, *Madras*, p. 128.
[16] J. P. Mencher, "Past and Present in an Ex-Untouchable Community of Chingleput District, Madras," paper presented at Wenner-Gren Conference on "The Untouchable in Contemporary India," Tucson, Arizona, April 21-23, 1967.

Looking at the social and ritual distance between the castes, one can see that there is hardly any change in the relationships between those at the top and those at the bottom. Whatever change has occurred is between castes close to one another in the hierarchy.[17] Nowadays, the Nāyakars and the small but slightly higher-ranking Naiḍus function as one group, except for marriages and funerals. Some of the barriers between the poorer Nāyakars and the Harijans have begun to break down, so that a poor Nāyakar and a Paraiyan might play cards together. But the change is not great. Relations between Paraiyans and Brāhmans still show the same distance as earlier, and there seems no reason to expect any change in the near future. I know of one case of a young Brāhman who claims that when his grandfather dies he wants to employ Paraiyans as tenants directly, but this is unlikely to make much difference to the Paraiyans themselves since it would merely be a variation (though somewhat more lucrative) of the old dependence relationship; in any case, Brāhmans own only 20 per cent of the land. The primary concern of the Paraiyans is to become economically independent. Paraiyans and Brāhmans hardly ever interact in any way, except at cremations. Paraiyan children in the village attend school with Brāhman children and are allowed to walk through streets which were formerly closed to them. But this is due to the laws of the state, and the Brāhmans are aware that any violation of the law would lead to agitation on the part of opposition political parties. However, Brāhman, Nāyakar and Paraiyan children return to their own residential areas after school, and play activity is largely intracaste.

Taboos on intermarriage and family interdining are as strong as ever, and there has not been any attempt to challenge them in the village, though the village teashops for the most part do serve males without discrimination. On the whole, it can be said that rules relating to ritual pollution are still as strong as ever, though to some extent the penalties attached to pollution are not as strictly applied as in earlier times. For example, children are not always made to take a bath on their return from school except among the most orthodox Brāhman families, or among Nāyakars making a point of their respectability. Though in the past the Nāyakars in some villages, including this one, gave up widow remarriage, enforcement of the ban is less strict than in former times,

[17] *Ibid.*

even though the practice is still not sanctioned. If, for example, a young Nāyakar widow runs off with a man from the village, gets married, and stays away for a few months, the ultimate return of the couple will gradually be accepted, the earlier marriage will be "forgotten," and the couple will be reintegrated into the caste group. In an earlier period, when the Nāyakars were trying to emulate Brāhmans, there would have been attempts to outcaste her. On the other hand, it is probably true that ritual ranking is coming to be less meaningful to caste groups than their economic status, though the groups at the bottom are acutely aware of their low position.

The continuity of the caste system can be examined not only with respect to intercaste relations but also with reference to intracaste solidarity. The general impression given by my data is that, if anything, caste solidarity is stronger than in earlier times. This is particularly true among the Paraiyans, among whom, in spite of their desire to improve their lot, there is no desire to identify with the upper castes or to imitate them in any way. Indeed, they tend to look for models to the members of their own caste who have "made good," and they will cooperate with each other to help individuals get ahead. A striking example of this is the case of a Paraiyan schoolteacher from the sample village who is soliciting help in order to send untouchable village girls to a school in suburban Madras. Though such activities often work on a family basis, they occasionally go beyond the limits of normal kinship obligations (as in the case of a village girl whose education was paid for by her mother's younger sister). Examples of this type of cooperation can be found also for other castes: for example, during my stay in the village, fishing rights for one of the local ponds were auctioned off by the government and were purchased by a group of Nāyakars who pooled their resources in order to keep the rights from going to outsiders.

In the area as a whole, caste solidarity shows up quite clearly in the tendency of Brāhmans to hire Brāhmans, Paraiyans to hire Paraiyans, etc. In the case of lower castes this has the function of helping individuals to get out from under the limitations imposed by the traditional structure. For the Brāhman, the opportunity to enter white-collar jobs denotes primarily entry into the higher ranks of the modern world and a means to continue his traditional social, economic, and intellectual position, as well as to maintain his traditional ritual practices. Thus with regard to opportunities for education and for new types of employment, it is clear that although these are aspects of social change, they also involve a reaffirmation and a reinforcement of caste ties. As yet, there is little direct effect on the village from these factors, though the implications for the future seem quite clear.

IMPLICATIONS FOR THE FUTURE

I have already suggested that one finds in the contemporary Indian situation a picture of variable adaptability, in which the response to change depends on the circumstances of particular groups. At least in the part of Madras State that has been observed, an individual's caste identity is one of the important social factors in determining this response. This point can now, on the basis of the foregoing, be illustrated more specifically with reference to the needs of different groups and their attitudes toward change, and the effects of orthodoxy and caste solidarity on the change process. From the point of view of planning for change, I would like to suggest that development will proceed most efficiently if programs are aimed at those groups which show the greatest receptivity to them.

The concern for economic improvement permeates all castes, though members of different caste groups in this area see diverse ways of improving their status. Those differences are due, at least in part, to different culturally disposing factors. Though low in the traditional ritual hierarchy, the Nāyakars see themselves as farmers par excellence. In many respects they share common cultural characteristics with traditional yeomanry the world over. Thus, they are more likely to reinvest any extra money in the land, to try and save all their money in order to buy more land or to invest in other agricultural improvements. The fact that they do not traditionally have the dowry system means that a Nāyakar farmer does not have to set aside large sums of money for a daughter's marriage. (They do pay a small bride-price, but on the whole expenditures for marriages are low compared with those of Brāhmans.) Apart from the very wealthy Nāyakars, the rest tend to be more poorly dressed than many of the Paraiyans, and families with 10-15 acres of paddy land lack many of the physical comforts which poorer Brāhmans may have purchased.

On the whole the Nāyakars do not focus their goals outside of the village. Whereas a Brāhman family usually saves money to see that a son has a chance for a white-collar job in the big city, a Nāyakar family will not take money from the land for a son's education. True, some Nāyakar boys have been educated and have jobs outside, usually technical jobs, but for the most part their education has been supported by nonfarm earnings. Some Nāyakars are currently educating their sons; indeed a few are now teaching in the village elementary and high schools, and one young man has become an automotive engineer in Tiruchirapally. On the whole, however, such education is rare, and many Nāyakar adults are opposed to educating their children beyond the fourth or fifth standard. Their feeling about the education currently available to them was phrased most cogently by the panchāyat president as follows:

What is the use of this education? The children learn to read and write and all that, but they are not able to work on the land and they cannot get such good paying jobs. Anyhow, who is to work the land if they all get educated? The teachers insist that if they are studying they cannot take care of the family cows, and who is to do that work?

Among the Nāyakars, two have set up rice mills, one in the sample village and one in a nearby village. Another set up a sari shop and tailoring establishment, first in the village (for about five years), and then moved it to a nearby road junction where there is more business. Strikingly, the sons of the two joint owners of the sari shop are the only young men who have had technical education. Their families also own land, part of which is let out to tenants (though previously they themselves cultivated the land directly). Despite the fact that they let out part of their land to tenants, these men belong to the group of most progressive farmers.

It is clear that the major focus of the Nāyakar community is on agriculture. Farmers with little or no education would ask for detailed information about fertilizers and would complain that the government had not determined the best kind for the local soils. The black market in fertilizers in this region is functioning on a massive scale. Any farmer who can afford to do so will buy fertilizer on the black market, rather than do without. They are the ones who are most concerned about the new seed varieties and are most eager to obtain them. There appears to be no lack of interest in trying new techniques or in learning about them, especially among the larger landowners who can afford to buy fertilizers. It is obvious that if one of the major focuses of the development program is on improving productivity, then it would be most fruitful to concentrate on members of the agriculturalist caste.

Programs of an educational nature, on the other hand, may well have a greater appeal to other castes. Apart from the Brāhman interest in education noted above, I have encountered a surprising eagerness for schooling among the Paraiyans in the sample village and other nearby villages. There seems to be a growing tendency among these people to look to education as the only way to achieve economic independence and improvement of their material existence. This is true of the lower castes in general, but particularly of those lacking a trade or skill. One Paraiyan from the sample village who qualified as an elementary-school teacher is to some extent regarded as a model by his castemates. As an illustration of current interest, one group of young Paraiyans asked me to speak to the authorities about arranging literacy classes for them at night. Their need was practical, based on the recognition that only the literate can make contact with the authorities outside the village. They had already spoken to a Nāyakar schoolteacher about this, but had been ridiculed. They expressed their feelings to me as follows:

If we can read and write, only then can we take full advantage of all that is available in the world around us, or go directly to the government. What good are special provisions for members of our community by the government if we do not know about them? The Nāyakar panchāyat President won't tell us about them.

An approach which ignores differences in socioeconomic position, motivations, and attitudes, and which insists on dealing with the village as a unit for all development programs, may well lead to a solidifying of economic and political positions within the caste hierarchy. When the emphasis in a rural development program is placed overwhelmingly on increasing agricultural productivity, the result is often to increase the wealth of the larger landowners without having much effect on others; thus, even if those lower on the scale remain in more or less the same economic situation, their relative position becomes worse. A new all-India program for small farmers, which is to be introduced in one model district in each state in early 1970, is intended to have a corrective effect on this situation, but will still leave out a considerable section of the population. (In Madras State the "small farmers" would be those with two to five acres, whereas in the area studied most of the untouchables, and many Nāyakars, own less than this minimum.) Thus this emphasis on productivity often turns out to be in conflict with one of the other important principles of the community development concept, namely, the need to change the fabric of social structure by the introduction of egalitarian reforms.[18]

It is also clear that a knowledge of local conditions is necessary in order to predict the benefits which would accrue from particular changes. This is true even in the case of obviously needed reforms, such as land reform. As compared with areas such as Tanjore, the potential value of agrarian reform would seem to be limited in the area under discussion here, where only 1 per cent of the landowners have over ten acres (with the large majority of these being owner-cultivators with holdings of less than twenty acres). Redistributing the land of the few large owners would probably be of some value, but would not be enough to help materially most of the villagers. Though I consider effective land reform an important measure (and believe that the ceilings could be even lower than presently advocated), it cannot in and of itself fulfill all the major needs of community development.

There might be many advantages if programs of rural social reform, linked with other types of reform, were in the hands of individuals who are aware of the fundamental socioeconomic barriers involved. If this were done, there might be some chance of eliminating dependence on certain stock notions of development personnel, which are based largely on ignorance and sentimentality. Two very prevalent notions of this type are the idea that the villager cannot change because he is too "tradition-bound," and the romantic notion of the unity of the village. With regard to the first, the excessive emphasis on the paralyzing effect of traditional patterns and values conceals the importance of the function of social class conflicts based on economic (and, consequently, political) inequalities. The widespread notion of the unity of the Indian village is supported by certain external appearances, but these appearances conceal a great deal of internal variation in needs, goals, and attitudes, which become most relevant as the village faces change. This notion of unity

[18] See Gerald Berreman, *Human Organization* (1963), for a discussion of this problem at the opposite end of India.

has, however, led to the official assumption that all innovations must go through the formal village government in order to be effective. The result is that, even in the face of genuine need, available help often fails to reach the people who need it. The approach suggested here would take explicit cognizance of the ways in which village social structure channels change, and would try to turn this knowledge to advantage.

HENRY ORENSTEIN

Gaon:

The Changing Political System

of a Mahārāshtrian Village

MOST OF THE THEORETICAL background for this discussion of the changing political system of a village in Mahārāshtra, based largely on the work of men such as Durkheim, Simmel, T. H. Marshall, and Max Gluckman, has been given elsewhere.[1] In brief, I hold that there are tendencies toward conflict for power within subdivisions of a group that prevent the subdivisions from being too sharply posed against one another, and that thus allow for the cohesion of the larger group. In this paper I mean to emphasize another aspect of political anthropology, that of shifts and conflicts in the means whereby domination is legitimated. In line with this I had, at the outset, turned to the typology put forward by Max Weber. However, in applying Weber's categories to my data I soon found that (however useful for a macroscopic historical approach) they yielded little of value for my purposes. Hence some effort was made to revise Weber's system, the better to grasp certain subtle conflicts that were generated by change. This revision, however, turned out to be extensive, so much so that it called for much documentation and defense. A full statement of it would entail an elaborate discussion, which would be inappropriate here. I shall therefore put my position very briefly, with little evidence or argument, in the hope that the reader will have the patience to await the more complete explication. I shall first outline

Henry Orenstein is Professor of Anthropology at the City University of New York and Brooklyn College.

[1] H. Orenstein, *Gaon: Conflict and Cohesion in an Indian Village* (Princeton, Princeton University Press, 1965), pp. 7-16. Most of the data in this article have been given in my book. The article represents, by and large, a difference of emphasis in analysis. The time for writing this paper was made available through a grant from the Tulane Council on Research.

briefly the categories I propose to use and then, after some general background on the village in question, attempt to apply them to the changing conditions found there.

TYPES OF DOMINATION

Two of Weber's categories have been altered. His "charismatic" domination has been changed only in emphasis. According to Weber, charismatic authority rests on a belief in the "extraordinary" personal qualities of the leader. While the adjective "charisma" may be applied to stable political phenomena—for example, the "charisma of office" or the "charisma of kinship"—these are, in Weber's system, so much "routinized" as, perhaps, more properly to be considered as traditional or rational domination. That is, charisma is a highly transitory political phenomenon, more a means of changing a social order than of sustaining one.[2] The change I propose is similar to that put forward by Edward Shils.[3] He has observed that charismatic domination should not be considered as quite so unstable, but rather as a kind of domination that is fundamental to all ongoing political systems. Great power constitutes "awe inspiring centrality"; the leader of great masses of people, because he is a leader, tends to embody the central values of the group, and thus he is, in effect, a charismatic authority.

This modification of Weber I find valid and useful. But Shils's emphasis is on modern Western societies, where the unadorned power, the order-producing function of high government officials, is indeed very great, and where, because of the large scale of the society, the official is so distant from ordinary people that he usually does inspire awe, sometimes even reverence. In small-scale societies, leaders and led are in close contiguity, and the means whereby order is produced is to be found to a considerable extent in ordinary social intercourse, for example, in the

[2] Max Weber, *The Theory of Social and Economic Organization*, translated by A. M. Henderson and T. Parsons (New York, Oxford University Press, 1947), pp. 358-73. My treatment of Weber is obviously far too brief to do him justice. For a summary of Weber's treatment of types of domination, see R. Bendix, *Max Weber: An Intellectual Portrait* (Garden City, Doubleday, 1960), pp. 289-449.

[3] E. Shils, "Charisma, Order and Status," *American Sociological Review*, XXX, No. 2 (1965), 199-213. I had been developing a position similar to Shils's, with some differences shortly to be discussed, when his work was brought to my attention.

constraints of reciprocity.[4] Thus, if dominators are to be recognized as such, social distance must somehow be created between themselves and the dominated. This is achieved, in part, by defining the dominator as someone different from ordinary people, someone with intrinsically extraordinary qualities, often inherited in a "pure" line. And this belief is very often bolstered by various restraints on interaction, as, for example, in Polynesia, where we find special modes of speech and gesture intended for chiefs, as well as taboos on contact.[5]

I propose an even more marked change in Weber's "rational domination." His discussion would restrict the use of this concept, in anything approximating "pure" form, to highly rationalized bureaucracies, that is, to its most elaborately developed form.[6] It seems to me useful to strip the concept to its most elementary and essential attributes. First, obedience must be to the office rather than the person. In "purest" form the office is filled by selection of the man best suited for it; but where the position is not very demanding it may be filled by other means, such as inheritance. Essential to this form of domination is that the limitations on the powers of office be understood by all, or most, participants in the interaction, and that the rules to be enforced by the officeholder be oriented to achieve the goals of the larger group (rather than, e.g., his own or his subgroup's interests).

I will not here employ Weber's category "traditional domination."[7] (Not only is traditional legitimation found in all societies, but it is, I believe and will later try to show, a secondary form of legitimation in all of them.) In its place I will substitute what I call "complementary domination." This concept is based upon the norm of reciprocity. A number of theorists have suggested that this norm may be an element of ethics

---

[4] For the emphasis on the constraints of reciprocity, see B. Malinowski, *Crime and Custom in Savage Society* (Paterson, Littlefield Adams, 1959), ch. III *et passim; idem,* "Introduction," in H. I. Hogbin, *Law and Order in Polynesia* (London, Christophers, 1934), pp. xxxv-xxxvi *et passim.*

[5] See R. W. Williamson, *The Social and Political Systems of Central Polynesia,* 3 vols. (London, Cambridge University Press, 1924), Vol. III, chs. XXXI-XXXII *et passim; idem, Religion and Social Organization in Central Polynesia,* ed. R. Piddington (London, Cambridge University Press, 1937), ch. XI.

[6] Weber, *Theory,* pp. 329-41.

[7] *Ibid.,* pp. 341-58.

found in every society at all times.[8] With this I agree; reciprocity is a universal moral imperative. Yet the norm is, in fact, often violated; indeed, complementary domination is based upon the fact of its violation. Thus, for example, among the Nambikwara, we find that the chief, having been given a prized (if difficult) position and at least some of the means to meet its demands, is conceived as in debt to those who bestow the status upon him, that is, the people of his band. He is, thus, continually subject to demands upon his services and his supply of goods.[9] A situation very like this is found among the Anuak of the Sudan, possibly also among the Santal in India, and, ironically, in Imperial Rome.[10] Similarly, as Weber has observed, in modern Western democracy, the elected official "becomes the 'servant' of those under his authority."[11]

This "democratic" complementary authority is, however, rather rare. Much more widespread is an alternative to it, indeed, a contradiction of it, which might be called "paternalistic" complementary authority. In this form we find the Nambikwara idea turned completely around. It is not that the position of dominator is of such great value that the bestowal of the position creates an everlasting debt to the dominated, but rather that because of the goods or services he distributes the dominated are his debtors and must obey him. This form of authority is very widespread. It is found in nearly pure form among some California Indians and in some Melanesian groups.[12] Mixed with other forms (often charismatic

---

[8] E.g., see M. Mauss, *The Gift*, translated by I. Cunnison (London, Cohen and West, 1954); Malinowski, *Crime and Custom; idem*, "Introduction"; C. Lévi-Strauss, "Reciprocity and Hierarchy," *American Anthropologist*, XLVI, No. 2 1944), 266-68; A. Gouldner, "The Norm of Reciprocity: A Preliminary Statement," *American Sociological Review*, XXV, No. 2 (1960), 161-78.

[9] C. Lévi-Strauss, *Tristes Tropiques*, translated by J. Russell (New York, Atheneum, 1965), pp. 278-79, 287-88, 302, 304-10.

[10] E. E. Evans-Pritchard, *The Political System of the Anuak of the Anglo-Egyptian Sudan*, London School of Economics and Political Science, Monographs on Social Anthropology, No. 4 (London, 1940), pp. 43-44; G. Lienhardt, "Anuak Village Headmen," I: "Headmen and Village Culture," *Africa*, XXVII, No. 4 (1957), 348-49. The Santal situation is less clear. See M. Orans, *The Santal* (Detroit, Wayne State University Press, 1965), p. 25. The Roman data, of course, are even more complex, and the system was by no means a "pure" case of complementary domination. H. Mattingly, *Roman Imperial Civilization* (Garden City, Doubleday Anchor, 1957), pp. 41, 139.

[11] Weber, *Theory*, p. 389.

[12] For California Indians, see C. Du Bois, "The Wealth Concept as an Integrative Factor in Tolowa-Tututni Culture," in *Essays in Anthropology Presented to A. L. Kroeber*, ed. R. H. Lowie (Berkeley, University of California Press, 1936), pp.

authority) it is distributed throughout much of the world, Ceylon, for example, and many African kingdoms.[13]

THE TRADITIONAL VILLAGE

THE SETTING

Gaon, the (fictitious) name of a Mahārāshtrian village of 1,554 people—265 households—is found in Poona District, about one mile from a market town, which I call Mot. In 1954-55, when the first part of this study was undertaken, over one half of the population lived out of the main settlement in houses built near their farms, a situation that had largely come to be since the turn of the century.

There were twenty-four castes in Gaon, but six of these were recent immigrants of little significance in village life. The most important castes were the dominant Rajputs, the Marāthas, who were dominant in the region but not in Gaon, and the Brāhmans. Rajputs and Marāthas had the same traditional occupation, agriculture. A number of Marāthas did not associate themselves with the village, and the caste had no traditionally assigned role in village organization; but many members of the caste were active in community life, and Marāthas, having the largest population in the village, remained an important force in village affairs. The village also included a number of service castes, such as Nhāvis (barbers) and Parits (washermen), as well as "untouchable" groups,

54-55; W. Goldschmidt, "Ethics and the Structure and Society; An Ethnological Contribution to the Sociology of Knowledge," *American Anthropologist*, LIII, No. 4 (1951), 512-13.

In Melanesia, a nearly "pure" case of paternalistic complementary domination is found among the Kapauku Papuans. L. Pospisil, *Kapauku Papuan Economy*, Yale University Publications in Anthropology, No. 67 (New Haven, 1963), pp. 45-46. This seems also to be true of the Malekula; see A. B. Deacon, *Malekula: A Vanishing People in the New Hebrides*, ed. C. H. Wedgwood (London, George Routledge, 1934), p. 47. This form of authority persists even in the face of local "legal" authorities appointed under Western hegemony; G. Oosterwal, *People of Tor: A Cultural-Anthropological Study on the Tribes of the Tor Territory* (Northern Netherlands New Guinea) (Assen, Netherlands, Royal van Gorcum, 1961), pp. 96-97.

[13] B. Ryan, *Caste in Modern Ceylon* (New Brunswick, Rutgers University Press, 1953), pp. 46-48. For Africa, see, e.g., J. J. Maquet, *The Premise of Inequality in Ruanda* (London, Oxford University Press, 1961), chs. VI-VIII. See also L. Mair, *Primitive Government* (Middlesex, Pelican, 1962), pp. 166-67, 176-77, 180-81.

such as Chambhārs (leatherworkers), Mahārs (scavengers) and Māngs (ropemakers).

SOCIAL STRUCTURE

Family organization in Gaon was much like that found in most of India. The family was joint in worship, in commensality, and in economics. While conflict among brothers was very frequent, they rarely partitioned during their father's lifetime. The ideal required that brothers remain joint after their father's death, but few did this. Brothers were approximately equal in status and were intimates hence could not help but measure status against one another. They were rivals; and as soon as paternal authority was gone, they separated.

Most of the long-standing castes of the village contained a main lineage (bhāuki),[14] which claimed descent from the original settlers of that caste in the community and which monopolized the caste's work in the village's traditional economy. Generally the main lineage held the majority of the population of each caste. However, castes of any substantial size also contained, in most cases, people affinally related to the main lineage; this had been the case as far back as village records reveal. The most important exception regarding the lineage situation was the Marātha caste, which, having no traditional roots in the community, contained fifteen lineages, none more important than the others.

Large lineages were divided into a number of maximal segments (ilānās), and these were sometimes further subdivided. Individual households aside, the smallest subdivisions consisted of a few, about two to four, closely related households, often called takśimās. The takśimās always invited identical people to weddings and other ceremonies. The other lineage subdivisions were generally of little importance.

The takśimās were in some cases highly solidary, but in many there was intense conflict. As we have mentioned, there was much conflict among brothers, and the takśimā consisted of brothers or inherited their quarrels. Indeed, the lineage as a whole was not an unambiguously solidary group. The lineage tie was very important in ceremonies, espe-

---

[14] The bhāuki differs from a lineage as ordinarily defined in that, in most cases, there are no genealogies, actual or fictional, and in that women who marry members of the group are incorporated into it. The latter feature would assimilate the group to Murdock's "clan," that is, a "compromise kin group." See George P. Murdock, *Social Structure* (New York, The Macmillan Co., 1949), ch. 4.

cially in marriage and death, and it was an important route along which
mutual support was channeled. For example, the Marāthā caste, which
was the most populous and one of the wealthiest in the village, had pro-
portionately little power; one important reason for this was that it had
no single main lineage within which lines of support might be clustered.
Nevertheless, it can safely be asserted that persistent and intensive cooperation was not a distinguishing feature of the lineage. The affinal bond
was at least as important in this connection, probably rather more so.
Cooperation was not more intense as one descended to less inclusive subdivisions, with the exception of some takśimās. There was often muted
hostility pervading the group, appearing, for example, as allusions to past
misdeeds perpetrated on an ancestor by his lineage member or as fear of
being poisoned by some (unknown) lineage member. The lineage was
an expanded version of the household and inherited its tensions. Less
intimate contact and less pressing obligations helped to lessen tension,
but the fact that there was little clear ranking within the group—in a
rank-oriented society—helped to sustain it.

Open conflict, clear-cut factionalism, existed only in the main lineage of Rajputs, whom I call by the fictitious surname "Koke." This feud
did not include the entire lineage; only, on the one side, a group of eight
main settlement residents, the "Bals," and, on the other, nine households from one Rajput hamlet, the "Annas." (The groups did not have
consistently used names. I base the Bal group's name on the fictitious
name of its leader; the Annas, which had no one leader, on the fictitious
name of their hamlet.) The Annas were the wealthier group and had the
sympathy of most "respectable" villagers, but few were openly allied with
either side. Most of the Bals were alleged to have a lower status than
other village Kokes.

The open conflict among Kokes is understandable in that they were
dominant as a group, and hence were more likely as individuals to assert
superiority. An allegation of inferiority among them was thus very likely
to, and did, produce severe antagonism.

The castes, considered in their extensions beyond the village, varied
in amount of internal organization and external definition. Some were
clearly defined and well organized. One such, for example, was the Rajput
caste, whose identity anywhere in the region was easy to ascertain. Many
castes, especially of low rank, held regular caste meetings taking in groups
of villages. But other cases were internally and externally amorphous.

The Marāthas were an extreme case of this, being composed of roughly ranked, vaguely defined bilateral kindreds and as a whole having ill-designated boundaries. The boundaries of the caste were especially rough because the term "Marātha" was used by a number of other castes (each of which had, in addition, a "proper" name) to indicate that they were of a high secular rank. One result of this was that there was probably a certain amount of individual upward mobility into the Marātha caste; a "Marātha" of, for example, the barber caste would not find it too difficult to become a "Marātha" of the Marātha caste.[15] This was probably the only group into which individual mobility took place, however. Even Marāthas maintained a fair amount of social control through occasional group meetings, for example, at weddings.

Caste rank was determined by religious and secular beliefs and practices. Castes without any especially pure or polluting customs were ranked by economic and political factors, particularly the latter. Secular rank was a function less of power within the village than of power in the region. Thus Marāthas were ranked by nearly everyone as higher than Rajputs, although everyone conceded Rajput dominance within the village. Probably as a consequence of this, the two castes were antipathetic.

For a number of castes, rank was determined primarily by ritual purity. Indeed, purity was fundamental to the entire system; whatever the basis of rank, it was ultimately translated into the "language" of ritual, for example, the assumption of the sacred thread and/or the alteration of food habits in upwardly mobile groups.

In a general way each caste was conceived as having an appropriate amount of ritual purity associated with it, largely determined by food habits and traditional (not necessarily actual) occupation. Those whose traditional occupations were associated with death or bodily substances were "unclean"; thus, washermen were unclean because they handled the clothing of women who had menstruated, and scavengers were unclean—"untouchable"—because they handled and ate carrion. This helped to integrate castes; they needed one another for services that they were too "pure" or too polluted to perform themselves.[16]

15 For a detailed discussion of this, see my article "Caste and the Concept 'Marātha' in Mahārāshtra," *Eastern Anthropologist*, XVI, No. 1 (1963), 1-10.
16 See Edward Harper, "Ritual Pollution, as an Integrator of Caste and Religion," *Journal of Asian Studies*, XXIII (June, 1964), 151-97; also published in Edward Harper, ed., *Religion in South Asia* (Seattle, University of Washington Press, 1964).

But this situation also forced castes apart, particularly the "untouchables." Ropemakers (who were traditional hangmen) and scavengers were conceived as so polluting that the notion of physical dirtiness and moral baseness was attached to them. A situation like this is bound to produce some mutual antipathy, and it did in Gaon.

At the other end of the scale, the "purity" of the Brāhmans, their proximity to the sacred, encouraged others to invest them with "extraordinary" qualities. Their religious practices were generally more rigorous, frequent, and elaborate; their knowledge of religious and moral rules allegedly greater; the ritual avoidances between themselves and the polluted more stringent. They were socially distinct from others and indisputably "above" others, thus potentially charismatic. But the consequences of this were not uniform. The community was small and intimate, hence the reality of individual Brāhman weaknesses was known. Laxity in religion, material ambition, and interpersonal intrigue were sharply disjunctive with the customary pretensions of the caste. Consequently the group as a whole was sometimes spoken of with contempt and sometimes with resentment. Nevertheless, individual Brāhmans who approximated the Brāhmanical standards were, in fact, highly respected and often followed. They were charismatic leaders.

Political domination within the village (in contrast to caste rank) was expressed largely through the *balutā* system (often called *jajmāni* in the literature). The system also helped to produced social solidarity within the village.

The system consisted of the provision of stipulated goods and services by village service castes and for other villagers, both service and agricultural castes. The defined goods and services were given in whatever amounts were needed and were paid for at a constant rate, a rough percentage of the crop. At harvesttime or just after sugar crushing, landowners sent word to *balutedārs*, those who served in the system, to come for their *balutā*, that is, their regular payment. If crops were poor one year, then *balutā* was less, but it was not smaller simply because fewer services were required and not larger if more were needed.

While outsiders could be included in the system, fellow villagers were much preferred. By and large, this meant not individuals or castes, but main lineages. In allocating work the lineages usually divided either village land or time, not landowners. For example, the ropemakers divided the land among themselves, and each man served the farmers on "his" land. Brāhmans rotated yearly among three lineage subdivisions. The tie was thus from the service lineage to the village at large.

The system ensured for service castes a measure of economic security (to the extent that such is possible for villages like Gaon). But their security was circumscribed by the village and bound up with that of the landowner, for there existed the belief, approximated in fact, that bālutā was proportionate to crop yield. Where a market system predominates, the income of a worker is determined by variations in production and consumption over a wide region, where he knows neither the land nor the people who work the land that decide his fate. Under such conditions social identification is not likely to be enhanced by economic exchange. Where the bālutā system remains strong, the bālutedār's condition is, in his own eyes, similar to the landowner's, in that it is inextricably bound up with the agriculture of the village in which he lives. He is given an obvious economic motive for identifying with the system of relations within his village.

Moreover, at the hub of the system there were the village landowners, especially the Rajputs. These were the ones for whom the system functioned. They, in their turn, needed the bālutedārs in order to express their domination.

THE TRADITIONAL POLITICAL SYSTEM

There were three formal political positions in the traditional village. One was the accountant (kulkarṇi), really a quasi-political status; another the revenue headman; and the third the police headman. In recent times the two headman positions were officially held either by a father and son or by two brothers, and one of the two men did the work of both offices.

The qualifications for the headman (pātil) were that he be educated through the fourth grade and that he be a member of the Koke lineage. The Kokes were divided into four maximal segments, and the right to fill the position was rotated among them every ten years. In the past the head of each segment—that is, the alleged lineal descendant of the founder—took one position, the other going to the oldest able male in the segment. Recently this method was changed to a simpler one, whereby the segment head appointed whomever he chose, usually himself and/or his sons.

When it came time to rotate the position, two men from each of the segments went to the office of a government official in Mot and attested to the qualifications of the incoming men. In fact, no unusual abilities were required for the job, and almost any mature Koke would have been able to handle it adequately. The duties of the revenue headman were to supervise the accountant in tax collection and in the maintenance of land and property records. He was, in theory, superior to the accountant, but the latter was always more competent in these matters and usually had a fairly free hand in his job. The police headman was supposed to report any crimes that took place in the village and to collect information on vital statistics. Actually, it was understood by both government officials and villagers that troubles should be settled within the village whenever possible. In this the police headman usually relied heavily on the influence of informal village leaders. An unusually strong headman might bring in outside authorities against the wish of the informal leaders, but he could not do so often, for he lived within the village and needed the village leaders' good will. Thus the laws of the state were reworked to fit village values.

The status of the headmen obviously constitutes "rational" authority as defined here. Although the positions were, in part, inherited, the power gained by the individual was modest; domination, to the extent that it existed, resided in the office itself, and the rules that were enforced were in accord with community values.

The office of accountant was inherited in the main lineage of Brāhmans. The descendant of the eldest son of the original village accountant had the legal right to keep the post permanently if he wished, but it was customary to rotate the work among the households every five years. The accountant's duties were to collect taxes and to keep village records, of which there were many different kinds. Although the rules associated with the office did not directly give power, they did so indirectly. Power derived from the accountant's knowledge of how to ensure transmission of property to an heir, how to secure loans, how to clear a mortgage, and so on. People not infrequently went to him for advice in disputes on economic affairs, for his knowledge of such matters usually surpassed that of others. Like the office of headman, the accountant's authority was "rational." Yet it also helped to enhance the charisma of the Brāhman; the accountant had access not only to sacred, but also to secular knowledge, knowledge of things that seemed beyond understanding, "mysterious"—and vital—to the ordinary villager.

By far the most power in the village resided not in formal statuses, however, but in informal village leaders. The overwhelming majority of these were Kokes. It should be understood that the Kokes, as a group, were conceived of as dominant. Although most of them did not actually serve as headmen, they were often addressed or referred to as *patil*; alternatively, they were sometimes referred to as *mālak*, that is, the "owners" of the village. This was done, in part, because they had the exclusive rights to the headmen's positions and because they all owned certain designated land (*inām* land) associated with the position. Most important, it was done because they were conceptualized as *the* village landowners; although others owned land, Kokes owned more than any other lineage in the village.

As has been mentioned, the bālutā system focused upon the Kokes. Payment within the bālutā system was asymmetrical, and it was recognized as such. In a survey of a number of villages of the region I found that all bālutedārs, barbers often excepted, were paid more bālutā by landowners than they could have received had they sold their goods on the market in Mot. That is, bālutedārs were, in a sense, overpaid, and thus were "debtors."[17] Moreover, there seems to have been a tacit recognition that this was so—even when it was not, as with the barbers. When specifically questioned on the subject, most bālutedārs answered (to me, at any rate) that the bālutā they received was "about right"; however, most said that other bālutedār groups, not their own, received very large payments, far larger than the market value of the goods and services they provided.

More important were parenthetical remarks made by villagers, not in response to specific questions on the subject. One ropemaker had just finished saying that all of his patrons continued to use his services. Then he corrected himself, saying that it was not quite all—"the very poor buy in Mot." A similar statement was made by a village barber. Some ropemakers had lost many patrons by 1954; these complained that they could barely live by selling in Mot. In the course of a survey of landowners, each was asked to name the bālutedārs who served him. A number of the landowners who were relatively poor said that they could afford no bālutedārs or relatively few.

17 For detailed documentation of this, see my article "Exploitation or Function in the Interpretation of Jajmani," *Southwestern Journal of Anthropology*, XVIII, No. 4 (1962), 302-15.

Landowners, and particularly Kokes, were conceptualized as "creditors." However, every Koke household head was not considered to be a village leader. There were but ten, by and large the wealthiest men. Moreover, three other men, one Marātha and two Brāhmans, were also considered to be village leaders.

I classify village leaders into three types, actually a continuum from passive, wherein there is little aggressive behavior, through active, to unsanctioned, in which the application of power is almost completely coercive.

An important characteristic of passive leaders is that their behavior nearly coincided with the ideal moral code of the community. For example, drinking intoxicating beverages was morally disapproved, but in fact most people considered it a forgivable fault; passive leaders were teetotalers. Without actually being otherworldly, they were more than usually religious. Generosity was a highly valued ideal, and leaders of this kind were unusually generous; however, unlike active leaders, they did not make a public spectacle of their generosity. Interpersonal conflict was, ideally, undesirable; but it was, in fact, expected to exist, especially among the powerful. Passive leaders, however, carefully avoided conflict. Their adherence to ideals was elaborately formal at times. For example, after the barber cut his toenails, one passive leader always "saluted" him —that is, a respectful apology was tendered: "It is as if I touched him with my foot."

There were three such leaders, one Brāhman who fully lived up to the criteria for passive leadership, another Brāhman who did so in part, and an elderly, religious, and highly moral Rajput, formerly an active leader. (The Brāhman population in Gaon was small; that there should be two leaders of this caste attests to the potential charisma of membership in it.) These three men, because they tended to act out the ideal moral code of the community, were charismatic authorities; they were somehow different from ordinary men. Their charisma, it should be observed, would have been greatly attenuated if they had actively sought positions of authority by the usual means of intrigue and aggression; these qualities were too common in village life, too "human" to inspire reverence. Thus they did not participate overtly in competition for power, but acted, upon request, as mediators in disputes and served as style-setters in behavior.

Active leaders were distinguished by wealth, public generosity, assertiveness, and pride. These men were deeply involved in status competition; for instance, they fiercely competed with one another for positions of honor at major village ceremonies. While their behavior was consistent with village expectations, it was much less so with moral ideals. Locally (illicitly) distilled rum found an outlet in many of their households. Many of them were present in the audience at a tamāśā, a traditional public show involving bawdy singing and joking. A few of these men kept women, sometimes women of untouchable castes, and many had casual extramarital sexual relations.

Active leaders directly ran the village. They were not usually employed to decide disputes in private, but along with passive leaders they considered such problems in public. Such leaders would, on occasion, directly order others about, for example, to disperse an unruly group in the village streets. If someone wished to have his way in a dispute, the most economical, rapid, and effective way was not to go to court, but to gain the favor of active leaders, who would put pressure on his adversary to yield. As was mentioned, headmen usually consulted active leaders before making important decisions. These were the men who organized the important village ceremonies.

The power of the active leaders was used not only to run the village, but also to ensure privileges for themselves. For example, when a well was constructed, allegedly for the village as a whole, it was placed at the edge of the village, inconveniently for most people, beside the home of one of the most powerful leaders.

I would emphasize that public generosity was essential for active leadership. For example, there was one rather boastful, aggressive, well-to-do, mature Koke who was not considered a leader. He was far from generous. On the contrary, he was known as a man too pleased to accept a handout of tobacco or tea. Hence, he was held in contempt, a "debtor" who did not need to be, who by lineage affiliation should not have been, a debtor.

To be an active leader one had to use one's wealth to exceed expectations, especially on ceremonial occasions. Weddings in the families of active leaders were always extravagant affairs, involving often two bands of musicians, sometimes professional dancers, and always enormous feasts, to which all the villagers, as well as outsiders, were invited. Some even plunged themselves into debt over such spectacles. Note that Brāhmans, including the passive leaders, invited relatively few people to their weddings.

Leaders of the active type were far more than ordinarily generous. They gave liberally to beggars. Their bālutā payments and tips to bālute-dārs were often larger than was considered necessary. They all used the village washerman's full services, although the service was considered poor and the fee high. Their contributions to village ceremonies and to collections for temple repair were always impressive. This generosity was a public matter. It encouraged the idea that others were indebted to them, that the village at large was beholden to them. Thus, by defining themselves as "creditors" they ensured their position of leadership. It is obvious that their domination was of the kind here called paternalistic complementary authority.

Although caste was not the sole determinant of leadership, all lead-ers were of high caste. Were this the end of the matter we might find lower castes to be nearly powerless and unprotected, their rights neglected. Abuses could easily occur, especially of untouchables, most particularly scavengers and ropemakers. Yet the rights of untouchables were not by-passed. This was partly due to the fact that power in the village was divided; village leaders did not act as a unit. Most important, the Koke feud created a political force, albeit an unsanctioned one, that helped the untouchables.

As has been mentioned, there were seventeen households involved in the feud, nine Annas and eight Bals. The Annas had more allies and were by far the wealthier of the two groups. To redress the balance the Bals used threats of physical violence, which were made more substantial through alliance with a small group of Harijans that had a reputation for violence. These Harijans were hated and feared by "respectable" vil-lagers, for they were said to be prone to steal or burn crops and to poison cattle. Their allegiance gave Bal, the faction leader, strength, for there was apprehension among "respectable" villagers, especially Annas, that Bal would call upon them for aid in case of an open fight. Moreover, it was said that Bal had, at one time or another, instigated the destruction of crops and cattle of some Annas (although proof of this was lacking).

Bal kept the allegiance of the Harijans by helping them. Thus a con-certed effort was made in 1954 to have four of the least reputable Hari-jans "externed" (required by court order to stay out of the district). A number of village leaders and others they persuaded to help testified that the four men were idlers who harassed the farmers. The Harijans turned to Bal. He and three of his kinsmen traveled to Poona to testify to their good character before a magistrate. The externment was not effected.

Moreover, Bal and his group kept the sympathies of Harijans in general by associating with them in a friendly fashion and by protecting them from abuse by others. Harijans recognized the assistance given to them by the Bal group, and many sympathized with it. Most Harijans, however, preferred to avoid giving open aid to Bal, for this would be tantamount to out-and-out defiance of sanctioned leaders.

It seems probable that Bal's support of untouchables was intended, not only to bind his allies to him, but also to give some moral sanction to his power. However, he cannot properly be called a sanctioned leader. The defense of Harijans had little relation to village customary values. His threats of force could not be justified by village norms or ideals. His relative youth, and, more important, his lack of wealth, helped to disqualify him as a "respectable" leader. Indeed, Bal himself seemed not to consider his power as entirely proper. His attitude when he was not actually involved in a dispute was mild and retiring. He never sought a central position in village ceremonies. He was neither boastful nor ostentatious, and his support of public ceremonies was modest, as were the feasts given by his household. His appeal, thus, was not to the community as a whole but to a single segment of it. The remainder of the community tolerated him, in large part, simply because they had no alternative.

While Bal's leadership was sustained by the belief that he might use violence, he did not in fact do so very often. "Respectable" villagers did not stand in constant fear of him, for he was not constantly active as a political force. More important, his political activities, while contrary to village properties, were limited by those proprieties. As was mentioned, he remained in the background in village ceremonies. He gave respect to sanctioned village leaders, excepting Annas, and even helped to maintain their authority. For instance, he was not averse to reprimanding Harijans who overstepped their "places" in relation to important villagers. Thus, because Bal accepted the system of relations and authority in the village, his power, though resented by others and not sanctioned by village norms, was accepted as a part of the scheme of things. If unable to handle Harijans, some villagers, even active leaders, turned to Bal for aid. He was tacitly allowed his sphere of influence, and other villagers, including leaders, worked within this sphere.

The fact that the Bals lived in or near the main settlement constrained most other residents to keep up an outward show of good relations with them. This held for leaders as well as for others. More than any other active leaders, those from the main settlement maintained a façade of good relations with the Bals, despite their sympathy for the Annas. For most of them this involved concessions to Bal's well-known attitude toward untouchables. They were almost all more careful and less overbearing than other active leaders in their relations with Harijans and were sometimes even helpful to them.

The Annas resented the main settlement leaders for their toleration of Bal. One Anna recited a Marāthi proverb intended to absolve the village at large, while condemning Bal and those who made concessions to him; it went something like this: "One rotten mango in a basket spoils a few around it, but it does not spoil the whole basket." The "spoiled" and especially the "rotten mangoes" formed a political force that worked apart from or even against the remainder of the village leadership, dividing and balancing power, and thus giving protection to the politically weakest elements of the village. The Bals, the core of this political force, while accepted as a necessary part of everyday life, had the active support and sought the consent of but a small segment of the community. Their power had no ideological support, neither complementarity, charisma, nor rationality. Fundamentally, the Bals exerted illegitimate power.

CHANGE, 1954-1955

In recent times a number of technological, ideological, and administrative innovations have taken place that have had a deep effect upon village life. One of the most important of these was the introduction of canal irrigation, which resulted in a greater emphasis on cash in the economy. Along with other factors, it stimulated the rate of immigration to Gaon, and newcomers were less concerned about village affairs. It also helped to bring about the dispersion from the main settlement to the fields—irrigated land requires more continuous attention—and thus less direct confrontation among villagers.

Irrigation also brought about more contact with government officials, and generally helped to broaden the villagers' sphere of interaction. Other factors were also important in this regard. For instance, government activity resulted in the formation of the village *panchāyat* and the Cooperative Credit Society. Government, the Congress Party, and the Scheduled Caste Federation (a predominantly Scavenger organization) campaigned against "castism," especially untouchability.

SOCIAL STRUCTURE

One effect of these innovations was a weakening of caste taboos. Organized meetings by castes had been discarded by most castes that formerly held them. Apart from this there had been little change in internal caste organization; although caste organization (in contrast to caste interdictions) had been strengthened in India at large, there were few signs of this in the region of Gaon. Scavengers and ropemakers were probably more overtly antagonistic toward "respectable" elements in the village, the former because of the new egalitarian propaganda, the latter largely because of a decline in the bālutā system.

Although bālutā remained a functioning system, there were signs that it was on the way out. Immigrants and even some old residents did not participate or participated but little. Some who used the full complement of bālutedārs gave smaller payments, and service castes reciprocated with fewer services. Bālutā payments, formerly considered by all to be a right, were being redefined as something akin to charity.

The decline of bālutā was one factor that weakened village ties. There were others. The community was becoming engaged more intimately than in the past with a network of relationships extending beyond its borders, especially with government. Government incursions included, for example, the village panchāyat and the Cooperative Credit Society. While not, in themselves, very effective, these and other government intrusions resulted in a widening of people's horizons; although there was some hostility toward government, people felt closer to it, less awed by its power.

THE CHANGING POLITICAL SYSTEM

One alteration in village politics was the substitution of a government-appointed official, the *talāthi*, for the Brāhman *kulkarṇi* as village accountant. This weakened Brāhman strength in the village. However, it was not a major change, for the activities of the Brāhman kulkarṇi were limited by village proprieties. Most important, the really significant power that Brāhman leaders had was charismatic authority, and this was little changed.

The introduction of the panchāyat, while representing a government intrusion on village soil, was of modest political significance in village life. The duties of the panchāyat were explicitly set down in law. It had charge of the repair of village streets, water facilities, and hygienic conditions. It was supposed to make provision for security against theft and violence. Its judicial committee had the power to try minor criminal and civil cases, including, for example, violation of the law requiring attendance at school and misuse of common village lands.

However, the panchāyat rarely acted. It was staffed primarily by informal village leaders. They ran for panchāyat office as a demonstration of their allegiance to the Congress Party, thus giving them an additional rationalization for the informal power they exercised. But they chose not to act through the panchāyat, where authority was "rational," and therefore limited. Most important, panchāyat offices, like those in the modern West, were positions for which one was supposed to campaign; once installed, one was supposed to act as a representative, a "servant," of one's constituents. That is, authority was, in theory, of the democratic complementary type. The men who filled the positions could not conceive themselves in this role vis-à-vis the very people with whom their normal relationships had taken the form of paternalistic complementary domination. The two forms of domination were not compatible in the same set of relations. Thus village leaders acted not through the panchāyat, but in the old informal manner, where they were the creditors.

Informal leadership had been little changed. Through propagation of the new egalitarian ideology by government and Congress, Bal's support of Harijans had been given some moral sanction, which he played upon to an extent; but within the confines of the village his power remained illegitimate. Thus, political relationships in 1954 were fundamentally those of traditional village organization.

CHANGE, 1961

The most important innovation since 1955 was an intensification of government activity. The first stages of an extension program had been laid down in 1961, preparatory to an intensive phase to be started in

1962. Apart from this, government officials were generally more active than in 1955, largely in encouraging the formation of "self-help" cooperatives. A group of people, a minimum of eleven, could get together for government aid and advice on what was deemed a worthy project, for example, dairying or housing; their initial financial contribution had to be but a very small percentage of the government's. The most important new cooperative ventures were two large sugar-processing plants started in the general area of Gaon. Each included members from a number of villages. Membership was profitable, and the cooperatives were popular. Ownership of one-half acre of canal-irrigated sugar-cane land gave eligibility, so all members were not necessarily well off. Members participated in regular meetings to elect officers to the board of directors and to discuss policy. Each member had one vote.

SOCIAL STRUCTURE

Caste organization was changing. In the general region of Gaon there had appeared in the six-year interval the new kind of formal caste associations that had been extant in other parts of India in the past. Such caste associations were familiar to members of six of the long-standing castes of Gaon, and some people from the village had joined. These associations were fundamentally different from the old caste structures. They were more broadly based geographically, were led by elective officials, and emphasized not primary, but secondary, relationships, such as communication by mail. The associations were intended to raise the status of the caste by encouraging education among members and, often, by finding ways in which members might get government aid.

These associations had probably diffused into the region from elsewhere, but it should be noted that they appeared at about the same time as the increase in government activity and that their goals were, in part, to gain access to government aid. It seems probable that government was a stimulus to the diffusion, a psychological blueprint for action in a formally constituted organization.

Although castes as social groups were gaining in strength, there were fewer signs of intercaste hostility. This was probably because such hostility was produced in the context of the intimacy of village interaction, and in 1961 the village had become less important.

By 1961 the bālutā system had been nearly completely destroyed.

Separate ceremonies were more frequently being held in hamlets instead of having a single ceremony in the main settlement. There were now four Cooperative Credit Societies instead of one, for conflicts within the old society had become intolerable. The membership of the new societies tended to divide along the lines of caste and faction. The village was being fragmented.

Attitudes toward government were less antagonistic than in 1955. There was a feeling that government was more accessible, that one could interact with it, possibly to considerable advantage. Thus people's mental outlook was being expanded.

The same held true of their sphere of interaction. The two sugar-processing cooperatives are examples, for they included people from a number of different villages. Members of some of the service castes, now nearly entirely deprived of bālutā, often went to Mot to sell their wares. Many others went to Mot frequently, some daily, for business or amusement. The 1961 talāthi established his office in Mot rather than in the village, an unprecedented move. One of the Cooperative Credit Societies moved its office to Mot "because people come here all the time. It is more convenient." Many people seemed to feel apathy toward the village; while the bond to it was lessening, a larger geographic area was increasing in importance.

THE CHANGING POLITICAL SYSTEM

The village panchāyat remained ineffectual. Indeed, it was of even less concern to villagers than it had been in 1955. For example, there were very few village leaders serving on it, and these showed little interest in it.

The small number of leaders on the panchāyat was indicative of a new attitude on their part. In the 1961 celebration of Independence Day very few leaders attended, and none gave speeches, although many speeches had been given in 1954. They were less concerned with village affairs, and the village was less concerned with them.

Passive leadership, based upon charisma, had been weakened, especially in the case of those who fully met the criteria for this form of authority. Some people still sought the advice of passive leaders; such leaders still embodied the ideal standards of the village in some respects, for example, regarding propriety in kinship behavior. But the old form of purely charismatic leadership was implicated with traditional village values, not with the new, increasingly important forms of organization that extended beyond the confines of the village.

Active leaders were in a dilemma. If they had chosen to respond to the imperatives of 1961, they would have led people toward opportunities created by government. But to have done this would have been, from their viewpoint, self-defeating; it would have bound the villagers to government, not to themselves. Government would have been the "creditor." Consequently, those former leaders who did not retire from leadership sought new positions, appealing to a wider audience in a different way, either in administrative divisions broader than the village or in other broadly based associations, especially cooperatives.

An important part of the interest of the villagers, including leaders, was in the new sugar-refining cooperatives. For example, the Brāhman who had been a leader approximating the passive type had adapted to the new circumstances and was seeking election to the governing board of a cooperative. One active leader was serving on such a board. These cooperatives functioned with relatively little reference to the old social factors of caste, feud, or neighborhood. Conflict existed within them, of course, but it tended to follow the lines of "rational" economic interest. The governing boards were composed primarily of wealthy men, who could afford to take time off for campaigning; but their power was limited by the nature of their appeal for office. They owed their prestigious positions to election by ordinary members, and the members were too dispersed, relations were too impersonal, for extralegal pressure to be applied with as much effect as within the village. Hence, the board had to attend to the wishes of members to a greater extent than did leaders on the localized, village level.

In the wider area of interaction involved in the sugar-processing cooperatives or in administrative areas beyond the village, men ambitious for power had to seek it by means of a different kind of appeal. The appeal had to be a claim that they could better serve the voters. In such wider spheres they were able to lay claim to democratic complementary authority without making the complete reversal of attitude that would have been necessary if they had wished to continue to dominate in the village, where paternalistic complementarity had been the main basis for power. The new form of domination required a new and different set of relationships.

YOGENDRA SINGH

Chanukhera:
Cultural Change in
Eastern Uttar Pradesh

THE VILLAGE CHANUKHERA is situated in the *tarai* (swamp) of north-eastern Uttar Pradesh, only ten miles from the border of Nepal. Its district headquarters, Basti, is about 35 miles to the south; a trunk road connects the village with the district headquarters and with the town Barhni to the north, which is a center of business and communication with Nepal. As the village is situated in the plains (*doāb*) between two rivers, the Budhi Rapti to its north and Rapti to its south, it recurrently suffers from the vagaries of floods. The climate here is moderate, not very humid, with an average rainfall of about 50 inches. The total cultivated area is 711.6 acres, of which about one third is single-crop area. In 1955 there were 296 houses; the number in 1965 had increased to 321. The total population in 1955 was 1,372; in 1965 it had increased to 1,475.

The social stratification system of the village is reflected in the location of major caste streets. There are six such streets, each named after the caste group predominantly inhabiting that area. All the streets slope downward to north, south, east, and west from a central plateau on which stand the big houses (*havelis*) of the Rajputs, the ex-*zamindārs* (landlords). Adjacent to the Rajput street in the southward direction is the street of Brāhmans; adjoining its eastern flank is the street of Āhirs. To the north of the Rajput street is the street of Banias, which, in the northeast, is surrounded by the street of Lōhars, Badhais, Kumhārs, etc., in the north by the street of Muslims, and to the far northwest by the street of the lower castes, such as the Dhobis and Chamārs. The contour of settlement and proximity with the Rajput street has traditionally been a mark of relative social status for the inhabitants.

Yogendra Singh is Associate Professor of Sociology at the University of Rajasthan, India.

The village was traditionally under the joint *zamindāri* system of land settlement and was dominated by the Rajputs. The gazetter of Basti and the village customs register (*sharayat-wajibul-arza*) provide some historical facts about the period of the establishment of power by the Rajput zamindārs. The Rajputs who belong to the Kalhans subcaste, settled in this village during the year A.D. 1544, after pushing out the local tribes, the Thārus and Domkatars. They had migrated from western Rajputana as an armed band. Until the establishment of British rule, this Rajput clan ruled over about twenty-five surrounding villages. Now the clan is subdivided and scattered into six villages of the region.

The social hierarchy and status of various castes can also be observed through the style and structure of their houses. The houses of Rajputs are bigger and more spacious than those of other castes; some stand two stories high and most of them have a sitting hall outside the main building. The houses of Banias and intermediate castes are smaller, stand on lower plinths, and generally have mud walls. The lower of the untouchable castes have very small houses with two or three rooms without plinths and are congested. Formerly, their houses used to be covered with straw but today most of them are tiled.

The transport facilities, which a decade back were very poor, have improved considerably. Chanukhera is now connected by regular bus service to the nearby towns. It has one primary school for boys, which was started in 1885; another primary school for girls was established in 1941. A post office was opened in 1945, which has now grown in size. A zamindār financed the establishment of a junior high school in 1963, which has been recognized by the State Department of Education.

Two crops, *khariff* (summer crops) and *rabi* (winter crops), are grown in the village. The khariff crops are sown in the months of June-July and harvested in the months of September-October. The main khariff crops are paddy, maize, pulses, and a coarse grain called *kodon*. The main rabi crops are wheat, barley, peas, mustard, and sugar cane. Most of the sugar cane is crushed in the village itself and converted into coarse sugar for consumption. Only a few big farmers cultivate sugar cane as a cash crop. Among fruits, mangoes grow in large quantities. There are six mango orchards covering about fifteen acres of land, all owned by Rajputs. Four other mango orchards are not of an improved variety. Guavas and bananas also grow in small quantities.

There are three temples, one mosque, and four other sacred spots in the village. The temples are devoted to the gods Rāma and Krishna. The mosque serves the religious needs of the Muslims. The sacred spots are located at the outskirts of the village boundary. The goddess Kāli, the serpent-god Nāga, the god Bhairon, and the evil spirit Nat are supposed to preside over these sacred places. Regular prayers and rituals are conducted at the three temples only. Seasonal offerings are made to Kāli and the god Nāga. In the past, when epidemics were frequent, collective prayers were offered daily or even many times during a single day, especially at the seat of the goddess Kāli. Now, only once in the year, that too according to the convenience of individual families, offerings are made at the seat of Kāli. Nat and Bhairon are the gods of the lower castes and they continue to be worshiped as in the past.

Important institutions which constitute the social system of the village are caste and subcaste, class, family, and panchāyats. All these foci of the rural social structure are welded together through an institution-alized complex of ritual structure, folkways, and the value system of the Hindu tradition. Both the formal and the folk version of the traditional Hindu ethic have deeper implications for the maintenance and regulation of the social system.

CASTE STRUCTURE

There are twenty-four Hindu and ten Muslim castes and subcastes in Chanukhera. Among them, Rajputs have always had the highest social status, honor, and power. They continue as the most influential group. Caste hierarchy in this respect represents the model of "Rajput domination"; unlike other parts of India, Brāhmans, especially in secular matters, are subordinated to Rajputs. All the Hindu castes can be arranged as follows in six status categories on the scale of the prestige and power they have in the social system:

    I. Rajput (12, 16) *; Brāhman (23, 32)

    II. Bania (32, 20)

    III. Āhir (30, 32); Kurmi (23, 28); Murao (5, 4); Sonar (5, 5); Halwai (3, 2); Thather (3, 2)

* The figures in parentheses show the number of households of each caste in 1955 and 1965 respectively.

IV. Kahar (14, 15); Bari (10, 14); Māli (4, 4); Badhai (3, 3); Lohar (3, 2); Kumhar (1, 4); Bhooj (2, 2); Dharkar (1, 5); Arakh (7, 6); Nai (3, 3)

V. Nat (3, 3); Teli (1, 1); Chamār (46, 52); Dhobi (4, 4)

VI. Hela (2, 2)

The sixty-one Muslim families are divided into ten subcastes which can be arranged in four status categories:

I. Pathān (4, 4)

II. Muslim (Shekh) (9, 9)

III. Kujra (17, 19); Ansar (10, 10); Manihar (10, 11); Nai (1, 1); Darzi (2, 2)

IV. Bhat (1, 1); Peelwan (1, 1); Faqir (3, 3)

The Kalhans Rajputs are widespread in the districts of Gonda Gorakhpur and Basti in eastern Uttar Pradesh. Their ancestor Keshri Singh was a powerful chief who ruled over vast areas in Basti. In course of time his estate disintegrated and his descendants divided the estate; they became less powerful and turned into zamindārs. All Kalhans Rajputs do not maintain close ties of kinship and ritual obligations throughout the district. The rule of subcaste endogamy is, however, strictly adhered to by all.

Rajputs in Chanukhera are organized into two patrilineages called *patti* or *thoka*. Pattis form the basis of ritual, kinship, factional, and economic relationships. The name of the patti is derived from the location of the patti households.[1] The two pattis are, therefore, called *poorab* (eastern) and *paschim* (western) pattis on this basis. Each patti has a separate tradition for celebration of life-cycle rituals. Each has a separate patti deity. All rituals are celebrated on a patti basis; a few members from the other patti are invited on such occasions if relations are cordial. Patti solidarity constitutes an important ingredient of the traditional social organization of the Rajputs, which plays a very important role in the intercaste relationship of the village. In 1965 the western patti consisted of three families and the eastern patti of thirteen families.

Rajputs practice hypergamy and there is a regional localization in their selection of brides and grooms which extends to a radius of about a hundred miles. Consequently, their interpersonal communication linkages and kinship ties are much extended, giving them additional influ-

[1] A similar pattern has been reported by Leigh Minturn and John T. Hitchcock, in *The Rajputs of Khalapur, India* (New York, John Wiley & Sons, 1966), p. 31.

ence and power. Traditionally they have been rulers and they continue to enjoy high prestige and power. The accept *kachcha* (raw) or *pucca* (cooked) food cooked by Brāhmans but do not accept kachcha food cooked at the home of any other caste. From the castes in categories II, III, and IV they accept kachcha food if it is cooked at their own households. They consider it beneath their dignity to accept kachcha food cooked at the residence of other clean castes.

The relationship between Rajputs and Brāhmans is of an ambivalent nature. Ritually, Brāhmans are respected and held as sacred. On ceremonial occasions Rajputs touch the feet of Brāhmans. The common style of Rajput respect toward a Brāhman is to announce "Palagan," which means "I touch your feet." But in secular matters Rajputs take precedence over Brāhmans. The basis of ambivalence or contradiction lies in the economic system and agrarian class structure. To some extent, the model of Rajput domination follows from the "kingly model" of the traditional Hindu structure of power and statecraft which offered Brāhmans the highest spiritual and normative authority but alienated them from the sphere of secular power.

Brāhmans are divided into two subcastes: Tripathi and Pande. Both claim caste status. Pandes are numerically stronger (eighteen families) and their main occupation is the priesthood. Tripathis engage primarily in supervisory farming. One Tripathi family has completely given up the priestly calling, since the head of this family serve as a secondary-school teacher and cultivates about ten acres of farmland. Brāhmans do not accept kachacha food from any other caste and follow strict rules of commensal purity. Ten years ago, none of the Brāhmans accepted service as priests for untouchables but today one Brāhman family is serving them; this is frowned upon by other Brāhmans despite its being tolerated.

Banias occupy the next higher position in the Hindu caste hierarchy. All of them belong to the Agarwal subcaste. A few Banias have traditionally enjoyed high prestige in the village owing to their wealth. Rajputs would treat a very wealthy Bania with a good deal of respect, because at a time of difficulty they may have to borrow from him. But the relationship changes with the fortunes of the Banias. The position of the Brāhman, on the other hand, does not undergo any such change, being based on sacred-normative rather than utilitarian considerations.

The Hindu castes in the third and fourth status categories are ritually clean. They can touch Rajputs, Brāhmans, and Banias and enter into their houses. Āhirs are by tradition a shepherd and cultivating caste. During the days of zamindāri, they worked as personal attendants and sepoys to zamindārs. Kurmis are agriculturists and are reputed to be good cultivators. Muraos sell vegetables. Sonars, though traditionally gold-smiths, now sell sweets and other merchandise. Halwāis, traditionally confectioners, maintain that occupation. Thathers specialize in the sale and repair of brassware. The traditional occupations of all the castes in the third status category, except for the Sonars, remain unchanged.

In the fourth status group are mainly the service castes. Tradition-ally, Kahars and Baris were domestic servants in the families of Rajputs. The subsidiary occupation of Kahars was fishing and of Baris making leaf-plates (pattals) for use at public feasts. Today, most of them have given up their traditional occupation. Kahars have opened betel shops and teashops and Baris work as vendors of sweets and other edibles. Mālis used to be village florists and attendants to the goddess Kāli. Traditionally, they were essential mediums for any rituals or sacri-fices offered to this goddess. As epidemics are now less frequent, the rituals at the altar of Kāli have dwindled. This has forced Mālis to take to cultivation as the main source of livelihood. Other castes, such as Badhais (carpenters), Lohars (ironsmiths), Kumhars (potters), and Dharkars (basketmakers), are artisans and earn through jajmāni rela-tions with the other castes. Nāis (barbers) are also related to other castes through jajmāni linkages but they mainly serve the Rajputs. Muslim Nāis, however, serve especially the lower castes.

The castes in categories V and VI are "untouchables." Among them, Chamārs are numerically predominant. Most of them are landless and work as laborers. When they have land, their holdings are very small, on an average less than an acre. In the past they worked as plowmen (halwahas) to Rajputs. Many of them still continue to do so. A number of them now also work as rickshaw pullers and road builders. Child mar-riage and widow remarriage is customary among them. They are divided into two subcastes, Utaraha (northerners) and Dakhinha (southerners), probably on the basis of the direction of their immigration. But a major cause for this subdivision is that Dakhinha Chamārs used to eat beef of carrions, which was not approved by the other Chamārs. This practice has now ceased. The traditional occupation of Bhoojs is the parching of grains; parched grain is a common form of food in this region. Arakhs were watchmen by tradition but now they have taken to agriculture. Nats, besides being snake charmers, manufacture and sell stone equipment. They are a nomadic group and their women go about begging, singing, and dancing. There is only one family of Tēlis in the village; they are oil crushers. While men press oil at home, their women go out selling oil to customers. Dhobis, as washermen, have not changed their main occupation.

Muslim subcastes are also endogamous and maintain social distance in accordance with caste hierarchy. Pathāns have the highest position among them and claim to be Rajput converts to Islam. Next in hierarchy are the Muslims or Shekhs. Pathāns and Shekhs deal in ready-made garments. Kujras (vegetable sellers), Ansars (weavers), Manihars (bangle dealers), Darzis (tailors), and Naīs (barbers) enjoy equal social status but maintain the rule of caste endogamy. Village endogamy is also common among the Muslims and some lower Hindu castes but not among the upper-caste Hindus. The Bhats (bards), Peelvans (elephant drivers), and Faqirs (mendicants) have the lowest position among Muslims. The relationship between Hindus and Muslims has always been cordial and harmonious. Muslims participate in Hindu festivals like Holi and Deepāvali; similarly, Hindus take part with enthusiasm in the Muslim festival of Moharrum. In the history of the village there has been only one case (in 1943) of tension between the Muslims and Rajputs (not between Hindus and Muslims as such) on account of a land dispute for Karbala, the ground where Moharrum is celebrated. It was, however, resolved peacefully.

Rigidity in the enforcement of caste rules was highest among Brāhmans, but they did not have a caste panchāyat. Caste norms were imposed and held together by consensus. Cases of caste deviance have been rare among them. Only recently (1963) a Tripathi Brāhman married his son to a girl from the Gossain (beggar-Brāhman) subcaste, as he was offered a substantial dowry. This caused resentment among the Tripathi Brāhmans, but barring one family (which still does not interdine with this family), others have accepted the deviant. Like Brāhmans, Rajputs, too, did not have a caste panchāyat. Each patti had a council of elders which before the abolition of zamindāri looked after matters relating to the caste norms as well as agrarian relations. But, unlike Brāhmans, Rajputs tolerated a great deal of laxity in personal moral standards. There was greater permissiveness, especially in the field of commensal and sex rules for the males. Relations with lower-caste or untouchable women never led to the ostracization of males from the caste. During the British rule, Rajputs often interdined with English officers or invited them to shoot game (*shikar*); some of them also used to dine at the residence of a local Muslim zamindār; all this was, however, tolerated.

Thus, it appears that Rajputs, before the abolition of zamindāri, were well on the way to westernization and liberalization. This mode of behavior was, however, confined only to the males; the females were kept under strict veil and authoritarian male domination. The very aged male members, too, used to regress to traditionalism, a feature which is so common in the Hindu mode of westernization.

Now, fifteen years after the abolition of zamindāri, when economically and socially there has been a sea change in the condition of Rajputs, they have given up the traditional pomp and show of the westernized mode of living. Rather, they show overcommitment to traditionalism. Most of them are supporters of Jana Sangha, a conservative and tradition-oriented political party. Their older style of control on the village having gone, they now rationalize their condition in terms of the fatalistic theme of the Hindu tradition.

Banias also had no caste panchāyat. They, too, are strict conformists to caste rules. Caste panchāyats played a very important role in the social organization of the cultivating and service castes. Disputes connected with marriage, divorce, payment of gifts or bride price, and those related to property subdivision used to be decided by these panchāyats. Caste panchāyats also cut across village boundaries and led to the "horizontal solidarity" of the system. These panchāyats offered protection against the excessive exploitations of landlords. When a lardlord became too tyrannical, caste panchāyats helped the victim to migrate and settle down in another village. Contrariwise, some less scrupulous members of a caste often attempted to evade the sanctions of a caste panchāyat by taking shelter under the authority of a zamindār. Such cross-shelterings, which Bailey calls "bridge actions,"[2] functioned as sources of dynamics or change in the traditional social organization of the village.

Today, caste panchāyats exist in name only. They seldom meet and very few people refer cases to them. This does not mean that caste solidarity has waned. On the contrary, new arenas have been opened in which castes function as solidary groups, such as village panchāyats, local

[2] F. G. Bailey, *Tribe, Caste and Nation* (Manchester, Manchester University Press, 1960).

political groups, and political factions. These developments have also been responsible for the decline in the interest of people in caste panchāyats. Caste leaders now try to occupy leadership in a formally organized panchāyat. Three fourths of the caste leaders of Chanukhera are now members of the executive committee of the village panchāyat, which is organized on rational administrative lines.

Caste, as a functioning system, has kept its major characteristics intact. Connubial rules are strictly maintained by all caste groups. During the last decade there were only two cases of violation of these norms. In one case an Āhir left his earlier wife to live with a Dharkar woman. In another case a Kahar started living with a woman from the Chamār caste. In both cases the deviant members were ostracized from their caste. The first event happened in 1949 and the second one in 1953. In both cases the women were from the lower castes and the men belonged to a higher caste; however, none of the castes were prepared to accept the deviants into their folds. The two families in the village exist alienated.

There is some relaxation in the commensal norms of various castes. Recently, a few teashops have sprung up in the village. These are run by Kahars. Except for a few Brāhman and Rajput members, villagers, irrespective of caste affiliations, take tea prepared at these shops. Although some discrimination and some social distance are still maintained in serving tea to caste members according to their hierarchy, a great deal of liberalization in commensal rules is implicit in this change. Untouchability, however, still prevails. Even at the teashops, the untouchables are not allowed to sit on the benches or cots. They must sit on the ground and take tea from earthen pots and not from cups and saucers. By law, untouchability is an offense, but in reality it persists. One element of the caste system, however, seems to have been more responsive to change—hereditary caste occupations. Many castes, such as the Sonars, Kahars, Baris, Mālis, and a few Brāhmans, have now given up their traditional occupations.

CLASS STRUCTURE

An important element in the social system of Chanukhera is its class structure. The big farmers (ex-zamindārs), small cultivators (ex-tenants), merchants, and landless agricultural laborers are the four major classes in the village. To a great extent the class structure overlaps with caste hierarchy. The farmers are Rajputs, most cultivators are Āhirs, Kurmis, Muraos, and Mālis. Merchants are mostly the Banias and a majority of the laborers belong to the Chamār caste. Nevertheless, in many respects, class relations also cut across caste ties. Recently, a few Brāhmans have purchased land and have become substantial farmers. Brāhmans also compete with Rajputs for power. Similarly, a few Kujras and Banias have started cultivation; Baris, Kahars, and Sonars have become shopkeepers and a few Āhirs and Kurmis have taken to working as laborers. Despite these changes, class inclusiveness of caste remains intact. The question arises: In what sense can we employ the concept of class as a relevant and viable analytic category for the description of the rural social system?

The reality of class as pointed out by Max Weber lies in the "market situation" and its accompanying features of polarization of economic interests and class consciousness.[3] The bonds of mutual relationship within the class are associative, defined by an identity of economic and, following from that, of social and cultural deprivations and standards of achievements. Communal and particularistic relationships, as in the caste, are external to the sphere of relationship within the class situation. On these criteria, historically as well as existentially, farmers, merchants, cultivators, and laborers constitute social classes.

Historically, a conflict between the tenants and zamindārs based on the contradictions of economic interests has persisted in Chanukhera for the last two or three decades; this conflict has taken diverse forms. Class consciousness was first generated during 1936-37 when the Indian National Congress established an office in the village under the leadership of a Brāhman, followed by three Chamār leaders (labor class), two Muslim merchant leaders, and one Āhir leader. This was the beginning of the agitations for land reforms, fair wages, abolition of begār (forced labor), security of tenancy rights, and legalization of land cultivated by tenants on a sharecropping basis and under oral tenancy.

Prior to 1937, the hold of the feudal pattern of class structure was strong on the rural social organization. Interclass relationship under this system was an ensemble of reciprocity and domination based, on the one hand, on caste values and, on the other, on the economic domination of Rajputs. Economic domination had, however, not been completely

[3] Max Weber, "Class, Status, Party," in *From Max Weber: Essays in Sociology*, trans. by H. H. Gerth and C. Wright Mills (New York, Oxford University Press, 1946).

differentiated from the interlinkages of caste relationships. Class relations were dominated by the jajmāni system as well as by zamindāri. Both these institutions together constituted the traditional rural social organization. The institution of zamindāri, however, deeply influenced the functioning of the jajmāni system.

The elements of reciprocity and domination in jajmāni relationships have been variously described by different sociologists who have worked in different regions.[4] In Chanukhera, however, jajmāni relations were dominated by the Rajputs. Rajput zamindār families, which were organized into two pattis, constituted the subunits through which many jajmāni relations were defined before the abolition of zamindāri. All households of the service castes, laborers, merchants, and cultivators were

[4] To the question whether the jajmāni system is based on reciprocal rights and responsibilities of partner castes, or whether some castes have a dominant position in the system, thus rendering it nonreciprocal, there does not seem to be a clear answer. Elements both of reciprocity and of domination have been found in jajmāni relations by Wiser, Gould, Beidelman, Leach, Pocock, Opler, and Singh. Oscar Lewis, too, comes to the same conclusions. In Wiser's village, Karimpur, Brāhmans are in the dominant position. Gould finds the upper-caste landowning groups in dominance in the village Sherapur. Beidelman finds a general pattern of somewhat nonreciprocal relations between the dominant-caste jajmāns and the lower-caste servants. Leach also emphasizes the role of "privileged elites" in the economic relationship among various castes. Pocock treats jajmāni as a religio-economic system but accepts the role of domination (ritual and economic) of the upper castes. He is critical about treating jajmāni as a mere economic counterpart of the caste system. Opler and Singh and also Leach mention not only the dominance of upper castes but also their dependence on the kāmins. The domination of Rajputs in jajmāni has also been described by Majumdar.

Greater elements of reciprocity in jajmāni have been reported by Orenstein and Ishwaran; for reference see W. H. Wiser, *The Hindu Jajmani System* (Lucknow, Lucknow Publishing House, 1936); Harold Gould, "The Hindu Jajmani System: A Case of Economic Particularism," *Southwestern Journal of Anthropology*, Vol. XIV (1958); T. O. Beidelman, *A Comparative Analysis of the Jajmani System* (Locust Valley, N.Y., J. J. Augustin, 1959); E. R. Leach, ed., *Aspects of Caste in South India, Ceylon and Northwest Pakistan* (Cambridge, Cambridge University Press, 1960); David F. Pocock, "Notes on Jajmāni Relations," in *Contributions to Indian Sociology*, Vol. VI (1962); Morris E. Opler and R. D. Singh, "The Division of Labour in an Indian Village," in Carleton Coon, ed., *A Reader in General Anthropology* (New York, Henry Holt, 1948); Oscar Lewis and Victor Barnouw, *Village Life in Northern India* (Urbana, University of Illinois Press, 1958); D. N. Majumdar, *Caste and Communication in an Indian Village* (Bombay, Asia Publishing House, 1958); K. Ishwaran, *Tradition and Economy in Village India* (London, Routledge and Kegan Paul, 1966); Henry Orenstein, *Gaon* (Princeton, Princeton University Press, 1966); see also Pauline Mahar Kolenda, "Toward a Model of the Hindu Jajmāni System," *Human Organization*, Vol. XXII, No. 1 (1963).

subdivided and their services shared pattiwise. The functionary castes within a patti were further subdivided into individual shares of zamindār families. Chamārs served as plowmen, the cultivating castes were tenants, the merchants paid house tax, and the service castes attended to the Rajput zamindār families in various capacities. In return each caste or occupational group was paid grains by the Rajputs, but often rent-free land was also allotted for cultivation. Usually, landlords gave some extra land apart from that as jajmāni payment; this used to be on oral tenure, on which rent was claimed. As jajmāns, if Rajputs were dissatisfied, they used to threaten the withdrawal of this additional land. Seldom did they withdraw land given in lieu of the jajmāni services, however, because of the scarcity of service castes and partly because these castes were well organized through caste panchāyats. Moreover, within the village itself each patti of Rajputs formed a faction which was too ready to help the service castes from another patti in escaping the retribution of its zamindārs.

A traditional rivalry between the Rajputs of the eastern and western pattis has existed. Originally, the property shares of both pattis were equal, that is, eight annas in a rupee each; but in a famine, when the Rajputs of the eastern patti were in difficulty, the western patti purchased two annas of their share and since then rivalry and animosity have existed between the two pattis. Moreover, up until 1953 the western patti consisted of only one family; therefore it was more prosperous and this, too, has been a cause for envy among the Rajputs of the eastern patti. Taking advantage of the inter-patti rivalries, tenants often crossed over from one patti to another, which was a major source of litigation or dispute in the past.

These factions and rivalries served as dynamic and counterbalancing forces in the social equilibrium of Chanukhera under the system of zamindāri. Each patti of Rajputs had a patti panchāyat consisting of zamindār heads of various households and the leaders of various tenant castes belonging to the patti. This panchāyat took decisions on matters pertaining to the tenant-zamindār relationship as well as inter-patti and inter-household problems among Rajputs. The jajmāni relations were, therefore, double-faceted: first, the relationship was class-dominated, especially where it referred to zamindārs as jajmāns and service castes as kāmins. The class relations even in this case were not purely secular, since there were many aspects of relationships which were particularistic and bound by noneconomic and quasi-ritualistic obligations. Many ceremonial forms of gift-payments were common between the zamindārs and the service castes and tenants. The element of domination, however, persisted in the intercaste relationship owing to the economic strength of zamindārs, and thus aspects of class exploitation were introduced into this pattern of relationship.

The second facet of the jajmāni relationship was reciprocity, particularly in the form the relationship took among the non-zamindār castes. At this level, definite rules of reciprocity for the mode of payment, as well as with regard to service obligations, prevailed. In case of conflict in this sphere, the caste panchāyat used to intervene; failing that, the panchāyats of the respective pattis arbitrated.

Today, the major class groups in order of the influence or power they command in the village are: the farmers or the supervisory cultivators, the merchants, the cultivators, and the landless laborers. The average farmholding of a Rajput farmer is 25.0 acres; for the Brāhmans it is only 2.4 acres. There are ten families of Rajputs with landownership of more than 20 acres and two families of Brāhmans having a landholding of more than 7 acres (one family has 7.3 and the other 10.2 acres). Both Rajputs and Brāhmans do supervisory farming, since tilling of the soil with a plow is considered to be sinful by them. Only four families of merchants are well-to-do (with monthly incomes of more than four hundred rupees); others live just above the subsistence level. Unlike other groups, however, merchants are more mobile and have greater initiative. The average landholding of cultivators is 2.1 acres; only three cultivators have a holding of eight to nine acres. The agricultural laborers, too, have some land in their possession, but on an average it is less than 0.5 acre per family; they, of course, cultivate some additional land as sharecroppers but on the whole most of them are still engaged in labor and depend upon wage earnings.

These four classes represent distinctive economic interests, which also to a great extent are mutually oppositional. Historically speaking, a long tradition of conflicts between farmers or ex-zamindārs on the one hand and cultivators and laborers on the other has existed. The bases of these conflicts were agrarian and political. In the existing class hierarchy, Rajputs are on the top of the scale of economic power, social influence and prestige. Education and literacy are highest among them. Next to Rajputs are the two households of Brāhman farmers. Brāhmans, too, are advanced in education and social awareness. Most agricultural innovations, such as the sinking of tube wells, the use of tractors, and modern plows, and the use of improved varieties of seeds and fertilizers, have been introduced either by Rajputs or by Brāhmans. In contrast to them, the standard of literacy and the motivation for new enterprises are less strong among the small-size cultivators. Much of this is due to their economic handicaps, which perpetuate the vicious cycle of their backwardness. Merchants, on the other hand, are more progressive and mobile. Twenty of their families, which were not doing well in this village, left between 1955 and 1965 for Nepal, where business prospects appeared better. Many of the remaining merchants have left their traditional street and have built shops on the outskirts of the village along the side of the road running to Nepal. Their motivation for enterprise seems to be stronger. In political matters, merchants have always played a neutral role and have rarely come into conflict with the Rajputs. The highly politicized groups in this regard are the ex-tenants and the untouchable laborers.

FAMILY STRUCTURE

Various regional studies have revealed a diversity of patterns in rural family structures.[5] The pattern of family differs on the basis of the caste and class levels of groups. Joint families are more predominant at the upper levels of caste and class than at the lower levels, where the frequency is of the nuclear types of families. Generally, the ideals of the joint family persist and are reinforced by the continuity of its traditional

[5] Morrison's study of Badalpur village in Maharashtra shows a predominance of nuclear families (552 out of 641). See A. Morrison, "Family Type in Badalpur: An Analysis of a Changing Institution in Maharashtra," *Sociological Bulletin*, Vol. VIII, No. 2 (1959). I. P. Desai associates "jointness" of families not so much with co-residence or commensality as with property interests and functional ties. See I. P. Desai, "The Joint Family in India: An Analysis," *Sociological Bulletin*, Vol. IV, No. 2 (1956). Kapadia writes: "The general presumption is that people in cities and big towns live in nuclear families and that towns and cities have disintegrative influence on the structure of family . . . . this assumption does not hold good for Navasari." K. M. Kapadia, "Rural Family Patterns: A Study in Urban Rural Relations," *Sociological Bulletin*, V, No. 2 (1956), 115.

normative themes through myths, legends, and epic stories perpetuated by the oral and *shāshtric* traditions. Some myths of the Hindu tradition have served as ideal patterns for family life. The idealized themes of family in the village are: (1) authoritarianism and high masculinism; (2) positive evaluation of age-hierarchical relations; (3) emphasis on horizontal spread of solidarity based on kinship ties; and (4) idealization of family jointness in terms of traditional honor and prestige. Each of these themes leads to many subsidiary norms; for instance, emphasis on masculinism leads to preference for male issue, low status of daughter in the family, low status of women and their subordination to males, segregation of females from a greater part of the cultural life of males, and development of a separate subculture of women in the rural society. Similarly, the other normative themes are also interlinked with a number of subsidiary norms. The expectation of conformity to these normative themes varies on the basis of caste affiliations, the conformity to them being highest among the upper castes and lowest among the untouchable and lower castes. However, the pattern exists as an ideal to be emulated by all groups if the existential situations permitted.

In Chanukhera we find a predominance of joint families among the upper castes (Rajputs, Brāhmans, and Banias) and among the intermediate castes (Kurmis, Āhirs, Muraos, etc.); the upper castes have joint families in 36.37 per cent of the cases, semi-joint families in 41.56 per cent of the cases, and nuclear families in only 22.83 per cent of the cases. Similarly, the cultivating and intermediate castes have joint families in 45.00 per cent of the cases, semi-joint families in 25.83 per cent of the cases, and nuclear families in 29.17 per cent of the cases. The structure of family among the lower (untouchable) castes is just the opposite of the pattern found among the upper and intermediate castes. In their case, 54.84 per cent of the families are of the nuclear type, 29.03 per cent are of the semi-joint type, and only 16.13 per cent are fully joint. The pattern among the Muslims tends to be closer to the lower castes than to the upper. Of their total families, 34.43 per cent are nuclear, 39.34 per cent are semi-joint, and only 26.23 per cent are fully joint.

Evidently, as we pass from the upper castes and classes to those in the lower hierarchy, we find a weakening in conformity to the traditional family ideal. The upper castes have the maximum number of joint families, presumably because they have the maximum number of cases of joint ownership and wealth and property. Their historical tradition also helps in the perpetuation of the joint family pattern.

Joint and semi-joint families are also common among the intermediate castes. In their case, too, the agricultural occupation and landholdings seem to sustain the motivation for jointness. The rules of marriage and the status of women in this group are much different than in the upper castes. Both men and women work in the field and enjoy greater freedom of movement and equality of status. Widow remarriage is common; as are marriage by exchange and the custom of bride-price payment. Payment of dowry was never practiced by these castes until recently when some rich Kurmis started paying and demanding dowry at the marriage of their daughters and sons, emulating the Rajputs in this practice as a mark of prestige. In marriage patrilocal rule of residence is common, but there are also two cases of *gharjamai* or matrilocal residence among the Kahars. There is one case of polygamy in a Murao family, where the husband has two wives who live in the village and look after his land and he, himself, does business in Calcutta. He has recently purchased some land from a Rajput in the village.

The predominance of nuclear families among the lower castes may also be due to economic reasons. As these castes do not possess sufficient land and have no substantial property to hold the interest of members to the joint family norm, the young behave more independently and break away from the parental family authority at the slightest provocation. Women, too, are independent; they leave one husband to live with another if they are not treated properly or if their marital life is not happy. Authority system within the family in these cases is rather equalitarian and presents a distinct contrast to the pattern found among the upper castes. Child marriage is still prevalent among the lower castes. Marriage by elopement is also accepted, after a feast is given to the elders of the *birādāri*, or the extended kin group of the husband, through the caste panchāyat.

Village exogamy is a norm in marital choices of all the Hindu castes. Muslims, on the other hand, do marry within the village. However, they follow the norm common in the rest of the village and marry within the village under rare circumstances' only. Most of them also live in joint and semi-joint families.

POWER STRUCTURE

The administration of the village is run by a village panchāyat, which has an elected executive committee consisting of the village president, vice-president, and twenty-eight members. The key office is the presidentship, which is held by an ex-zamindār Rajput. He is about forty and a member of the dominant faction of Rajputs. His election to this office was, however, unanimous. The panchāyat system was established formally in 1949 by a legislative act to replace the system of administrative control during the period of zamindāri. Zamindāri was subsequently abolished in 1950. There have been three elections of this new panchāyat, one each in 1949, 1953, and 1962. Rajputs were completely out of power in the panchāyats of 1949 and 1953. In both these elections, a Brāhman leader associated with the Congress movement, about whom mention has been made earlier, led the panchāyat. He was a leader of the ex-tenants, who were solidly supporting him against the Rajputs.

The present Rajput domination, after a lapse of power for about a decade, has resulted from the economic vulnerability of the ex-tenants and the successful maneuvering of the situation by the Rajputs. It has come about after a long-drawn period of conflict, but the present reconciliation, though in some respects coercive, was achieved smoothly. As we have mentioned earlier, seeds of conflict in the village were sown in 1936-37 with the growth of a Congress leadership supported by three Muslims, three Chamārs and one Āhir and Brāhman each. The Brāhman who owns a substantial farm and teaches in a secondary school, was the leader of this whole movement. The Rajput zamindārs were opposed to the Congress for two reasons: (1) The Congress was mobilizing tenants for agrarian reforms, and advocated the abolition of begār (forced labor), the payment of low wages to persons working on the zamindār's farm, and permanent tenancy rights on sharecropped land and on land held under tenancy at will, which were sources of power to zamindārs. (2) All Rajputs with the exception of one family were members of the Aman Sabhā (committee for peace), an organization created by the British government that violently opposed the struggle for independence.

These differences polarized the tenants and zamindārs into two opposite groups in the arena of power politics of the village. The conflict in one form or another continued until 1955-56 and finally subsided only in 1962, with the unanimous election of a Rajput and ex-zamindār as the village president. What happened in between this period offers a meaningful case study in the dynamics of rural power structure.

A series of conflicts took place between 1937 and 1956, each one having its basis in the agrarian movement and tensions resulting from tenant-zamindār relations. Curiously, these conflicts united the Rajputs of both pattis irrespective of their factional animosities. Similarly, they also united all other castes simply on the basis of their being tenants. These various conflicts could be classified according to the following types: (1) between service castes and zamindārs for better wages; (2) between Brāhman leaders and zamindārs on account of land disputes and political differences; (3) between tenants and zamindārs during correction of land records; (4) between ex-tenants and ex-zamindārs on the election issues; (5) between the same parties on the issue of consolidation of landholdings.

A brief account of these conflicts in a chronological sequence follows. In 1937, just after establishment of the Congress office in the village, a Kahar family, working as domestic servants in the household of a zamindār of the eastern patti, refused to work unless, in addition to the existing land of 1.6 acres, they were granted more land or salary. The zamindār tried to put pressure on the Kahar but failed because of the unity of all other service castes. The same year, a Chamār plowman of the western patti also demanded more wages and in this case, too, succeeded in getting an increase after a few days of hartāl (strike). Two similar cases of tensions between the Chamārs and Rajputs also took place in 1938. In 1939 a conflict ensued between the Brāhman leader (Congress worker) and his zamindār, since the latter, angered by the political activism of the Brāhman, withdrew the land he had given him for sharecropping. The Brāhman, however, forcibly occupied this land, which led to a protracted litigation between the two parties.

These conflicts only prepared the grounds for more organized and large-scale conflicts between tenants and zamindārs later during the Land Records Operations in 1945 and 1947. These operations were meant to correct ownership rights to land; during the course of the operations, revenue officials checked from plot to plot and entered the names of those who claimed ownership on the basis of oral witnesses on the spot. So it was easy for any united group to contest the ownership of zamindārs to the land cultivated or possessed by the group. This was done quite thoroughly by the tenants in 1945 when they claimed about 100 acres of Rajput land. For every case of contested ownership, zamindārs had to bring suits to protect their rights. Since the tenants were well united, it was difficult for zamindārs to find witnesses in support of their rights except from among themselves, which they did. Following this movement, 108 law suits were registered; only three suits had tenants as both the contesting parties; in the rest, the concerned parties were the zamindārs and the tenants. Of these 108 suits, tenants won in 53, and in this manner about 20 acres of land passed from the zamindārs to the tenants. In 1947 the same pattern was repeated, but this time, since the zamindārs were also prepared, out of 52 claims, tenants could win in only 18 cases.

The panchāyat elections of 1949 and 1953 were held under the shadow of these conflicts. In both elections zamindārs tried to capture office but failed. The new panchāyats were entrusted with many responsibilities which were of deep concern to the zamindārs. Panchāyats could levy taxes, auction common pastures and ponds, and report cases of sharecropping and oral tenancy for formal land records; in addition, they held the responsibility for all improvement works in the village. All applications for government loans were to be forwarded through the president of the village panchāyat. Hence, the Rajputs were keen to have control over this organization.

But as their attempts to control the village panchāyat failed, they adopted the tactics of foiling the work of the panchāyat; they would not pay the taxes and levies imposed by the new panchāyat; they refused to contribute for the improvement of roads; rather, they fanned or created disaffection among the ex-tenants by exploiting the interfaction and interstreet rivalries. Most of all, they involved about seven key persons from the ex-tenant group in false law suits and victimized many others by refusing them land for sharecropping. They offered economic patronage only to those who supported them in various maneuvers for securing power. The economic disparities between the Rajputs and the non-Rajputs being great indeed, these economic sanctions had a telling effect on the morale of the ex-tenants. Nevertheless, until 1956 ex-tenants resisted the pressures exercised by the zamindārs.

In 1956 another land reform, consolidation of landholdings, took place in Chanukhera. Once again the ex-tenants planned to take advantage of the correction of land records, which preceded the actual consolidation. This time, however, false claims were made on the holdings of each other by both the ex-zamindārs and the ex-tenants. This deterred many ex-tenants from bringing forward false claims. Also this time the ex-tenants as well as the Rajputs were sufficiently divided among themselves. Each one of them was anxious to secure better plots through consolidation. Most benefits, however, accrued to the zamindārs, since they had the biggest holdings in the village.

The failure of ex-tenants to secure benefits through consolidation, and simultaneously the division that this caused among both Rajputs and non-Rajputs, changed the form of intergroup relationship in the village. Between 1956 and 1962 (when the village unanimously elected a Rajput as the president of the village panchāyat) the populistic orientation of the ex-tenants had considerably subsided. The Rajputs, too, had by then realized the need for a redefinition of their scale of values and expectations. The years of conflict had disrupted the equilibrium of the economic and cultural life of the village. Rāma Līla, Moharrum, Holi, and a host of other festivals, which in the past were jointly organized with the good will of all, had, during the interim period, deteriorated and were being used for factional ends. Many ex-tenants were suffering losses because they were not given land for sharecropping or on oral tenancy.

To sum up, the causes of these changes were: (1) a redefinition of the expectations and aspirations of the ex-tenants and ex-zamindārs in view of the changes in the social situation; (2) failure of the populistic movement of the ex-tenants due to the lack of economic power; (3) absence of external (Congress Party or other political groups) help to the ex-tenants and their consequent apathy toward further conflicts; (4) failure both of the abolition of zamindāri and of the ceiling on land-holdings, as measures of land reform, to bring about a radical improvement in the economic and social status of the ex-tenants; and finally (5) continued economic and social superiority of the Rajput ex-zamindārs.

CULTURAL STRUCTURE

Hinduism and Islam are the two cultural streams which flow side by side in the life of Chanukhera. Over the centuries, both have interacted and formed a blend which is clearly evident in the cultural practices and beliefs of the two communities. The important rituals and festivals of the 243 Muslims, who belong to the Sunni sect of Islam, are Moharrum, Meelad, Giarahwin Shaif, Shabe-barat, Ramzan, and Id. Among the important Hindu festivals are Rāma Navami, Krishna Ashtami, Deepāvali, Dasehra, and Holi. Apart from these a number of other festivals also are celebrated. Among the Muslim festivals, Moharrum is celebrated by both the low and intermediate caste Hindus. A fair is held on this day in the village and *tazias* (paper models of coffins) are displayed and ceremoniously buried in the memory of Hassan and Hussain, the two brave descendants of Prophet Mohammed (A.D. 680). Some twenty years ago even the Rajputs and Brāhmans used to make tazias, but since a conflict between Muslims and Rajputs in 1943, in connection with the land for *karbala* (where tazias are buried), they gave up this custom; they still, however, patronize this festival by helping Muslims celebrate it. Other Muslim rituals are not shared by the Hindus, since they have to do with Islamic religious beliefs. Among the major Hindu festivals, Muslims participate in Dasehra, Holi, and Deepāvali. During the period of zamindāri, Muslims, too, presented gifts to the Rajput zamindārs on Dasehra; now they only help in the organization of the Rāma Līla (a religious dance-drama) enacted on this occasion. They also decorate their shops for this festival and help in making the paper effigy of the demon king Rāvana, which is burnt at the conclusion of the Rāma Līla. During Holi, a festival of colors at the dawn of spring, many Muslims visit their Hindu friends and participate in color ceremonies. In Deepāvali, a festival of lights, Muslims also decorate their shops with lights. Despite these interactions, Muslims do maintain a distinct culture of their own. They have a mosque located in their street and hold most of their cultural and religious functions there.

On Rāma Navami, the birthdate of the god Rāma, and Krishna Ashtami, the birthdate of the god Krishna, two major dance-dramas on the adventures of these heroes are celebrated; they are Rāma Līla and Kamsa Vadha, which are major sources of recreation for the village folk. The Kamsa Vadha drama is played during the month of Shrāvana (July-August) and Rāma Līla in the month of Chaitra (March-April). Both dance-dramas are connected with legends from the Hindu epics and are enacted by Brāhman actors, since the roles are often those of gods and deities. These roles being sacred, lower castes are not supposed to play them. Holi is a highly equalitarian and joyful festival in which everyone participates without much distinction of traditional status. All indulge in revelries and throw colored dust on one another. Finally, sweets and food are distributed. Deepāvali is celebrated by all Hindus with a display of lights, but it has a special significance for the Banias, who worship the goddess of wealth, Lakshmi, on this day. Similarly, Dasehra is a special festival for Rajputs, who attach martial significance to it and spend the day in worshiping weapons and the family deity.

The lower and untouchable castes celebrate these festivals but keep a discreet distance from the upper castes. They receive gifts on the occasion of these festivals from their upper-caste patrons. One difference between upper- and lower-caste ceremonial practices is that, apart from the above shāshtric or Hindu calendric festivals, the lower-caste Hindus also have some ceremonies and rituals connected with the worship of ghosts and spirits. The Chamārs and Helas worship Bhairon and Nat (an evil spirit) and practice many magico-religious rituals. Once or twice a year these spirits reveal themselves by possessing individuals of these castes. One Hela and one Chamār are known for being such mediums, and when they are possessed, the men and women from their castes offer them drinks and victuals and in return receive omens. In the past, these omens carried great sanctions with them. Now, with the people's growing faith in modern medicines and the control of diseases such as cholera, malaria, and plague, through modern medical means, the omens of the mediums carry much less sanction for the villagers, and there are many in the village who look at this spectacle with unbelieving amusement.

Despite these changes, the belief in the traditional values of karma, rebirth, and moksha and the sacerdotal character of all beings still persists. The various life-cycle rituals (samskārās) are strictly performed by all Hindus. Yet, there are changes taking place. A Brāhman priest has given up the traditional calling; he holds a university degree, is highly politicized, and teaches in a secondary school. Other Brāhmans no longer send their promising sons to traditional pāthashālas or religious seminaries but to modern schools, colleges, and universities. These college-educated youths look down upon the traditional priestly occupation and covet professional and white-collar jobs. Slowly, changes are also taking place in other values of the people, especially those related to the concepts of pollution and purity and the outlook toward modern education and science. In due course, a new equilibrium of the value system might emerge through a synthesis between the new and the old values.

ELEMENTS OF PERSISTENCE IN THE SYSTEM

Major changes have taken place in the social and cultural life of Chanukhera. Nevertheless, many traditional forms of relationships and values continue. The changes may be analyzed, as Linton suggested, through the logic of the "cores" and "the fluid zones" of cultural forms and their structural interlinkages. Making a distinction between the folk and modern culture on this basis, Linton writes:

The difference between folk cultures and modern civilizations or between genuine and spurious cultures, as Sapir calls them, is primarily a matter of the proportion which the core of Universals and Specialities bears to the fluid zone of Alternatives. Folk cultures are borne by small, closely integrated social units which have already worked out satisfactory mutual adjustments. In such cultures, new items are not appearing with any great frequency and the society has plenty of time to test them and to assimilate them to its pre-existing patterns. In such cultures the core constitutes almost the whole.[6]

In our context, the above formulation of Linton's may be accepted with two qualifying statements: first, that the village constitutes a "part culture"; second, that the "core" of its cultural tradition is institutionalized as an extension of the Great Traditions, primarily the Hindu, sometimes the Muslim, Christian, and other traditions. In Chanukhera, we find two major cultural-religious traditions interacting and persisting together, the major Hindu tradition and the minor Muslim tradition.

Elements of persistence may be found in the institutional ramifications of both traditions. Intercaste distance and conformity to caste or subcaste norms persist among Hindus as well as among Muslims. All the major caste rituals are observed. Pollution as a value frame of the caste system still persists. Despite the fact that untouchability is now an offense by law, it is observed and the untouchables acquiesce in it, if not willingly, yet with indifference. The functioning of the caste system shows a great degree of persistence in respect of the connubial and kinship norms and regulations. Occupational and jajmāni obligations associated with caste have undergone only slight modification. Persistence may also be found in the substantive nuclei of power. Rajputs continue to maintain their position as the traditional power group. The basic

[6] Ralph Linton, *The Study of Man* (New York, Appleton-Century, 1936), p. 283.

economy of the village remains subsistence-oriented and continues to be dominated by the ex-zamindārs.

Traditional patterns also persist in the form and functioning of the family system. Extended and semi-joint families are common among the upper and intermediate castes. This form of family is the most predominant in the village. In six cases, where people have migrated to cities with their nuclear families, they invariably maintain functional links with the traditional joint family; they visit it regularly, contribute financially for agricultural development or purchase of land, and consult as well as are consulted in marriage negotiations of their members and on other important decision-making processes. The savings made through earnings in the city often go into purchase of land, which reveals the extent to which familistic and agrarian values are dominant among the villagers. That among the lower castes there is a predominance of nuclear families and lack of familistic authoritarianism is no new phenomenon. In fact, probably owing to the exigencies of economic situations, such a family pattern among the lower castes has persisted through the Hindu tradition.

Similarly, the core values of the Hindu world view have still a hold on the psychology and behavior of the people. The themes of predestination, cosmic unity of all life, otherworldliness, and religious asceticism continue to be expounded and extolled not only by the upper castes but also by the castes in the lower hierarchy of the Hindu tradition. All these norms, however, are not quite translated into action, but they serve as ideal patterns or ideal value-themes. They provide reinforcement to the perpetuation of traditional values through fostering psychological continuity of attitudes. Although at the metaphysical level the structure of the Islamic tradition differs from the Hindu tradition, in actual life many themes or value structures prevailing among Muslims are identical to those of the Hindus.[7] This may be a result of their centuries-long

---

[7] Similarities in value themes of the Hindus and Muslims have been pointed out by many sociologists; Ishwaran writes: "The three main religious groups are the Hindus, the Jains, and the Muslims, although the last of these functions as a caste group as well. Though in matters of theology and doctrine these groups may differ, yet they are knit together into a single working system thanks to the all-pervasive Hindu outlook. Thus, one may see how all three groups resemble one another with regard to their value system and ritualistic forms." (Ishwaran, *Tradition and Economy*, p. 12.)

interaction in an identical existential situation, which has survived the forces of religious schisms and contradictions.

THE ELEMENTS OF CHANGE

Broadly speaking, the structural changes in the social system of the village have not been as profound as changes which could be called institutional, or developmental. The positional framework of the system of social stratification remains unchanged. Rajputs and a few Brāhmans continue to dominate the power structure and prestige hierarchy. Significant role differentiations and an adaptive "upgraded" institutionalization, which are the necessary preconditions for structural change, have not been much in evidence. Nevertheless, it would be a mistake to assume that the system has remained static.

The abolition of zamindāri itself has contributed to some changes in the intergroup relationships which are structural in essence. It has automatically led to the abolition of certain important roles from the village social structure. For instance, the offices of village headman (mukhia) and revenue headman (lambardār) have been abolished. The structure and mode of functioning of the panchāyat have been reorientated, rationalized, and interlinked with the national judiciary. This has brought about radical changes in the nature of the sanctions behind this institution. In this process the network of relationships of the reciprocal services group has also been uprooted to some extent. For more than a decade the Rajputs, who held power traditionally, were out of power in the village panchāyat, and even when they regained it in 1962 the return was not to the traditional-authoritarian but to a somewhat consensual-democratic pattern.

Another aspect of change is in the occupational structure. Kahars and Baris, traditionally a servant caste, have now taken to shopkeeping; the Chamār plowmen are now pulling rickshaws; goldsmiths have become vendors; and Brāhmans, supervisory farmers. These changes, though more symptomatic than statistically significant, reveal the facts of gradual diversification of occupational roles.

Even more significant than occupational changes are the changes that have taken place in the development fields. Compared to 1955, in 1965 many more children were going to schools. The number of urban migrants had gone up, communication had improved, and there were visible signs of betterment in the housing condition of the lower castes. Taking 1955 as the base year, we find that the number of boys and girls going to school doubled in 1965 and the number of urban migrants increased sixfold. The village has been electrically connected and a number of shops of Banias now have electricity. The method of cultivation has improved. Two Rajputs have tractors for cultivation; three tube wells have been constructed; chemical fertilizers are accepted by all the cultivators and farmers and are increasingly being utilized. Winnowers, chaff cutters, and meston plows are now a common sight in the households of farmers. Ten years back, about 80 per cent of the houses of Chamārs were covered with straw thatch; now about 70 per cent of them are tiled and a few also have brick walls.

Major changes have taken place in the values and attitudes of Rajputs and non-Rajputs. Now the men and women from the lower and untouchable castes openly chew betal leaves and wear chappals (sandals) and silver ornaments which they were proscribed to use in the days of zamindāri; the lower-caste men ride on bicycles openly and can use umbrellas in the presence of a Rajput, which a few decades back would not have been possible. Rajputs look at these changes with tactful indifference and always try to win the support of the non-Rajput castes. People in the village still address Rajputs with respect but the traditional attitude of servility and impotent humility has disappeared.

Many traditional festivals are now organized on a rational and collective basis. For Rāma Līla, Kansa Vadha, and Moharrum the respective communities raise subscriptions. In these festivals the use of sound amplifiers is quite common. Playing records of film music is now popular on the occasions of marriage, birth, or other joyful ceremonies and festivals. Thus, modern media of communication have been adopted for the perpetuation of traditional ways of life.

The nature of withdrawal from or commitment to tradition is not identical for the Brāhmans and Rajputs; on the contrary, in some respects the two are in contradistinction. Thirty years ago Rajputs were more modernized; they invited British officers for hunting parties; they used to play tennis and had a tennis court built in the village; they also possessed motor cars and wore Western-style dress. Now Rajputs have given up their attachment to Western clothes and a Western way of life. On the contrary, they profess overcommitment to the traditional Indian values and rationalize their loss after the abolition of zamindāri in terms of traditional doctrines of karma or destiny. Most of them support Jana Sangha, a tradition-oriented political party. Brāhmans, on the other hand, are rapidly westernizing. With increasing prosperity and education, they tend to develop apathy toward their traditional callings.

In the sphere of values, an important change has taken place with regard to magico-religious beliefs, which have declined. Traditional medicine men or *ojhas* are still consulted for illness or possession; but in most cases the villagers' first choice now is a medical doctor and a dispensary, and only in the second place are medicine men consulted.

To sum up: Chanukhera remains traditional, but the nature of traditionalism has itself undergone major changes. Behavior patterns have ceased to "continue from generation to generation" without change, as is characteristic of a traditional society.[8] People's attitudes toward work and nature are changing. Motivation for acceptance of development innovations is high. Persistent jolts that intergroup relations have received through class conflicts have also weakened, if not abolished, the hold of authoritarian-hierarchical values on the pattern of social relationships. The relatively closed social structure of the village is gradually being rendered more open to the inflow of new values and opportunities and may well be on the path to rapid change if existential factors do not controvert the process.

ANALYSIS

In conceptual terms, innovation and diffusion are the two basic "prime movers" toward social change in the village. The initial diffusion was of the new values of nationalism and populistic-agrarianism, and the first innovators of this order of values were the peasant leaders. It may be noted that the populistic leadership was headed by a Brāhman who had traditionally been an ally of Rajputs. The Rajputs themselves were self-alienated from this movement owing to their class interest. Hence they served as an anti-force to resist the movement, not because it was

---

[8] Everett E. Hagen, *On the Theory of Social Change* (Homewood, Ill., The Dorsey Press, 1962), p. 55.

nationalistic but because it was antifeudal and egalitarian. In other regions, where the nationalistic movement did not immediately threaten the interests of zamindārs, they supported the freedom movement.

An immediate consequence of this phenomenon was the growth of a new class solidarity, a "horizontal cleavage" in the social structure.[9] The horizontal solidarity of class was, however, superimposed on the horizontal solidarity of caste, which preexisted in the social structure. The solidarity of class resulted from a temporary and partial coalescence of intercaste vertical cleavages, as well as from horizontal solidarity of individual castes. Class solidarity was, however, not stable, since it was oriented to economic issues and was dependent on the support of cultural-political movements external to the system. Consequently, it withered away whenever the external variables were not in existence, such as Congress support and land reforms. The horizontal caste solidarity has, in contrast, been more stable, being integrated with kinship and marriage ties. The fact may, however, be noted that major upheavals and readaptations in the social system of the village have followed from the spasmodic character of class conflicts (as a form of horizontal cleavage in the social structure) rather than from caste solidarity, which at no stage operated as a political force. This calls for a review of the significance attached to caste as an analytical category for the explanation of social change.

At the vertical level, too, many change-producing processes have been observed. The Rajput "model" of culture is being emulated by lower castes following a change in their economic and existential situation. But such emulation or imitation is a consequence rather than a cause of change. Most of the changes (payment of dowry, betel chewing, use of ornaments, etc.) are not sacerdotal in character. On the other hand, a few of the emulated customs resemble "conspicuous consumption," for the intermediate and lower castes are imitating the Rajputs (ex-zamindārs), formerly almost a "leisure class"!

[9] A distinction between vertical and horizontal cleavages is drawn by Julian H. Steward in the following words: "There are two principal types of socio-cultural segments. First, there are locally distinctive segments, such as communities, rural neighborhoods and ethnic minorities, which may be considered vertical cleavages within the larger society. Second, there are horizontal cleavages, which separate segments following occupational or class lines and in some cultures, caste lines. These may cross-cut local cleavages." Julian H. Steward, *Theory of Culture Change* (Urbana, University of Illinois Press, 1955), p. 66.

In the case of the Rajputs, the traditional rural elites, we observe a regressive process of cultural change toward "traditionalization" and away from "modernization" or "westernization." This reveals the limitation of continuum models in the study and analysis of social change, and calls for the use of historical and ideal-typical models for the understanding of change in all its ramifications and trends. Formulation of the processes of change in terms of dichotomies implies a type of conceptualization which may not be truly diachronic. Moreover, such models have all the limitations of a "contextual" rather than a historical approach to social change. Assuming that continuum models recognize the possibilities of evolutionary changes, their inherent bias for unilinearism renders them methodologically weak.[10] The view that change may always proceed from a stage of traditional society toward modernization or westernization may often be oversimplistic or even historically false. In many new nations in Asia and Africa, changes are not only nonunilinear but show trends toward rejection of Western cultural styles and symbolisms. It should also be possible to account for such regressive phases in the process of change and modernization in a conceptualization of change. There are breakdowns in modernization itself which must be explainable through such categories.

This necessitates analysis of the theoretical significance of the concept of "levels" in the understanding of social change. In this context Abraham Edel writes:

The concept of levels, which was sharpened primarily in evolutionary philosophies, refers initially to the emergence of qualities in the process of historical development. . . . Philosophically, the concept of levels involves the idea of some continuity of the new with the old, a maturing causal process which constitutes the emerging, a field of novel distinctive qualities with some order of its own (hence an element of discontinuity with the past), some degree of alteration in the total scene and its modes of operation because of the new. *Methodologically, a new level requires new descriptive concepts and, many believe, new empirical laws, independent of the old level.*[11]

Thus, in the analysis of social change, the concept of levels should introduce a dynamic-historical element, since this model is adapted to the description of social process in the setting of both historical indi-

---

[10] *Ibid.*, Chapter 1, pp. 11-29.
[11] Abraham Edel, "The Concept of Levels in Social Theory," in Llewellyn Gross, ed., *Sociological Theory* (Evanston, Ill., Row, Peterson and Co., 1959), p. 197.

viduality and integrative cumulative qualities. Continuum models, on the other hand, turn out to be less viable as explanatory categories of change, and in reality their significance as diachronic models may also be doubtful. Moreover, most of the continuum models take a consensual view of society and put undue emphasis on the process of acculturative diffusion. Elements of conflict and intergroup contradictions of material and existential interests—in other words, structural dilemmas of change —are not taken into consideration. The approach tends to be *culturological* rather than *sociological*.

The primacy of values or ideas as symptomatic indices of change, which continuum models emphasize, cannot be doubted, but what is needed is an addition of motivation in such processes of change. Emphasis should shift from "what is being emulated" to "why it is being emulated." This would lead us to the study of change in the context of differential existential situations of various classes and other social categories; it would also lead to emphasis on historicity of the individual contexts of change.

STEPHEN A. TYLER

Koya Social Organization:
Change and Persistence
in Andhra Pradesh

ONE METHOD FOR THE study of persistence and change begins with an assumed or demonstrated base-line description of some system. This description is then compared point for point with another description of the same system made at some subsequent time. These two descriptions are then united by a statement of the "directional" processes responsible for bringing about the differences between the system at time one and time two.[1]

Basically simple as this program is, it is difficult to employ. Reliable base-line descriptions are rare, the units of the system may no longer be coordinate, or the boundaries of the system may be so altered that it is almost impossible to demonstrate a relation between the two descriptions. Even more troublesome is the whole problem of process. Concrete data on the processes involved are often lacking and are usually only inferential. It is frequently difficult to isolate sequences of different processes where one process follows as a result of some other process and then by feedback influences the direction and force of the original process.

Despite these difficulties, it will be the purpose of this paper to analyze some of the characteristics of change and persistence among the Koyas of Bhadrāchallam tālūk, Andhra Pradesh, India, using this basic model.[2] The paper consists of two parts: (1) a reconstruction of Koya society prior to 1800; (2) an analysis of processes which have created

Stephen A. Tyler is Associate Professor of Anthropology at Tulane University.

[1] E. Z. Vogt, "On the Concepts of Structure and Process in Cultural Anthropology," *American Anthropologist,* LXII (1960), 19-22.

[2] Data for this paper are derived from fieldwork carried out in India during 1962-63. Field research was supported by a Foreign Area Training Fellowship granted by the Ford Foundation.

changes in that system. The theoretically more interesting problem of persistence is left unanalyzed. A feeble explanation for some of the persisting elements in Koya society is the general idea of the functional linkage between elements in the structure. Given a particular process of change, only those elements most directly affected by the process are subject to change. Those elements most intimately tied by a functional linkage to the initially affected elements are subsequently influenced, and so on. In this view, the "ordering" of relations between analytic elements in a structure is assumed to be the crucial factor in the explanation of both persistence and change.[3] Thus, for example, Koya clan and sib ceremonies persist because there is only a weak partial ordering of relations between the clan and sib and the processes of ecological adaptation and population development. On the other hand, ceremonies associated with the cycle of shifting cultivation have disappeared or been modified owing to the strict ordering of relations between these ceremonies and the processes of ecological adaptation and population development.

Since adequate base-line data do not exist for pre-1800 Koya social organization, I have attempted to reconstruct this organization on the basis of data derived from mythologies, scanty historical sources, variations occurring in present-day Koya society, and conjecture. The methods, data, and explicit techniques on which this reconstruction is made are left implicit. Consequently, much of the reconstruction can be taken only as conjectural history. I am not concerned about this for three reasons: (1) conjectural history is better than no history; (2) in a longer paper I am confident that most of the data, procedures, etc., could be made explicit; (3) such a conjectural history has a useful heuristic purpose, functioning in much the same way as any ideal type construct. On this last point, I would even argue that a conjectural history can be superior to the type construct if it is closer to the known empirical facts of the system.[4]

One further caveat should be entered. I have talked of changes in the structure of a system, and this is somewhat misleading, for with the

---

[3] Cf. S. F. Nadel, *The Theory of Social Structure* (Glencoe, Ill., The Free Press, 1957), pp. 63-96.

[4] F. G. Bailey, *Caste, Tribe and Nation* (Manchester, Manchester University Press, 1963), advances a reconstruction for the Kui similar in many ways to the one given here for the Koyas. The Koyas and the Kui are linguistically and culturally related. The major point of difference in the two reconstructions concerns the nature of large territorial groupings.

exception of the problem of tribal integration and the structure of authority relations in the village, most of my data pertain only to rather simple aspects of structure, for example, the presence, absence, and complexity of structural elements. The basic structural problem of the ordering of relations among these elements has been left relatively untouched. Thus, it is conceivable that no real structural change has occurred, for the same ordering of relations may occur between elements which appear to be totally different from, or more complex than, those of some other system.[5] A case in point is the structure of authority relations in the village. Despite the much greater complexity of present-day Koya villages, it is doubtful that there has been any substantial change in the structure of authority relations simply because the same kind of orderings occur now as in the earlier system.

KOYA SOCIETY

HABITAT

The Koyas occupy a 200-by-40-mile stretch of land on either side of the Godāvari River in Andhra Pradesh and Madhya Pradesh. This area is a wide alluvial plain of fertile soil which gradually slopes away from the river to hills ranging from 200 to 4,000 feet above sea level. Coursing down from the surrounding hills and cutting through this plain at numerous points are short, swift-flowing streams which, though dry for most of the year, are impassable during the rains.

One third of this area of approximately 3,600 square miles consists of reserve forest. These are areas which have been set aside by the government of India and in which it is illegal to reside permanently. The use and exploitation of products from these forests is strictly controlled by the Forestry Department.[6] Of the more important forest plants only teak, bamboo, and ebony are exploited under license from the government by Hindu timber merchants and Koyas. The harvested timber is floated 200 to 300 miles down the Godāvari to the saw mills and paper mills in Rajahmundry.

[5] Cf. A. F. C. Wallace, *Culture and Personality* (New York, Random House, 1961), pp. 29-41.
[6] K. N. K. Ayyar, *Gazetteer of the East Godavari District* (Madras, Superintendent, Government Press, 1935), II, 36.

A band of fluvial alluvium lies near the river, on its islands, and along its tributaries. Adjacent to this is a broad belt of light sandy soil stretching from four to ten miles to the interior of the plain and interspersed with pockets of red ferruginous and heavy black soils. Where the ground rises above the alluvial plain this light sandy soil begins to give way to a very light rocky soil or a red ferruginous variety. The latter two, with pockets of sand, heavy black soil, and alluvium, predominate on the hills and in the valleys of the remaining area.

Rainfall is usually abundant, but dependent on the monsoons, and consequently is concentrated in only a few months of the year. Beginning in late May or mid-June and lasting until August-September, the southwest monsoon provides over half of the yearly total of 43.56 inches. The northeast monsoon in October-December contributes most of the remaining moisture, with scattered showers in April and May providing the remainder. Scattered cyclonic storms sometimes occur in February or March, and heavy winds usually precede each of the monsoons. During the heavy rains in June-July, floods occur and villages along the river banks occasionally have to be evacuated. During the early part of the monsoons, travel and transport are nonexistent.[7]

Popularly, the seasons are divided into the hot weather (April-June), the rains (June-November), and the cold weather (December-February). Daily temperature readings for these seasons indicated an average high of 89 degrees (Fahrenheit) during the day and a low of 41 degrees at night for the cold weather; a high of 105 degrees during the day and a low of 93 degrees at night during the hot weather; and a high of 96 degrees during the day (broken by showers) with a low of 82 degrees at night during the rains. The highest temperature recorded was 121 degrees in the hot weather and the low of 34 degrees during the cold season.

Within the area, communications are poor. There is only one major road paralleling the river for about 150 miles, but it lacks bridges across most of the Godāvari tributaries and is practically unusable when it rains. Above the Dummagudem locks, the river is useless for navigation from December to June, and during June and part of July is extremely dangerous for small boats. Accessibility from other areas is limited by the fact that the Godāvari is unbridged and no major road cuts through the chain of hills on the north bank to connect it with Central India. There are,

[7] *Ibid.*, p. 284.

however, numerous cart trails cutting through the hills and surrounding jungle.

Perhaps even more significant in isolating the area is its bad reputation. It is regarded as a center for endemic malaria; its forests are reputed to abound with man-eating tigers and its houses and fields with poisonous snakes. There is some justification for these fears. Malaria is endemic, cholera frequently assumes epidemic status, smallpox is frequent, and tuberculosis, leprosy, beriberi, black-water fever, yaws, and filariasis are prevalent. In areas where water supply is poor and the inhabitants rely on shallow wells or ponds for water, the guinea worm thrives. In addition, there are a host of minor irritants ranging from the "itch" to dysentery. Recently, these diseases have been relieved to some extent by government sanitation and health teams, but much remains to be done.

HISTORY

The Koya habitat prior to 1500 probably did not extend into the alluvial tracts of the Godāvari valley, though scattered settlements of Koyas may have occurred. Koyas were probably largely concentrated in the hillier areas of Bastar. Koya mythology asserts that Koyas began migrating into their current habitat 200-300 years ago. To some extent this is confirmed by external sources. Genealogies of Koyas now resident in Bhadrachallam tālūk eventually go back to a lineage founder who is reputed to have migrated from a specific village in Bastar. That this is an accurate indication of migration is supported by what little historical data exist for the area.

Historically, it is known that the entire area of current Koya habitation was in the hands of the zamindārs of Albaka, Cherla, Nugur, Bejji, Chintalananda, and Bhadrachallam. In Bhadrachallam tālūk, the zamindāri belonged to Anapa Ashva Raavu, who received the grant of the estate (consisting of 137 villages originally) from the Emperor in Delhi in 1324.[8] Shortly after this there was apparently considerable population increase, since the number of villages is reported as approximately 250 by the nineteenth century when the British first began touring the area. There were even more villages than this in the area which had not yet been incorporated into the zamindāri, and these were included under the revenue settlement administered by the British. Approximately one

---

[8] H. Morris, "Descriptive and Historical Account of the Godavari District," *The Presidency of Madras* (London, Trubner, 1878), p. 42.

fourth of the villages were included in the British settlement, indicating that there were approximately 300 villages at that time. This continued growth is reflected in the figures for 1921, which indicate that there were 334 villages in Bhadrachallam tālūk.[9] Since the majority of these villages are inhabited by Koyas, this increase since the fourteenth century is probably attributable to Koya migration and subsequent population growth. These data lend strong support to the traditional origin myth of the Koyas as a group derived from an area outside their current habitat.

AGRICULTURAL METHODS

Within both that habitat and their premigration habitat, the Koyas practiced a form of swidden agriculture. An area of forest was cut down, allowed to dry, the brush stacked in windrows, and burnt. The ashes were then scattered, the soil plowed, and seeds planted. After a given field was cropped for three years it was abandoned and allowed to revert to jungle. It was not cropped again for at least seven years and more usually fifteen years.

While population density remained low, it was possible to allow the full cycle of fifteen or more years. Since a settlement might consist of as many as five extended families, this practice entailed shifting the dwellings to locations near the new fields as those located adjacent to the dwellings gradually reverted to jungle and the distance from the dwelling to the field became too great to ensure adequate protection for the crops.

It is not certain when Koyas began using plows and draft animals, but their mythology asserts that they did so before they migrated to their present habitat. Prior to this event, the soil was not tilled, but seeds were planted in the ashes with a dibbling stick.

In addition to swidden cultivation, there is some evidence to indicate that from an early period Koyas kept fairly large herds of cattle and goats, and in addition raised a few pigs for consumption. Both agriculture and animal husbandry were supplemented by hunting and gathering.

Associated with swidden agriculture was an annual cycle of agricultural ceremonies. These included rites for the village mother or earth mother, various first fruits festivals, rituals associated with selecting swidden sites, and special observances designed to protect the new crops. The religious functionaries necessary for all these ceremonies were the village

[9] Ayyar, *Gazetteer*, p. 1.

headman and village priest. Since villages consisted of agnatic relatives, the village headman and priest were the same as the lineage headman and priest.

SOCIAL ORGANIZATION

Prior to 1800 the evidence indicates that Koya villages were small, shifting settlements comprised of a single exogamous patrilineal local descent group (clan). These groups were doubtless occasionally supplemented by affinal or distant cognatic kin, but the general pattern ideologically was for a village to be composed of agnatic kin of probably no more than three generations in depth and a narrow collateral spread. These settlement groups were highly fissiparous and tended to segment readily so that clans retained a minimal size. In all likelihood, this size was just sufficient for members to trace actual genealogical relation to some known group founder. The solidarity of this group was based on annual rituals for the ancestors, cooperation in exploitation of natural resources, and defense of clan territory. Clans were also fully corporate in the sense that membership in the clan guaranteed a right to a share in the produce of the land. There was probably no organized concept of ownership in the sense of the right to alienate land. Rather, one had a right to exploit the natural resources of a given area as a function of being a member of the lineage in control of that area.

These clans were bound together by common membership in patri-sibs tracing their origin to some mythological founder or circumstance. Unlike clans, the sibs were noncorporate except in a religious sense. Each sib had its own set of sib deities who were worshiped annually in the home territory of the sib.

Each sib was also semicorporate in the sense that it had a traditional territory. Yet, all evidence indicates that sibs were not territorially organized. They consisted of dispersed segments occupying noncontiguous tracts of land. The sib territory was an ideological concept which may have reflected a real population distribution at some remote period, but which ceased to exist so long ago that details in the mythology are no longer consistent with such a distribution. Sibs probably have never functioned as jural organizations. To some extent the annual lineage festival functioned as a jural association, for the shaman had the power to divine the case of death of sib members. Should this cause have been attributable to another sib member, the elders and the sib priest could pass sentence and secure its implementation. Yet, since the festival was an annual event and it is doubtful that the whole sib ever convened at one place for it, the sib could hardly have sufficed as the only form of jural authority.

Patri-sibs were grouped into five exogamous patri-phratries. These were probably late inventions, but were certainly in existence before the Koyas migrated to Bhadrachallam tāluk. Attached to each phratry was a unique set of phratric deities. Of this set of deities each sib in a phratry was more closely associated with some subset. Since the number of deities associated with any one phratry appears to have been rather small, some lineages probably shared similar constellations of these deities. The phratry was even less of a corporate group than the sib. Even in its religious function the phratry was weak. Its members never convened at any set period for the purpose of worshiping the phratry deities. At two-year intervals, representatives of the phratry deities were carried to villages inhabited by phratry members and a special ceremony was held. The phratry was only mythologically associated with a specific territory, and the mythological founder of the phratry was given no special ceremonial significance except in the traditional tales told at the time of the sib festival.

Phratries and sibs were not united into a larger tribal framework by any specific set of officers. The ordering of intertribal relationships was not a feature of phratry organization. There were, for example, no officers recruited from each phratry to form a tribal council. Instead, tribal integration was based on a weakly connected set of overlapping marital relations. Mythologically, each phratry was linked with at least one other phratry or sib as a marriage partner. But, since phratries had so little formal organization or territorial integrity, the significance of this feature is ideological rather than organizational. The same argument applies as well to the sib. It was, then, only at the lowest level in the hierarchy that marital relations could serve as a mechanism for tribal integration.

Each clan regarded itself as linked to some other set of clans as wife-giver and wife-taker. To the extent that real cross-cousin marriage was operative, this would have resulted in a closed system of exchanges[10] among a limited set of clans and would have served only a limited integrative function. The system seems, however, to have been more open-ended than this. Exchanges certainly took place as they do now, but in

[10] Cf. C. Lévi-Strauss, Les structures élémentaires de la parenté (Paris, Presses universitaires de France, 1949), pp. 85-135.

all probability they were limited to a single instance sufficient to renew an old affinal tie. Subsequent marriages were made with other "new" clans, and old affinal ties were probably allowed to lapse as situations warranted. Consequently, even though each local clan regarded itself as affinaly related to some other set of clans, there was still room for variation. Further, local clans of the same sib did not have marital relations with the same set of affinal clans. Thus, from the point of view of any sib, there was a large number of other sibs in other phratries to which it might be related by affinal ties. The following diagram illustrates this rather loose network of intratribal ties.

The relationship of A to I, for example, is given by the sequence of interrelationships: A-B-G-F-H-I; A-C-D-F-H-I. The relationship of A to D, on the other hand, is given by the fact that they are members of the same sib and share affinal relations with clan C.

In addition to marriage and sib ceremonies, relations with other clans seem to have been largely limited to cattle lifting, territorial raids, and acquisition of captives for human sacrifice. In the earlier period these activities seem to have had no organization larger than the clan, but in later periods there seems to have been broader organization based on the village composed of more than one clan. This is an important transition, for all of the mythology indicates that raiding, warfare, and human sacrifice were aimed at affines who occupied tracts of land contiguous to one's own. Activities of this type conducted by groups comprised of individuals from various clans seem to indicate the development of some kind of formal organization, and a broader object than retaliation and harassment of affines. Unhappily, the sources provide no information on this subject.

Crosscutting categories of occupational specialization other than priests, shamans, and headmen could hardly have been a feature of Koya social organization in the period prior to 1800. There were probably no specific groups engaged solely in such occupational specialties as blacksmithing, weaving, basketmaking, oil pressing. To the extent that these occupations were existent, they were probably part-time activities carried on by some members of each isolated hamlet. The major occupation of all members of the tribe was essentially limited to swidden agriculture supplemented by hunting and gathering. The division of labor was probably based on sex and age.

There were other occupational specialists of a religious and jural nature. These would have included a shaman, a village priest, and a village headman. Not all villages had a resident shaman, but the village or clan priest and headman were undoubtedly present in every village. Even so, these specialists were only part-time, their principal occupation being agriculture. Whether such occupational specialists as bards and funeral singers were present at a very early period is dubious.

RELATIONS WITH NON-KOYAS

At no time were the Koyas ever completely isolated from other non-Koya groups. At all times they have been in contact with other tribal groups and Hindu castes. The main agents of this contact have been Hindu and Muslim merchants and government officials. There was also sporadic contact with religious mendicants and various other religious performers, but this was hardly systematic.

The pattern of weekly markets located in the foothills to which merchants bring their wares in exchange for Koya produce is probably an old one. This would imply that Koyas were more than subsistence farmers even at an early period, although the amount of grain surplus was relatively slight. The majority of trade was probably confined to such subsidiary products as turmeric, tamarind, twine, and chillies, supplemented by occasional surpluses of rice, millet, and livestock. In exchange for these items the Koyas received cloth, salt, oil, dried salted fish, bangles, and other spices and condiments.

Koya migration from Bastar was stimulated by local famine and the availability of relatively unoccupied alluvial land in the Godāvari valley. The period of Koya migration roughly coincides with a period when there was minimal political control exercised over the region by the zamindārs. The Koyas were migrating into a depopulated area which had just been devastated by one of the recurring wars between opposing zamindārs. Political control was apparently loose for a period sufficient to allow fairly large numbers of Koyas to settle in the area unopposed.

Thus, prior to 1600, the Koyas, because of their isolated and remote habitat, probably had limited contact with government officials, but as more and more Koyas settled in lowland areas, the reextension of political control over these areas by petty zamindārs increased the amount of such contact. The pattern of contact seems to have been largely exploitative. For revenue purposes, the zamindāri was divided into administrative districts (samutus) under the authority of a Koya headman (samutu dōra). It is doubtful that this administrative subdivision corresponded to a prior Koya system. It was probably imposed on the Koyas as a means of exacting revenue and servants. The administration of the area under the zamindār was carried out by the zamindār's ministers and was enforced by a mixed army of Rohillas (a military caste group), Koyas, and Mādigas (an untouchable caste). The last were primarily servants, and the Koyas were recruited for a month's service at the rate of 100 men per month. During this period of service the Koyas had to provide their own subsistence, to which there was apparently some resistance. Since the Rohillas were paid very little, they supplemented their income by looting and pillaging Koya villages on the slightest provocation. Refusal to provide the proper number of conscripts was certain to lead to coercive action from the Rohillas. Koyas apparently lived in great fear of them, and are reported as hiding their grain and wealth in caves and holes of large trees.[11]

The British arrived on the scene in the early 1800s in the form of geological surveyors. They were followed some years later by a team of engineers and Tamil laborers who constructed an anicut canal and lock at Dummagudem as part of the Godāvari navigation scheme.[12] Christian influence in the area dates from this time. The Tamil laborers were Christians and began converting the Telugus and Koyas hired to work on the anicut project. As a consequence, the Church Missionary Society began missionary activities among the Koyas and Telugus sometime in the 1860s.

After a promising early start, missionary work was not particularly successful and was largely limited to the more accessible Koya villages in Bhadrachallam tālūk. The explanation of this failure, as given by the Koyas, is that feuding began early between Mālas (an untouchable caste), Koyas, and other Hindu castes over the issue of taking communion from a common cup. The Koya church at Pedda Nallaballi was burned, the

---

[11] E. Thurston, *Castes and Tribes of Southern India* (Madras, Government Press, 1909), IV, 39.
[12] Morris, "Descriptive and Historical Account," pp. 42-46, 109-40.

Koyas blamed the Mālas, but the Mālas bribed the witnesses, and several Koyas, including my informant's father's elder brother were jailed for the crime. While they were in jail the Godāvari flooded, trapping the Koyas in the jail. Subsequently, nearly all of the Koya converts apostatized and reverted to the tribal religion. Today, the number of Koya Christians is relatively small, owing partly to this tragedy and partly to the decreased activity of the mission since its heyday in the 1900-1930 period.

From the 1860s onward, the British extended their control over the area, making a revenue settlement, establishing courts, and demarcating reserve forests. With the reservation of the forests, restrictions on swidden agriculture were imposed. Not only were the Koyas prohibited from cultivating swidden tracts in the reserve forests, but the British also attempted to discourage swidden cultivation even outside the reserve forests. This was the final blow to an already disintegrating swidden system.

CHANGE AND PERSISTENCE

As a consequence of influences encountered in their new habitat, there have been many changes in Koya social organization, yet certain patterns have persisted in almost unaltered form or have assumed new dimensions.

One of the most notable changes has been in the settlement pattern. Koya villages are now permanent semi-nucleated settlements. This seems to have been a direct result of four factors: (1) changes in the system of landholding; (2) changes in agricultural methods; (3) population growth and changes in population structure; (4) government policy.

As has been indicated previously, Koyas did not have a system of individual land "ownership." The system seems more to have been one based on the right to the produce of the land. Land rights were derivative of membership in a descent group occupying a given area. As such, land was not individually alienable. When Koya villages were incorporated into the zamindāri, they were regarded as the property of the zamindār in the sense that he had a right to a portion of the produce in the form of revenue, and a limited right of alienability. This entailed assessment of the area under cultivation and of standing crops. In itself, this system was not in direct conflict with Koya practice—with one exception. Villages which failed to pay revenue could be alienated to a tax farmer by the zamindār. In essence, this meant that Koyas became mere renters of land. Right to a share of the produce of the land was no longer a simple function of membership in a descent group. This right was now conditioned by an obligation to pay taxes and/or rent as well as other informal charges.

Obviously, such a system is predicated on the assumption that some surplus must be produced over and above the villagers' needs, and the amount of such surplus must be at least sufficient to pay the cost of its collection and hopefully realize some profit for all concerned. Consequently, Koyas must have been engaged in some form of agriculture that would be productive enough to produce a reliable surplus. It is doubtful that a system of agriculture based solely on shifting cultivation could achieve this end, and even if it could, the problems of revenue collection would be extremely difficult. Thus, the Koyas by this time were either already to some extent permanent field cultivators or were forced into settled communities by the zamindār's troops. It seems most likely that both processes were at work. But ultimately the transformation in Koya agriculture was brought about by changes in the population pattern.

The evidence is sketchy, but there appears to have been a definite increase in population in Bhadrachallam tālūk since the fourteenth century. This increase probably reflects two processes: (1) migration; (2) increases in the local population. The former represents not only the Koya migration but a countervailing migration of Hindus and Muslims from the south. Both groups were moving into an area which had been previously only sparsely populated. It may well have been that both waves of migration were encouraged by a deliberate policy of the zamindār, but concrete evidence is lacking.

The revenue figures for settlements in the Bhadrachallam area indicate that the substantial increase in villages between 1400 and 1800 could not have been entirely the result of migration. Evidently there was a period of natural population increase. It seems quite likely that this was related to a mode of production capable of supporting a larger population on the same area of land. Therefore, it is probable that the Koyas had already begun to practice permanent field agriculture where soil and water conditions were favorable.

This tendency was reinforced and accelerated by the presence of a growing non-Koya population which not only practiced permanent field agriculture but settled the land permanently, thereby alienating the richer alluvial tracts from Koya cultivation. The desertion of a field in the swidden cycle simply resulted in its being appropriated by a non-Koya cultivator who would settle permanently on the land. Since production from permanent fields, especially those under regular irrigation, is higher and more dependable than production from swidden fields, non-Koya cultivators were probably aided and abetted in this process of alienation by revenue-hungry zamindārs and their subrenters. If this process were allowed to continue along with an increasing population, the land available for swidden would gradually decrease until the swidden cycle became too short for the soil to regenerate itself or until the Koyas were left only with the poorer, rocky uplands. As a consequence, Koyas, in order to protect their richer tracts of land, were forced into permanent settlements, thus accentuating and reinforcing a pattern of change that had in all probability begun when Koyas first migrated into the area.

Associated with these changes were new agricultural methods. Not only is there a shift from swidden agriculture, but there is also a shift from basically dry-land to wet-land farming, and a consequent change in the cropping complex. Rather than the earlier swidden pattern of millets and grams grown in cleared jungle patches, dependent entirely on the monsoon rains and produced largely for subsistence, there is a new pattern of fields permanently cleared, with some measure of control over water resources, and production of rice as a surplus profit-making crop. For subsistence purposes, there is still a dependence on millets and grams grown in permanent or shifting dry fields.

Resulting from this change in agricultural method has been a decline in the importance and frequency of the ceremonial cycle geared to swidden cultivation. Although the major ceremonies still occur in most villages, the cycle is usually incomplete or aspects of it are adapted to rice cultivation, and in some cases swidden ceremonies have been assimilated to non-Koya festivals. Since most of the swidden ceremonies were at the same time village ceremonies in which all village members participated, the pattern of change in village composition has reinforced the decline in swidden ceremonies. In contrast to swidden or village ceremonies, those observances associated with the local descent group and the sib are still maintained.

Changes in population structure and agricultural methods brought about changes in the relationship of the Koya cultivator to the wider regional economy. The Koya cultivator is no longer a marginal producer of occasional surplus products which are exchanged for a minimum of manufactured goods. He has become a producer of a fairly reliable surplus crop which can be sold for cash. The cash returns for this surplus can be expended for further capital improvements, such as tanks, bunds, and oxen. They will also buy larger amounts of manufactured goods. As a result, the Koya cultivator has now become more dependent, and systematically so, on a wider group of non-kin for realization of his wants.

Production for a market has created a pattern in which differential distribution of acquired wealth is possible. Consequently, in place of the rough equality of swidden cultivators there is a growing tendency toward greater and greater disparities in the distribution of wealth. Those who have been able to retain control over land or exploit new opportunities arising from the contact of Koyas and non-Koyas have been able to acquire wealth.

Market production and contact with non-Koyas have led to the development of occupational specialization. Today, even though the clan, sib, and phratry system persists, these vertical genealogical segments of society are cross cut by groups based on occupational specialization, the most important of which are blacksmiths, bards, and funeral singers. Blacksmiths now constitute a subgroup within each of the phratries. Although their principal occupation is blacksmithing, most engage in subsidiary agricultural pursuits. Similarly, bards and funeral singers are also agriculturalists, but their degree of emancipation from sole dependence on agriculture as a source of livelihood is much less pronounced than that of the blacksmiths. Perhaps more significant than occupational specialization is the tendency toward endogamy and hierarchy. Genealogies for these groups indicate a high frequency of marriage with other members of the same occupational specialty. Some villagers argued that intermarriage between Koya agriculturalists and bards or funeral singers was, if not actually prohibited, regarded as incorrect. Associated with this was a further indication that these groups were "lower" than other Koyas. This disability did not apply to the blacksmith group.

There is some evidence to indicate that all three of these groups have been recruited as Koyas from other originally non-Koya groups. Bards, for example, do not have sibs and phratries of their own. Koyas regard them as belonging to the sib for which they work.

In addition to the groups having both occupational specialization and endogamy, there is now a Koya Christian community which is highly endogamous, but which has no particular occupational specialty. Intermarriage between Koyas and Koya Christians is now practically nonexistent, though such marriages occurred frequently in the earlier phases of missionary work. Koya Christians share with the occupational groups a tendency for greater emancipation from dependence on agriculture. Unlike the situation with the occupational groups, this independence arises from a higher degree of integration with the wider Indian society. Koya Christians tend to find new jobs outside the tribe as teachers, truck drivers, mechanics, and minor government officials, largely as a result of education. Almost all of the educated Koyas in the area are the products of mission schools, and the majority of Koya teachers in the new schools are descendants of the small group of Koyas who did not give up their faith. The descendants of my informant's father—one of the early Koyas Christians—alone account for fifteen of the Koya teachers in Bhadrachallam *tālūk*. Aside from teaching, there is little opportunity for educated Koyas in the tribal area, and more and more of them are migrating to urban areas. The offspring of my informant are typical of this development. Two of his sons are lorry drivers in Nagpur, one is a clerk in Hyderabad, and another is a village level worker in the government's Community Development Program in another part of the state.

The Christian Koyas are now a part of the general Indian Christian caste and no longer intermarry with tribal Koyas. Marriage is endogamous within the Christian caste. Interestingly enough, commensal rules do not apply, and Christian Koyas still interdine with tribal Koyas, though physical separation occurs with the Christian Koyas living in separate hamlets in tribal villages. The modern generation of Christan Koyas no longer participates in the sib sacrifice, but those of earlier generations still take part in most of the sib functions. In fact, up until the current generation, the pattern of marriage alliances between lineages still persisted. Christian Koyas of one lineage continued to marry their cross-cousins in other Christian Koya lineages. Even in the early generation, however, there were a significant number of Christian Koya marriages with Christians who had originally been members of Hindu castes. One of the more general patterns was for intermarriage with a caste new to the area, and which consequently had no previous marriage obligations or connections. These alliances are partially responsible for the migration of educated Christian Koyas. The presence of affinal relatives in urban areas, particularly Nagpur, Hyderabad, Khammamet, and Masulipatam, where there are sizable Christian populations, provides an avenue of introduction and temporary support for a young man migrating to a new area.

All of these changes have produced far-reaching alterations in the composition of villages. Villages now contain several local descent groups from at least two different phratries, and many villages contain such non-Koya groups as Koya Christians and Hindu and Muslim castes. Each of these groups is spatially isolated and separate hamlets in villages are named for their dominant population. Thus, there are Koya local descent group hamlets named for the clan which founded the hamlet or for the dominant population in it; there are Christian hamlets, Vaddera (a stone-working caste) hamlets, etc. The Christian hamlets are also separated further depending on whether the hamlet is a Māla or Mādiga (untouchable castes) Christian hamlet or a Koya Christian hamlet. The two Christian groups keep physically separate and infrequently intermarry.

This transition from a small, homogeneous village based on kinship and common descent to a larger, multiple ethnic-group village based on individual rights to land has exerted an important influence on the structure of authority relations within the village. Although the village headman continues to be recruited from the clan which is considered to have founded the village, his authority is now limited by the new government panchāyats and more importantly by noninstitutionalized patterns of power and authority deriving from the differential distribution of wealth and countervailing ethnic-group identifications. This lack of centralized authority is not entirely a function of change, for in part it represents the persistence among Koyas of a pattern of cooperation and authority distributed in terms of descent group membership. Among the Koya population the clan still functions as the major cooperative group and is largely responsible for disciplining its own members.

Increased village size and changes in village composition have attenuated the earlier pattern of tribal integration based on overlapping affinal ties. Now that villages contain more than one clan from more than one phratry, it is no longer necessary for the village to be exogamous. It is evident from genealogies that, among the Koya population, village endogamous marriages have increased in the last two generations. Former affinal ties with distant villages have been dropped and new alliances have been formed with other descent groups living in the same village. The integration of the tribe, always a tenuous thing at best, is probably less now than it was even a hundred years ago, since no new organizing principle has yet replaced the earlier one.

There is some evidence to indicate that a new pattern of marriage reflecting the differential distribution of wealth is emerging. Wealthier families attempt to maximize their range of kinship ties by contracting marriages with other wealthy families in the surrounding area. Yet, since they must also maintain ties in their local village, the pattern of alliance with other descent groups in the village is also kept up.

These patterns of change are very unevenly distributed among villages in the Koya area. In general, change is most pronounced in those areas which are most accessible. The more remote and inaccessible a village, the less likely that it will have non-Koyas as full-time residents. In addition, contact with agents of change will be much less frequent. In such areas, the major changes are simply those of settlement pattern and the presence of local descent groups from a phratry other than that of the founding descent group. In many of these villages where population density and availability of land permit, a restricted cycle of swidden agriculture supplemented by monsoon-fed, irrigated rice culture is practiced, and the ceremonial cycle associated with swidden agriculture is still maintained. By contrast, in villages where access to agents of change is maximal, the pattern of change has been even more thorough than that documented here.

In addition to the acculturating influences of government and mission, the more subtle but older influence of Sanskritization still persists. Many aspects of Koya ritual and mythology attest to a long-standing influence from nontribal Indian sources, but recently the influence in plains areas where access is relatively easy has taken on a different complexion. Formerly it seems that Indian elements were incorporated into tribal religion and social organization without much altering their basic character. Now there seems to be a pattern of incorporating the Koyas into the caste hierarchy. At two of the marriages in Chinna Nallaballi, for example, the Brāhman priest from Dummagudem officiated. This would indicate that some Koyas are being admitted into the local caste hierarchy at a level approximating that of the other landholding cultivating caste groups for whom the Brāhman also officiates. This process is far from complete, since the cultivating caste groups do not recognize Koyas as a "clean" caste. They refer to them as a *jāti* (species, kind, caste), but add that they are not a "clean" jāti, and point to their different religion, language, and habit of cow sacrifice as an indication of the difference. Status in the hierarchy is conditional on the number of Koyas present in a given village and their comparative wealth vis-à-vis the non-Koya population. In villages where the tribal population predominates, the Koyas are regarded as the equals of other landholding cultivating castes, but where Koyas have lost their lands and Hindu populations predominate, there is a tendency to include Koyas with lower-caste groups. This is more true of Koyas in Burgumpahad tāluk and especially in villages near the Singareni collieries and sawmills of Kothagudem. Except for a few of the larger villages in Bhadrachallam tāluk (e.g., Bhadrachallam, Dummagudem, and Kunnavaram), the Koyas are still the dominant group.

With independence, the Indian government has inaugurated a wide variety of tribal welfare schemes, and though their influence is still relatively slight, they have made some changes, particularly in disease prevention. Here, too, the usual pattern prevails: only those villages which are not too inaccessible receive aid of this type and villages in the hinterlands are relatively untouched by it.

That the activity of both Christians and government agents will increase in the next few years is a foregone conclusion. A bridge is being thrown across the Godāvari at Bhadrachallam, an all-weather road paralleling the river is under construction, and the Christians are planning to renew their efforts among the Koyas with increased vigor. All of this indicates that the processes of change, particularly in the plains villages, will be accelerated.

CONCLUSION

Arising primarily from the interaction of various reactions to processes of ecological change, Koya social organization has changed considerably in the last two or three hundred years. It has been transformed from a structure based on relatively isolated local descent groups, living in impermanent settlements, practicing a form of subsistence agriculture, and only loosely integrated with other local descent groups, to a structure still based on local descent groups and still only loosely integrated with other local descent groups, but now living in permanent settlements and practicing a form of agriculture posited on the existence of a market for surplus crops. In addition, the structure, from the point of view of the tribe, has become more complex. The ordering of all important relationships is no longer given in terms of kinship relations only, but is now partially ordered in terms of separate occupational groups and market obligations. Even though tribal integration remains weak, there is now a shift from tribal integration based on marital relations and the protection of territorial rights to an integration with the wider regional society consisting of both tribes and nontribes and based in large part on participation in a regional and national political and economic system.

The current structure of Koya society is but one of the transitional states in what is undoubtedly a larger and more complex process of assimilation to Indian society. Many plains Koyas now appear to be but a few short steps from being integrated into that society as simply another caste whose eventual status in the hierarchy will ultimately depend upon their ability to retain landed wealth or to take advantage of the new opportunities which will hopefully be available to them as a result of education and a changing Indian society.

Index

Adaptive response, 24, 28; adaptation, 272
Affinal relative, 83; tie, 279, 286
Aiyappan, A., 131n
Alegālu, 190
Artisan, 38, 77, 181
Astrologer, 142-44
Attitude, 49, 50, 52, 54, 70, 86, 182, 183, 187, 190, 201, 211, 214, 234, 239, 266-67
Āya, 176, 190-91; āyada kula, 176
Ayyar, K. N. K., 273n, 276n

Baden-Powell, B. H., 202
Bailey, F. G., 248, 272n
Bālutā, 230, 236, 239; bālutedār, 227-28, 230, 236; payment, 233, 236; system, 15, 227-28, 230, 236, 238
Barnett, Homer G., 97, 161n
Barnouw, Victor, 251n
Beals, Alan R., 4, 12, 14-15, 17, 30n, 57-72
Beidelman, Thomas O., 123, 251n
Bendix, Reinhard, 6, 9, 11, 220n
Bennett, John W., 39n
Bennett, Wendell C., 101n
Berkeley Union Reading Room, 62, 64, 66
Berreman, Gerald D., 4, 14, 15, 16, 17, 73-103
Béteille, André, 32n, 210
Bhajan, 174, 188
Bhūtam, 138
Bloomfield, Leonard, 90n, 100n

Bourgeoisie, 160, 163
Boyd, W. C., 100n
Brāhminocentric, 8
Bride-price, 77, 95

Capitalism, 157-58
Caste: association and organization, 27, 30, 34, 131-32, 135, 141-42, 145, 198, 200, 236, 238; dominant, 8-10, 22, 50-51, 56, 129-30, 157-86, 195, 209; group, 28-30, 32, 92, 138, 199, 200, 202, 209, 213, 249; hierarchy, 78, 87-88; lower, 15-16, 49, 51, 77, 87-89, 91, 114, 117, 129-30, 138-40, 142, 145-47, 151, 159, 162, 172, 200, 243, 246, 255, 262, 266, 289; solidarity, 16, 199, 213, 268; structure, 77, 238; system, 22, 26, 38, 93, 197, 199, 263; upper, higher, 15-16, 47, 49, 75, 77-78, 87-89, 111, 115, 118, 130, 134, 136, 138, 145-47, 159, 174, 255, 256, 262, 264
Center and periphery, 31; periphery, 30-32, 34
Ceremonies, 78, 87, 107-8, 118, 121, 130-32, 136, 138-39, 143, 151, 154, 170, 189, 191, 224, 232, 234, 239, 245, 261-62, 272, 276, 279, 284; betrothal, 174-75; religious, 65, 85, 182; wedding, 58, 77-78, 114-17
Change, 2, 4, 6-9, 12-18, 22, 25,